# LIFE on the LINE

## The heroic story of Vicki Moore

Matilda Mench

The Bluecoat Press

# Contents

A Feeling ... ... ... ... ... ... ... ... ... ... ... ... ... ... ... ... ... ... 7

In Love ... ... ... ... ... ... ... ... ... ... ... ... ... ... ... ... ... 8

Donkey Work ... ... ... ... ... ... ... ... ... ... ... ... ... ... ... 16

Baptism of Fire ... ... ... ... ... ... ... ... ... ... ... ... ... ... 28

Run for Your Life ... ... ... ... ... ... ... ... ... ... ... ... ... 35

Spanish Lessons ... ... ... ... ... ... ... ... ... ... ... ... ... ... 42

Coria ... ... ... ... ... ... ... ... ... ... ... ... ... ... ... ... ... 49

Bloody September ... ... ... ... ... ... ... ... ... ... ... ... ... 53

Judas Day ... ... ... ... ... ... ... ... ... ... ... ... ... ... ... 56

A Dog's Life ... ... ... ... ... ... ... ... ... ... ... ... ... ... ... 60

Mother ... ... ... ... ... ... ... ... ... ... ... ... ... ... ... ... 67

Travel Companions ... ... ... ... ... ... ... ... ... ... ... ... ... 70

The Leaping Goat ... ... ... ... ... ... ... ... ... ... ... ... ... 73

Water Bulls ... ... ... ... ... ... ... ... ... ... ... ... ... ... ... 78

Pepa and Magdalena ... ... ... ... ... ... ... ... ... ... ... ... 85

Fame ... ... ... ... ... ... ... ... ... ... ... ... ... ... ... ... ... 88

Riots ... ... ... ... ... ... ... ... ... ... ... ... ... ... ... ... ... 95

Friction ... ... ... ... ... ... ... ... ... ... ... ... ... ... ... ... 99

The Colombian Connection ... ... ... ... ... ... ... ... ... ... 106

Searching for John Major ... ... ... ... ... ... ... ... ... ... ... 109

Thirty Pieces of Silver ... ... ... ... ... ... ... ... ... ... ... 113

Scapegoat ... ... ... ... ... ... ... ... ... ... ... ... ... ... ... 116

Dolphins in Distress ... ... ... ... ... ... ... ... ... ... ... ... 121

Dirty Fighting ... ... ... ... ... ... ... ... ... ... ... ... ... 124

The Battle of Brightlingsea ... ... ... ... ... ... ... ... ... ... 129

Life on a Thread ... ... ... ... ... ... ... ... ... ... ... ... ... 132

Going Home ... ... ... ... ... ... ... ... ... ... ... ... ... ... 144

Inner Demons ... ... ... ... ... ... ... ... ... ... ... ... ... ... 151

A Class All by Herself ... ... ... ... ... ... ... ... ... ... ... 155

A Close Call ... ... ... ... ... ... ... ... ... ... ... ... ... ... 158

Mysterious Ways ... ... ... ... ... ... ... ... ... ... ... ... ... 163

New Arrivals ... ... ... ... ... ... ... ... ... ... ... ... ... ... 165

Into the Firing Line ... ... ... ... ... ... ... ... ... ... ... ... 168

What the King Saw ... ... ... ... ... ... ... ... ... ... ... ... 172

Living Target ... ... ... ... ... ... ... ... ... ... ... ... ... ... 175

Sparky ... ... ... ... ... ... ... ... ... ... ... ... ... ... ... ... 177

Goodbye ... ... ... ... ... ... ... ... ... ... ... ... ... ... ... 181

What Happened to Sparky? ... ... ... ... ... ... ... ... ... ... 184

A Rough Beginning ... ... ... ... ... ... ... ... ... ... ... ... 190

"When I became aware of the immensity of the problem of the Blood Fiestas, I was confronted with an almost metaphysical awareness of being given a cross to carry, like the penitents of Semana Santa. A cross called conscience was put before me, and I hesitated before picking it up. In August 1987, I shouldered the burden and within days, witnessed a bound and screaming 'fire bull' dragged to its death down a street called the Calle de Calvario (Street of Calvary) in Canet de Berenguer, after hours of terror, pain and torture. My true initiation into the calvary of the animals had begun."

Vicki Moore
1945 – 2000

# A Feeling

"I'm being followed wherever I go. I've come out of the fiesta now and I'm not actually sure where the bull is … I don't know what to do … I don't know whether to go back, or stay away, because I don't feel it's safe at all … Something's very, very wrong."

Down the line Tony could hear the roar of the crowd in the background and the familiar screams of, "Fuera! Fuera!" (Out! Out!), aimed at the British film crew; unwelcome intruders in their village, hellbent on thwarting their fiesta, their valued traditions. He could also detect the fear in Vicki's voice, but neither was unusual. Danger and risk came with the job and angry mobs were an occupational hazard.

"Are you still there, Tony?" came her voice again, more urgently now. "What should I do?"

Despite her courage, Vicki had certainly been afraid before – she had found herself in endless tight spots in pursuit of her campaign against animal cruelty, particularly in the Spanish blood fiestas – but it was not normal for her to behave like this; to look for a way out. She and Tony were often forced to embark on missions alone, usually because of financial constraints, and then they would telephone each other for advice on what strategies to adopt in the often frightening situations in which they found themselves.

And so it was that Tony said what he now considers to be the fatal thing and which he has bitterly regretted ever since.

"You know, I'm not there. I can't tell you what to do. It's up to you whether you can go back or not. You have to make a decision on that one, I'm afraid."

He remembers that towards the end of the conversation she suddenly began speaking in Spanish – not very good Spanish, but enough to say, "Erm … it's quite interesting … I'm having a good time." Tony realised that they must have come right up close to her and she quickly ended the call. As he replaced the receiver he suddenly remembered what Vicki had said to him just before she left for Spain. "I don't want to go. I think there's something wrong. I just don't feel safe."

He had paid little attention to her words at the time, putting them down to her superstitious nature, but now they reverberated around inside his head and he was filled with a terrible foreboding. He anxiously paced up and down, unable to think of anything else.

An hour later the telephone rang again, and with a sinking feeling, he lifted the receiver. "Señor Moore?" said a voice in a thick Spanish accent.

"Yes … speaking."

"Your wife is dead …"

# In Love

Like so many successful relationships, on the surface Vicki and Tony seemed to have little in common. For a start, he was twelve years older than her and their backgrounds were poles apart; she the product of a wild and feckless mother, who led a colourful life, unerringly putting her own needs ahead of her daughter's; he the beloved middle son of two loving and conventional parents. Yet together, they forged a formidable partnership, devoted, above all else, to the protection of animals; a devotion for which she would pay the ultimate price.

Lucille Eva Valentine Seel Haywood, later known simply as Vicki Moore, came into the world as a Christmas present, on 24 December 1945, in Western Favel, Northhamptonshire, but her childhood was not always to be like Christmas. Her mother Louise was already forty-three when she became pregnant with Vicki and the doctors feared a risk of severe health problems for herself and her child and suggested she consider a termination. Having chosen to proceed with the pregnancy, Louise forever reminded Vicki that she had saved her life.

When she was two or three years old, Vicki was placed in a foster home and put up for adoption, because her mother wanted to advance her career as a professional ballet dancer unencumbered by a child. Vicki's foster mother expected her to call her 'mother' and when she refused, she was locked away in a wardrobe for hours at a time. This happened repeatedly.

One day they took her to the post office to sign some documents and Vicki believed that they were signing the adoption papers. She could not bear the thought of never seeing her real mother again, so she ran out of the post office and grabbed hold of a passing policeman's leg and clung on like a limpet. She created a great disturbance and would not let go, crying out that these people were trying to take her away from her mother.

She must have put on a very convincing show, because the policeman took her kicking and screaming, along with her foster parents, to the police station, to clarify matters. Having established that they were indeed her legal guardians, he then tried to persuade Vicki to go home with them, but she flatly refused. A terrible row ensued and in the end Vicki's real mother was forced to come and get her. The subject of adoption was never mentioned again.

Reunited, they moved to Brontë Country for a short time, the home of Louise's latest husband. Born in 1902 she had been married and divorced four times. She married her first husband, James Yale, at the tender age of seventeen. They had a child, whom they also called James. Louise later told Vicki that the reason for divorcing James was a little delicate; he was caught with a young liftboy in one of the exclusive London hotels in which he frequently stayed. In the 1920s homosexuality was regarded as highly improper, as well as illegal, behaviour. Louise was deeply shocked, but when she had to take the stand in the High Court, she defended him, if that is the right word, by claiming that he had always been a womaniser. His family succeeded in keeping the case out of the public eye and James was able to carry on with his profession as a lawyer unscathed. The family begged Louise to stay with them on their Welsh estate, but she insisted on a divorce and took little Jimmy with her.

The next husband was a Russian sculptor, who lived in London. When the lease on his Notting Hill studio expired in 1930, it was acquired by Marie Rambert, as the main rehearsal room for the Ballet Rambert. When the sculptor died of a heart attack, Louise married their good friend, another Russian. He was a wealthy oenologist and they travelled together through the vineyards of France. However, when the second World War loomed on the horizon, being a Jew, he was desperate to leave Europe. He sent all his belongings, including cases full of jewellery and share certificates, to Australia, on board a ship. Unfortunately, the ship sank, and with it all his wealth and hopes for the future. They were both devastated and the strain must have caused his already weak heart to deteriorate even further, because he died of a heart attack shortly afterwards.

Louise's penchant for professional men landed her a fourth husband, said to have been an archaeologist, who frequently travelled abroad on expeditions. Vicki was encouraged to believe that he was her father, but most likely she was the product of an extra-marital affair with a Spanish sailor, whom her mother met whilst they were living in London for a time, which would explain Vicki's darker looks. Louise dropped various hints and promised to tell her the truth before she died, but she never did. In later life, during her trips to Spain, Vicki would always be mistaken for a Spaniard. Louise soon tired of her archaeologist and her fourth marriage broke up. Money was tight without a husband providing for her and she was now forced to work for a living.

Due to the huge age difference, Vicki was raised like an only child and knew her half brother James only vaguely. However, her lack of siblings was made up for by the world in which she became immersed, which had much to offer a young child. When her mother worked in musicals in the West End, she used to wait behind the scenes, meeting many famous actors and learning plays and musicals by heart. Sometimes she would be wilting with exhaustion but she still had to wait for her mother to take her home after the show. Needless to say, she was often sleepy in school the next day.

The intriguing world of theatre did not make up for the one thing that Vicki missed terribly in her life. In an interview she said, "Although I loved animals I was unable to have any pets, because my mother was in the ballet and we used to tour everywhere in Britain and Europe." She was deeply affected by an animal story from her mother's childhood. Louise had been the second youngest of the 'Seven Little Lancashire Lasses – the only seven real sisters performing together anywhere'. There were also two brothers, and at times, unbeknown to the audience, one of them would be made to dress up as a girl to make up the seven. Together they formed a troupe which toured the country, singing and acting in Vaudeville style. Once, Louise's father, Sergeant Parsons, Army Ordnance Corps, found a stray dog and integrated him into the show by tying a drumstick to his tail and making him beat a drum. The animal grew quite attached to them, but after the season was over, he was abandoned on a train platform. Louise tried to persuade Vicki that the dog would have found a place to live, but she was not convinced.

Eventually, Vicki's mother drifted into alcoholism, and Vicki developed a co-dependent relationship with her, common in families containing alcohol abusers. At the age of thirteen, when they lived in Brixton, Vicki dropped out of school for good. Even though she had been a precocious child, for whom teachers had predicted an academic future, she felt a pressing need to earn money, since her mother had become increasingly unreliable. Always terrified that the school inspector would find her, she took on odd jobs, such as addressing envelopes.

She trained to become an actress, playing small parts in the theatre and as an extra in films, but eventually gave it all up to be close to her mother, who wanted to move up north. They settled in Southport, where they shared a flat and Vicki initially worked in an electrical factory. Then, in the early 1960s, she started working as a waitress in a nightclub, because the money was better, and that's how she met Tony.

Tony was born on 2 January 1934 in a nursing home in Paddington and spent the first years of his childhood in Kilburn. He too showed an early concern for animals, but there the similarity with Vicki's early years ends, for he enjoyed a far more secure childhood. He remembers his father, William Earnest Moore, or Bill, as he was called, as a brilliant mathematician with an analytical mind. When Bill was eleven years old he passed an exam for people a lot older than himself. He came top in the whole of London and was awarded a prize in the London City Hall. Because they were a family of seven, and in need of money, young Bill, who wanted to be a professional cricketer and had been offered a place at Lords, was set to work for little pay in a factory producing mercury-in steel thermometers used in aeroplanes.

Tony's mother Phyllis, whom he adored, was a well educated woman with a good sense of humour, who stayed at home to raise him, his younger brother David and his older brother John. Her culinary skills were way ahead of her time; she understood nutrition and cooked with olive oil, even when it could only be obtained from pharmacies. She was virtually vegetarian for moral reasons and was especially disgusted by veal, because of the way calves were abused in its

10

production, and pork, because she thought pigs were so closely related to humans.

Tony loved to read Jack London's tales about wolves roaming the country in packs. On his first visit to London zoo he was shocked to find wolves trapped behind wire in a narrow, featureless run. "They were poor scabby things with yellowish fur, like poor dogs in a shelter, smelly and wet." He also read Rudyard Kipling's *Jungle Book*. "When I saw the monkeys swinging about in compounds, the lions and tigers in cages, it looked wrong, but it didn't register. But the wolves did ... I never wanted to see wolves in a zoo again."

His parents moved out of central London to the edge of the green belt near Heathrow. The airport was very small then and he used to climb on top of the control tower, which was not much more than a little shed with a flat roof, to watch the planes take off. He went to school in Ealing, passing the Film Studios every day. Through the fence he glimpsed another world of soldiers with bleeding head wounds and their nurses, African tribesmen and white people wearing safari hats. On his own, he frequented art exhibitions and the Opera. Drawn to this exciting new world, he decided to become a make-up artist, an idea which did not meet with his parent's approval. In fact, they strongly objected to him becoming a member of the arts world in any capacity.

Tony also loved the outdoors and spent hours in the woods on his own and in the summer he used to live in a tent in the garden and disappear for days on his bike. His mother complained that he used the house like a hotel, just going in for meals. When Tony was fifteen, his father was offered the job of running the branch of a factory in Cumbria and the family moved. His first ambition having been quashed, Tony decided that he would like to work outdoors, so he took a job as a helper on a farm in Egremont, West Cumberland. His older brother was away in public school and his other brother was still very young.

He knew nothing about animal husbandry, or the hardships of farm life. In the 1950s, many farms lacked electricity and there was neither a tractor nor a milking machine on his farm. He had to get up a 6 o'clock in the morning to milk the cows. His first experience of milking was with Snowdrop – a huge, sixteen-year-old white beast. He could hardly get his hand around her teats. He also looked after the horses and learned to plough with them and cut hay with a scythe.

At seventeen, Tony wanted to explore life on another farm and went to Lorton, about ten miles away; still no electricity, but they did have a generator to operate the milking machines. There was a river close by and he learnt to poach salmon, sometimes using a friend's fishing licence as a cover. They would sell the salmon to the local hotels during the season but his regrets are deep. "Getting a salmon out was great. The skill of knowing how to do it by tickling the salmon was a good feeling, but then after getting it out of the water, feeling dirty and horrible, not really wanting to know. I wanted to put it back in, but it was too late. I always had that feeling about it. It was a bad feeling."

11

The farmer was heavily involved in hunting and at the end of the season used to take in hounds from the pack, disappearing two or three times a week and occasionally returning with a fox's brush. "He was totally involved in it, but I wasn't. If the hounds came through, I followed to see what was going on, but I didn't actually take part." The more he learned about hunting, the more his opinions crystalised.

One day the farmer told him they would have to move a vixen and her cubs because another farmer, on whose land they had their den, was about to kill them. Tony soon realised that this was not done to protect the animals, but because they needed something to hunt. Paraffin was spilled around the den's entrance forcing the vixen to take the cubs out and move them elsewhere. "I remember seeing them digging some cubs out on the farm next door and these horrible terrier men arrived. I couldn't believe the brutality of it. Digging these little helpless cubs out – a cross between a kitten and a pup. The men were laughing and hitting them on the head with a shovel. It sickened me totally."

Shortly afterwards, Tony had an experience that finished him with hunting for good. It was late summer, before the hunting season had started, and the farmer and a few others who kept hounds decided to go hunting. Tony was asked along and they set off for the fells with eight hounds running ahead of them. The farmers stayed at the bottom of the fell, while Tony was sent halfway up and it was then that he saw a fox racing away from the hounds. "The next thing I knew it came towards me. It was wet with sweat, tongue hanging out. It was exhausted. It came within just a few metres of me and stood there, like a little dog, looking at me. What I should have done was call up the hounds. But I thought, I can't do this. So we stood there and just stared at one another. After a while, the fox trotted past me into the bracken. From that moment on I thought, this is terrible, this is not right."

He never went to hunt balls again.

In 1960, after two years working in Germany in the army as a weapons instructor, he returned to England to work on a farm in Wigton for a year, before deciding that this was not enough for him. Having saved some money, he was able to put himself through agricultural college in Penrith. The effort was worth it, he finished with good grades and became a farm manager and soon found himself married to the farmer's daughter. Despite three children, the marriage did not last. After an agonising separation and subsequent divorce, Tony wanted to embark on a new career, which did not include breeding and selling animals for food.

In the mid-1960s, Tony's family had moved again, this time from Cumberland to Burscough, near Southport. Tony moved nearby and worked on plant-hire and building sites. His brother David was about to get married and was having a stag party. In the course of the evening they visited various pubs and by the time they entered Southport's Kingsway Club, some of them were already the worse for wear. Girls dressed in bunny costumes served in the club. They were sort of straight-laced bunnies and many of them looked decidedly uncomfortable in their outfits.

David had taken a liking to a particular bunny girl. She was short with a nice figure and a beautiful face. He was pulling her tail and making silly comments. To stop him making a fool of himself, Tony pulled him away. He apologised for his behaviour and added, "So what are you doing tomorrow?" The girl did not seem particularly interested, but they chatted for a while. She had not yet adopted her stage name, Vicki, so Tony got to know her as Lucille. He was taken by her dark brown hair cut very short, and her warm hazel eyes which matched her dark complexion perfectly. He was also impressed by her well educated voice and wondered what she was doing in a place like that.

Nothing happened that evening, yet he couldn't get her out of his head. For a month he visited the club whenever he could. Admission was quite expensive, as were the drinks and he couldn't afford to keep going there, so he finally summoned up the courage to ask her out. She agreed to meet him for lunch outside the club the following day. She stood him up and after half an hour of waiting he went home, dejected.

A week went by, after which he could no longer resist going back to the club. She seemed genuinely embarrassed and immediately apologised. "I should never have made an appointment to meet you at 12 o'clock. I'd only just got to bed really." Tony decided to give it another go and they agreed to meet when she next had a night off. Over a period of months they got to know each other by going out for meals, walking and talking. Their relationship seemed promising, or so Tony thought, but he was in for a nasty surprise. One day, Vicki suddenly announced that she was engaged and that her husband-to-be was an Australian sailor in the merchant navy. Tony met her fiancé and took an instant dislike to him, but nevertheless agreed to be best man at their wedding. He realised immediately afterwards that he should have asked her to marry him instead. But it was too late.

Vicki's husband soon had to go back to sea and she and Tony continued to see each other as good friends. He fetched her migraine prescription when she had one of her debilitating attacks and supported her when she needed respite from her mother. Vicki soon realised that she was not happy when her husband was on leave and that she did not really love him – she loved Tony. A few months into the marriage, they became lovers. She left her husband and fled to Manchester with Tony, renting an apartment in Sale. A few days later Vicki's mother moved in with them.

They lived in Manchester for three years and during that time Vicki talked Tony into taking up music. He bought a guitar and taught himself to play within ten weeks, accompanying Vicki who had a good singing voice. Pub talent competitions helped them gain experience in front of an audience. "I only had an unamplified nylon-strung guitar. I was terrified at first. Vicki had a little stage fright too, but she was far more nervous for me."

They were approached by several agents, one of whom called herself Madame Ace and offered a letdown service, which meant that every weekend Tony packed his gear into the car and around 7pm called her to find out whether there was a letdown. Later on they had a proper agent and formed a double act called 'Victoria and Albert'. They played in nightclubs in the UK and Ireland. Travelling to Ireland with his guitar, amplifiers and other technical equipment was a problem, so Tony learnt to play the banjo, which was easier to transport.

Some time later, the Harry Gunn Agency booked them to play in South Africa where they would stay for a longer period of time. At the last minute, when everything was packed and ready, Vicki's mother created a scene and scuppered their plans. She had decided that she wanted to live in Southport again, so they rented a flat and continued to tour the country, sometimes even taking Louise with them. By the time they were leaving a club, she had usually passed out from drink. Had she not, there was trouble on the horizon, because she was jealous of Vicki. Often, after Vicki came off stage, people would flock round her saying what a wonderful voice she had and how come she was working there. Her mother would butt in, "You think she's good! You haven't heard me. I'm her mother."

Louise deteriorated mentally. Once, while Tony and Vicki were asleep in bed at around 5 o'clock in the morning, a noise disturbed them. Grabbing his dressing gown, Tony went to check out the situation and found a stranger standing with Louise in the middle of their flat. "Here he is – the policeman!" she announced. The 'policeman' was just a normal, if very bewildered person. She had dragged him into the flat telling that him Tony had murdered Vicki in their bedroom. Obviously Vicki was very much alive and the man shuffled out, deeply embarrassed.

Louise was also becoming more vicious by the day. Vicki bought her some slippers for Christmas and asked her to try them on. With one shoe off and one shoe on, Vicki tried to put the slipper on her foot. Without warning she lashed out and kicked her in the face. By this time, Louise no longer needed alcohol to act crazily. She always left the house carrying two plastic bags full of the things she valued, in case the house was burgled while she was out. Her brain was destroyed and she should have been in an institution receiving medical help but she insisted on having her own flat, which she hardly used. She would hang around at Vicki and Tony's place instead, sleeping in the living room most of the time. Even at this late stage, her manipulative skills were still intact and she managed to run their lives by emotional blackmail, until her death in 1989.

Vicki and Tony had always been animal lovers, but only in the late seventies did they get actively involved in animal welfare. In 1977 they found a stray puppy on the beach, which was very ill with distemper. After taking him to a vet they nursed him at their small home. Tony even slept with him on the kitchen floor but he was beyond rescue and eventually died. Later on, they joined the Southport committee of the RSPCA. Vicki fed stray cats and raised funds for them.

In 1980, while Tony was building and running the Southport RSPCA shelter, a dog came in who had been found running the streets. He was a cross between an Alsatian and an English sheep dog. He loved people and especially children, but he hated male dogs. Nobody claimed him. "I think we've got a dog," he told Vicki. "He's got a lovely nature. We can't let him go, because people will want him as a guard dog for his looks. He likes our cats. I think we can look after him." So they did. Tony tried to find out his name: Bruce, Rover, Rascal, Prince – all the usual names. Eventually he came up with Fritz. The dog pricked up his ears as if to say, "Hello! Yes, that's my name." So Fritz it was and he lived to be seventeen.

A few months later, Susie came into their lives. Vicki was alerted by a member of the public that there was a dog locked up in an empty house, the occupants having moved out three weeks earlier. It was not exactly love at first sight. She was hostile when Vicki went to pick her up, but soon settled down on her knee in the car. She also threw up in her lap! She took the ugly creature home and when Tony came back from work she told him that there was a friend waiting to see him. The little thing was like a whippet, she was so thin, her hairless tail like a rat's. She went straight for Tony's throat, snarling savagely. He just sat down calmly and Susie slunk back underneath a chair. Eventually, she came over to him and pushed her head into his hand. From then on she used to follow him round, wrapping herself around his feet whenever he stood still, or jumping up on to his lap when he sat.

Most of the animals in Vicki and Tony's unconventional household had been rescued – either from cruel situations, or from the threat of being put to sleep – and each one became a treasured member of their family. Tony had found Mimi, the first of their ten cats, as a kitten in a fairground, shivering with cold. When a beloved pet dies, it is like a death in the family; it affects people profoundly, and when Mimi died, Vicki actually lost her voice. She cried non-stop for nearly three days, until Mimi was buried. On New Year's Eve, they had a gig in Southport. Suddenly, in the middle of singing 'The Lady is a Tramp', Vicki's voice crackled to a halt and she was no longer able to perform. She managed to get an emergency appointment with a voice specialist but he could find nothing wrong with her vocal cords and suggested a psychological cause.

Vicki remembered having seen an invitation for a faith healing session in the local paper. She was desperate, since her voice meant their income, so she went to see the healer. She was told to lie down on a couch and when his hand approached her, without actually touching her, she felt her neck becoming warm. Back home she was relieved to find that her voice had returned. With Vicki back on stage, their normal life should resume. Or so they thought …

# Donkey Work

When Vicki bought the *Today* newspaper for her mother on 16 February 1987, she did not expect that one small article would change their lives forever. It was about a donkey that would be crushed to death in a Spanish village fiesta. The article gave few details but she could not stop thinking about it. She showed the piece to Tony and suggested they do something to save the animal. His response was typical of most people, "It will be stopped now that it's in the paper. One of the big groups or someone else will be dealing with it." This answer was unacceptable to Vicki. She would not be deterred that easily. Having contacted the big organisations and been met with negativity – this was not UK business – they decided to start a letter campaign, which was joined by the World Society for the Protection of Animals (WSPA), to put pressure on the Spanish Government. These were, of course, pre-internet days.

They visited their local papers, the *Southport Visiter* and the *Southport Star*, to try to get them to include a piece about the fiesta and invite people to write letters of protest. As they were leaving the *Star* newspaper office, the chief reporter ran after them and asked what they were going to do if the campaign failed. Out of the blue, Tony replied, "Go over there and try to stop it."

For three consecutive days the campaign dominated the front page of the *Southport Star*. Other media picked up the story and the Spanish Embassy was deluged with letters and phone calls. But it did not appear that the fiesta would be stopped. The British Government did not wish to get involved, the thinking being that questions of animal welfare were matters of internal policy for the Spanish Government. There was no support from the Church either. Vicki and others appealed to then Archbishop of Canterbury, Dr Runcie, to extend his compassion to the donkey of Villanueva by protesting to the Spanish authorities. She was dismayed to receive a circular in which the Archbishop simply accepted the assurances of the Spanish Embassy that the story was completely false.

Even though neither Vicki nor Tony had ever been to Spain before, they decided they must go. The village was about 100km west of Madrid, in the Gredos mountains. The central theme of the Pero Palo fiesta seemed to be the burning to death of a man, but establishing the identity of this legendary figure was more difficult. One version suggested that when all the Jews were cast out of Spain, he had stayed behind and turned into a bandit, raping the village women, another that he was a warrior from the time of the Reconquista. Or, according to the village's official leaflet, the fiesta was simply the re-enactment of the trials at the time of the Inquisition. Strangely, there is no picture of the donkey and his rider in the leaflet.

Whatever the murky historical justification for the event, every year, on Shrove Tuesday, a puppet which had previously been made by the villagers and stuck on a pole in the town square, was sentenced to death by a tribunal of locals. At this point, the donkey made his appearance, ridden by someone reading out the death sentence. The pronouncement was celebrated by gunshots and in the evening Pero Palo was burned.

Because of their pets and because the cost would be too great, Tony and Vicki could not travel together. It was decided that a woman would probably be perceived as less of a threat than a man, but they were wrong, as I was to find out myself as recently as 2003. It is right to accuse the villagers of Villanueva de la Vera of animal abusive and xenophobia, but they definitely treat women and men with absolute equality. Never before have I been so roughly handled in Spain.

Vicki started to study as much Spanish as she could in the short time prior to her trip. Until now she had only sung popular Spanish songs with Tony's band, without really understanding the words. Louise had to be put into a nursing home for the time of her absence. Her alcohol abuse had taken its toll on her brain and nobody else but Vicki was able to handle her anymore.

News of a British girl's attempt to save a donkey from being crushed to death in Spain spread quickly. The *Sunday Express* was the first to report death threats by the villagers to Vicki. The Devon Donkey Sanctuary contacted her, offering to help fund the trip with a donation of five hundred pounds, in return for being mentioned in the media. They also demanded a written statement absolving them from any responsibility should she be harmed. She found this a bit strange, but accepted the conditions in exchange for the welcome donation. She did not appreciate then, that for some people in Britain, donkey welfare means serious business. Newcomers are regarded as competitors in the battle for donations and not necessarily welcome. Had she been aware of this, she might been more circumspect in involving other people.

As active members of the RSPCA, Tony and Vicki sought their support but were told by their local branch secretary that someone at headquarters had told her they were not to go. To back this up, they were given the name of the head of the Spanish Federation of the Societies for the Protection of Animals and Plants. She spoke good English and warned them on the phone that it would be too dangerous to go, it was bandit country! This seemed so ridiculous that it only served to strengthen their resolve.

The death threats kept coming but Vicki stuck to her plan and on 28 February Tony took her to Manchester Airport. In Madrid she was to meet with members of the Spanish animal rights group Asociación para la Defensa de los Derechos del Animal (ADDA). They recommended the most expensive hotel in

Madrid, but her budget forced her to find a cheaper one which happened to be near a red light district.

The next day Vicki met with the ADDA people and told them she wanted to go to Villanueva de la Vera as soon as possible. Since the fiesta was due to take place on Tuesday morning she wanted to be there no later than Monday midday, but nobody was willing to assist. She would have to resort to public transport. Then, out of the blue, reporter Don McKay and photographer Stan Meagher of the *Daily Star* appeared at the Hotel Menfis in the evening and offered her a lift early the following morning. Vicki wrote in her report on the fiesta: "The *Star* team made their offer to transport me to Villanueva and do all in their power to assist me to save the donkey. They had already hired transport and could, if I agreed, arrange for the services of a freelance journalist – very fluent in Spanish, and with an excellent comprehension of the Spanish character – to accompany us to Villanueva de la Vera. In the circumstances, their offer of assistance seemed to be a gift from heaven, so albeit with some reservations, I accepted." They also said that Tony had asked them to put her complete trust in them, because they would look after her, that is, if she stayed with them exclusively. He had made no such request.

They left Madrid very early the next morning and set off for Jarandilla, about five kilometres from Villanueva, where they arrived at 7.30am. They were to stay in the Parador, an old castle-type building which had been turned into a hotel. Journalist Ed Owen, who spoke fluent Spanish, joined them. The Parador would soon be buzzing with press people from the UK.

Tony's suggested plan was to buy the donkey. Even though it could not be spared the fiesta, it would have to be handed over in good condition, if money had changed hands. The Donkey Sanctuary advised a top price of no more than fifty pounds, but the present owner would take advantage of the situation.

When they arrived in the village they were surprised by the unbearable stench of alcohol and urine permeating the picturesque passageways and town square. Wherever they went they were eyed with suspicion or open hostility. Firecrackers exploded around them and insults were hurled. One of the journalists even thought they were being shot at and dropped to the ground. It was abundantly clear – Vicki and the other foreigners were not welcome!

They tried to find Mayor Gonzalo Marcos Tomé, or his deputy to negotiate the purchase of the donkey. Vicki would later tell *Womanpost*, "At the time I was naïve enough to think I could just go and speak to the local mayor and point out how cruel this sort of festival was and that he would understand and put a stop to it." The town hall was locked up but they were told they would find them in a certain bar. When they arrived at the bar, they were directed to another bar and yet another, all crowded with people singing and beating frantically on drums which fell silent when they entered. They were not talked to or served in several bars. An increasing number of drum beating youths started to follow them wherever they went. As Don Mackay wrote in his article, "From bar to bar youngsters swigged local red wine to the beat of drums … which soon turned into the drums of hate."

Whilst they were in one bar the village youths hanging around outside grew impatient and crashed into the bar. "We were standing in a small bar, like a cube with a long counter fronting the shelves of liquor, a few rickety chairs and tables stood around, the atmosphere rank with old smoke. One of the round tables was petalled by a pair of stout women, an old man with a white stubbled chin and a fractious over tired child of some four or five years, in fancy dress. Apart from these and ourselves the place was empty. It was also reverberating with the frenzied banging of drums, the clamour of the shouting drawing nearer by the second.

"The doors burst open and we were overwhelmed and half suffocated by a surge of a hundred people, or more, pushing into the cramped space. The thudding of the drums was earsplitting. 'Don't worry, my dear. I went all through Korea. I'll look after you.' Kindly meant as it was, when I compared the speaker – slight, elderly and dapper in his canary Pringle sweater – with the men and youths pouring in with soot-daubed faces, some sporting livid red and purple bruising round their eyes and jaws, all in various stages of drunkenness and all very angry, I felt less than reassured. We were being pushed against the wall by the press of scowling, gesticulating humanity, intent on giving us the full benefit of rough music! Somewhere in the din and melee the child was sent flying and her terrified shrieks were added to the cacophony. One of the leading percussionists, wild eyed and stale breathed, shoved his drum into the chest of my protector, and in a flail of drumsticks broke one against his head. Firecrackers exploded, choking us with the acrid fumes. And the same snatch of song that had been hurled like a threat at us for the last hour or so, during the cat and mouse troupe round the village, again punched our eardrums.

"Face after face with spittle-flecked lips drawn back against bare teeth were shoved into us. The large, hollowed-out gourds dried and formed into knobbled clubs, à la Flintstones, were swung in clumsy arks and brought down thrashing the air around us. Following a childhood injunction to sip, not slurp, I raised my glass with its wildly thrashing contents to my lips and endeavoured to drink without spilling … the stamping, shoving, screaming mob surging around. I felt a bit like the Eddystone [lighthouse] in the midst of a gale. Buffeted, shaken, but still thankfully standing. My companions reading to their internal directions maintained a similar demeanour.

"When their pyrotechnics and war dance had little or no effect on these peculiar strangers in their midst, they, as though by some unheard word of command, broke their line. The majority ambled out, while some formed little muttering groups. The girl, retrieved from the melee and dusted down by her relatives, made loud accusatory noises in the direction of some of the wild black daubed figures and in the hiatus of this welcome diversion, we slipped out. 'I think we should be out of this place before dark.' The speaker was a Spanish-based journalist employed by the *Star*. He had accompanied the other two *Star* men in our fruitless track around the village in search of the mayor, who, it transpired, had absented himself from his municipality deliberately."

By now, it was nearly 4 o'clock in the afternoon. Finally, they were directed to a café near a shop belonging to the deputy mayor. The barkeeper assured them that he would open his shop soon. Meanwhile, the village youths milled around menacingly outside the café. When, after quite a wait, the shop still had not opened, the two reporters set off for the deputy mayor's house. His wife seemed terrified and obviously did not wish to speak to them, but she told them that she had not seen him since early morning and that he would be at the fiesta.

Vicki and the *Star* team, whom she now jokingly referred to as her 'guardian angels', returned to the town square, followed by the youths. Again firecrackers were thrown at them and shouts of "Fuera!" (Get out!) could be heard. The town hall was still locked. A group of elderly people advised them that they would neither get to see the mayor, nor the donkey, whose whereabouts were secret. And the donkey could not be bought, because it was illegal to sell it while the fiesta was already in full swing. Vicki still insisted on buying the donkey, so they followed the senior citizens, who were not aggressive towards them, to a bar.

Over a glass of wine it was explained to them why the villagers were so upset by their presence. The previous year's donkey had indeed died in the fiesta – crushed to death by the crowd. According to a paper issued by ADDA, this was not an isolated incident; previous donkeys had either been drowned in the fountain, or thrown from balconies on to the cobbled streets. It appeared that over the years the fiesta had got out of control. In former times the villagers themselves had used their own donkey for the fiesta but over the last few years they had had to buy a new donkey each year. Since the donkey was not going to last, they bought ones that were old and sick, because they were cheaper. Spain's *ABC* newspaper reported, "When the poor beast can no longer get up, the youths jump on it, while they chant, 'Finally the donkey which brought the vinegar is dead'."

However, the village was in denial, even though there was a picture of a dead donkey in the fountain in the bar. The bar's owner, Emilio San Miguel, was quoted in *The Observer* as saying: "I have lived here for fifty-six years and never has a donkey died during our festival. Okay, unless of course it is a very, very infirm donkey and then it would be a terrible accident. We never kill donkeys deliberately." Another villager said that the animal was a bag of bones, no use for anything, so it didn't matter what they did to it.

ADDA alerted foreign animal rights groups to protest to the Spanish Government and when the fiesta of 1987 came closer, they alerted the international press. They also placed a full-page advertisement in the Spanish newspapers, condemning the people of Villanueva de la Vera for their inhumanity. "Are we really part of Europe?" it asked. The villagers felt publicly shamed. Indeed, in a meeting held on 24 March 1986, the municipal authorities admitted that that year's donkey had been mistreated and it was decided that in 1987 the necessary measures would be taken, so that those 'deplorable acts' would not be repeated. In a letter to ADDA the mayor wrote: "The acts that unfortunately happen are a result of the degeneration of some of the aspects of the Fiesta of Pero Palo, which, due to the few means all of the small villages, are difficult to avoid, however, one must not come to the conclusion that our fiestas are of a cruel and uncivilised nature."

Prior to the 1987 fiesta he issued a statement asking the villagers not to commit acts of cruelty towards the animal. It was also forbidden to throw firecrackers at people.

Vicki felt it was better to leave the village, because with nightfall, things might get completely out of hand but she was desperate, because she had not managed to improve the situation for the donkey. A whole day wasted sitting around and getting nowhere. Anxious that someone might harm the donkey from spite, she felt somewhat reassured knowing that a British journalist was mingling incognito in the village, spending the night there and watching out for the donkey. The donkey would have at least one friend in the village that night.

Back at the Parador in Jarandilla, journalists from the *Sun*, the *Daily Mail* and the BBC were checking in, and another journalist from the *Star* had arrived. There were incessant calls from print media and radio stations from the UK, demanding an interview with Vicki. The *Star* people would not allow her to speak to any other publication, but she was allowed to do short radio interviews without giving out much information.

Travellers to Southern European countries know all too well that food and drink can make you ill. Vicki and her entourage had been offered refreshments in the bar with the elders. Their polite acceptance soon took its toll in the form of stomach cramps and diarrhoea that evening. Of course, they could not prove anything, but they suspected that something had been added to their food.

Vicki hardly slept that night, afraid of what might happen the next day. Should the many death threats received at the hotel be taken seriously? On the way back to the village the next morning, workers in the fields stopped working and stared at them. Some even shook their fists. The centre of the village was packed and the previous day's stench was even stronger. When they reached the town square, the donkey had already been taken into the town hall – a rather undistinguished little building with a tiny lobby. There, according to press witnesses, the donkey had three bottles of spirits forced down his throat and was generally knocked about. This year, apparently to make a point, a thin, angular man had mounted the animal. In former years it was reported that the chosen rider was the heaviest man in the village.

The women and the band wore very colourful costumes, while the men surrounding the donkey wore blue smocks. Nearly all the men were armed with medieval-type weapons, such as cudgels, halberds, or billhooks. Normally a long rope, knotted at intervals, would be attached to the donkey's neck and it would then be dragged through the village by some hundred to one hundred and fifty youths. This year, the rope was not attached to the donkey, but carried around by the youths.

It was barely possible to see the donkey in the crowd, but Hugh Whittow from the *Sun* managed to squeeze through the crush. Fearing for his own safety, he joined in the leaping and chanting and was able to see that the men closest to the donkey seemed to function as security guards. They were armed with clubs and tried to fend off the crowd's attacks on the donkey. But firecrackers were still being thrown beneath the terrified animal and shotguns fired close to his ears. The donkey's legs were repeatedly kicked, causing him to collapse several times before being rudely yanked back to his feet. He was pushed and shoved through the narrow streets for at least an hour and a half.

Vicki's attempts to follow closely, were hampered by the village youths' hostile behaviour. At one point they charged at her with the rope. Luckily, an elder intervened and they let her go. The procession eventually made it back to the town square, where the crowd tried to snatch the yellow vinyl poncho from the rider. His face was blackened and he wore dark sunglasses and a pair of huge wooden dentures. Once the poncho was off, the fiesta was over and the donkey was led back inside the town hall. He seemed to be uninjured, but was covered in sweat and visibly shaking.

A young couple in normal dress introduced themselves to Vicki as Spanish animal rights people and told her that what she had witnessed that day was not authentic, being arranged to mislead the international observers. In previous years the donkeys had suffered far more, so much so, that, if they did not die in the fiesta, they invariably died a few hours later. The greatest problem was finding a way to discredit the lies the authorities spread around. Several villagers told a similar story. The previous week, no lesser person that the mayor's wife, when her husband had to take a phone call in another room, had confided to a journalist, "Do not believe that the donkey is not harmed. They do terrible things to it, but I dare say no more."

Vicki and the *Star* team set off to try and buy the donkey from its owner, Felix Cantalejo, who ran a small hostal and a beer kiosk at the top of a steep hill. He was also a donkey dealer and had bought 'Morenito' especially for this year's fiesta. He would now be sold on to a slaughterhouse. They waited in a bar, out of the way of the inflamed crowd, while Derek Ives from the *Star* negotiated the price of the animal. Stan Meagher suddenly rushed in. He had positioned himself outside the town hall to wait for the donkey to leave the building. Morenito had just left and was now on his way to a field outside the village, accompanied by the villagers, but protected by the many press people snapping pictures every second.

When they arrived, Felix Cantalejo had agreed to sell the donkey to the *Star* for fifty-five thousand pesetas (two hundred and eighty pounds). This, of course, was much more than he would have got from the slaughterhouse. However no money had yet changed hands, as the journalists were short of cash. So Vicki lent them forty-two thousand pesetas. The cash was handed over and a bill of sale given to the *Star*. Morenito's name was translated into English and Blackie the donkey made history.

But this is not where the story ends. Suddenly the *Sun* people waved a paper in front of the cameras bearing Cantalejo's signature, claiming they had bought the donkey. As so often with tabloid journalism this was not strictly true. It was Cantalejo's signature, but he had done some extra business by making them pay for taking Blackie's picture. This was enough for the *Sun* to raise doubts about the true ownership. The battle for the claim of who had saved Blackie, and the plot to cut Vicki out of the story, had begun!

Vicki and the *Star* people managed to drive to Cantalejo's place without being followed by the *Sun* team and other journalists. When Cantalejo brought Blackie out of a barn, he punched him repeatedly to make him hold his head up. The donkey seemed to have recovered a little and Vicki had her picture taken with him. One picture showed a smiling Vicki leading Blackie down a lane together with *Star* reporter Don Mackay. Under the headline "Off to a New Life" this picture appeared in the paper the next day. There was also a box entitled: "The Facts Not the Fiction – Other newspapers may try to claim the credit. They may even say *they* have bought Blackie. Don't believe a word of it. They are just a bunch of jack-asses …" The *Sun*, however, claimed: "We Save Blackie". They too carried a picture of Vicki, but did not show her with the donkey. Instead, there was a picture of reporter Hugh Whittow with a donkey of the wrong colour being ridden by children. As in the *Star*, she was quoted as thanking the *Sun* for bringing Blackie to safety, which, of course, was not true. Surprised at the competition between the two papers, she had diplomatically thanked everybody involved.

Meanwhile, a village youth, who had been very prominent in their rough treatment, arrived at the place with his girlfriend. He pointed at Vicki and started shouting verbal abuse. He was angry with her for accusing the village of treating donkeys cruelly. His girlfriend eventually managed to calm him down, but he continued to shout at Vicki from a wall to which he had retreated.

Vicki had thought they would take Blackie with them to a stable in Jarandilla. "I was worried that the youth in his drunken temper at the donkey killing being thwarted, would in some way try and harm him at a later time, and tried to impress on Don Mackay the need to remove Blackie from the environs of the village at once." She and the photographer volunteered to stay with him until he had rested and then walk him the few kilometres to Jarandilla. But Don Mackay was becoming paranoid, fearful lest the *Sun* should try to kidnap the donkey on the way. Vicki offered to pay for his transportation that afternoon, so that he would be out of reach of the villagers by nightfall. But to no avail! She was told he would be taken to Jarandilla the next morning.

After a restless night and eager to see Blackie, she went to meet the *Star* people and found the atmosphere considerably altered. They refused to tell her the animal's whereabouts, saying the *Sun* team had been lurking outside the barn in the early morning. In a car chase, they were tricked into going in the opposite direction, while Blackie was brought to Jarandilla.

Vicki had not come all this way and risked her life for this farce. "I found it rather strange, ridiculous, that his well-being should rely on the efforts of journalists who hardly knew one end of an animal from another, whilst I who have spent twelve years of my life involved in the care of animals, was totally prevented from seeing him. I asked them to be careful not to overfeed him, and to watch the condition of his bowels. This last they received with great amusement. I tried to explain the harm that can be done by overstuffing the wrong quantity and type of food into an animal that has existed in semi-starvation."

Back in Southport, Tony waited for news. When radio and television widely reported the fiesta, he understood that Vicki had managed to get out safely and that the donkey now needed a home. He contacted his Southport RSPCA branch and it was agreed that Blackie could live in Southport. The local RSPCA inspector agreed to go to Spain and deal with the formalities. Tony rang everybody he could think of who could help finance the trip, but a few hours later he had a call from the inspector, saying that he had been in touch with RSPCA headquarters to arrange his absence and they had forbidden the trip because it was too delicate and political a situation. They did not want to get involved. Mike Smithson, campaigns director at the RSPCA, put it like this on BBC Radio 4: "Well, we are occasionally faced with very, very difficult choices, as in the case of Blackie the donkey in Spain. We looked at this and we felt, our vets felt, that the best thing for this donkey was for it to stay in its natural environment in Spain provided their were proper controls for it, eating the diet that it knew and so on."

Tony felt disappointed and let down. Since the *Star* wanted to bring Blackie to England, he suggested the Devon Donkey Sanctuary, which had sponsored part of the trip. When Don MacKay heard this, he was furious. "Who the f****** hell are they?" he exclaimed, adding that it was no longer urgent that Blackie make it to England quickly. Someone had come up with a wild scheme to have Blackie travel around the Spanish holiday resorts carrying an advertisement for the newspaper. Vicki nearly lost it when she heard this. She would never let this happen and threatened the *Star* with the worst publicity they had ever had, should they go ahead. The plan was abandoned.

The *Star* managed to keep Vicki isolated during her last few days in Spain, held virtually incommunicado by Don Mackay, who even intercepted and diverted her phone calls. Even Tony was prevented from speaking to her on one occasion. When he found out what was going on, he made a very explicit phone call to their Manchester office and from then on the situation improved considerably. At this point Vicki wrote, "To summarise, I must concede that despite the unfortunate element of Fleet Street journalistic practices that manifested themselves after the fiesta, on the day prior to and during Pero Palo itself, the *Star* team played a very courageous and helpful role in the rescue of Blackie, and rendered me the greatest assistance to this end." Little did she know that she was merely a pawn in their attempt to beat other newspapers and as such was now considered an obstacle rather than an asset.

She did manage to discover Blackie's whereabouts, hidden away from the *Sun* in a little stable. She even managed to escape the constant supervision of the journalists to see him twice. He seemed to be doing fine. Two employees of the Donkey Sanctuary were en route, and would take Blackie to a farm near Madrid, while he waited for his travel permit. She was not allowed to meet the inspectors, nor could she find out the farm's exact location.

The *Sun*, meanwhile, had started a campaign to keep Blackie in Spain. With the customary misspelling of foreign names, they wrote:

*The Sun had paid farmer Felix Contalato £250 to give the donkey a good life. But another newspaper then bought Blackie with the aim of bringing him to England – in defiance of animal experts who said it would be cruel to make him leave his homeland. You can join the Sun's campaign to keep little Blackie in his native land. Show the world you don't want any unfeeling newspapers dragging him away from the home he loves by sending for your own FREE 'Keep Blackie in Spain' badge ...*

A few days later, on the *Pamela Armstrong Show*, the editors of both newspapers engaged in a fierce fight over Blackie, a battle which would continue for some time and allegedly even resulted in a fist fight in a Fleet Street pub and the firing of one of the journalists involved. *Time* magazine even picked up the story:

*Although the claim of donkeycide was hotly denied by villagers, Fleet Street papers outdid one another to 'save' this year's donkey ... commented the daily Independent, which had stayed out of the great donkey stakes: 'Fleet Street's Finest Finally Save their Ass'.*

In a letter to Vicki dated 1 May 1987, *Star* deputy editor R A J Mills wrote:

*... it is a suitable time to thank you for all your help and co-operation during the protracted negotiations to get Blackie back to Britain. I am sure you found it something of a revelation, and I can tell you that even in the sometime cynical newspaper industry, the case of Blackie has been unique. I have no doubt you watched the situation with increasing amusement and amazement as The Sun desperately tried to claim the credit. You now have an insight into the reality of tabloid newspaper competition, and I hope you don't think too badly of us as a result. But at the end of the day the only thing that matters is that Blackie is now safe and sound in Devon, and I am sure you will agree that the ends more than justify the means. On behalf of Don McKay, Stan Meagher and The Star, I would like to thank you again for all your assistance during this extraordinary episode.*

And so Vicki returned to Southport and waited for Blackie to come to England. Tony made repeated calls to the Donkey Sanctuary to find out what was going on. There was a problem with African Horse Sickness in Spain, even though this did not really affect donkeys, and he was promised they would be told when Blackie was coming to England. When the phone call finally came, towards the end of April, there was no way they could make it on time; a rather obvious and deliberate ploy to keep them away. It worked! The *Star* turned the donkey's arrival into a huge media event. Emblazoned on his red travel rug were the words 'Blackie' and '*The Star*'. The *Southport Star* reported on this manoeuvre, "Despite Vicki risking her life to rescue him, the Donkey Sanctuary in Devon, where Blackie is staying, didn't bother to invite her to attend the welcoming celebrations." Vicki was delighted that he was safe and well, but would have dearly loved to have been there to welcome him.

As promised, Vicki typed her report about her stay in Villanueva de la Vera and sent it to the sanctuary. She also forwarded a donation which someone had sent for Blackie, thinking that would be the end of the matter. She was wrong! In a rather peculiar thankyou letter from headquarters, dated 6 May 1987, the circumstances surrounding Blackie's arrival were described to her as follows:

*As you know, The Star had asked to accompany us, to which we had agreed, and they were insistent that no one else was invited and I found them very difficult people indeed to work with. I am sure you will appreciate my problems on this score. We had what could nicely be described as a 'few words' with regard to a press release that I was putting out and which they were almost fanatical in trying to prevent, unsuccessfully, may I add, as we required more publicity than that given by The Star, which tended to give credit to nobody – yourself, ourselves included – except their own two people and paper.*

In a letter to one of their supporters, the manipulations of the *Star* were described even more explicitly:

> ... *The Star wanted to be totally involved in Blackie's return and as they had purchased him and passed to us, we felt this only fair and they insisted on total secrecy for Blackie's sake. They specifically asked that Vicki Moore not be asked, as this would draw the press attention to Blackie's imminent return...*

In both letters the charity complained of not being mentioned enough by Vicki in the media, even though she had done her very best under trying circumstances to promote them. This first foray into direct action to stop animal cruelty had taught her some hard lessons about the duplicity of the press and the risks, as well as the benefits, of dealing with organisations concerned with animal welfare. She would need support from many different sources to effectively carry out what would soon become her's and Tony's campaign, but experiences in Villanueva and back home, would make her far more wary of offers of help in the future.

# Baptism of Fire

Scribbled on the July page of Vicki's personal organiser is the famous Gandhi quote: "The greatness of a nation and its moral progress can be judged by the way its animals are treated." Having been made aware by Spanish animal rights people that any conceivable species was used in Spanish village festivities, they felt it right to draw the world's attention, not only to the plight of the donkeys in Villanueva, but to any animals abused in a similar way. They sought the involvement of several large British charities, some of whom also operate internationally, but were told they were wasting their time in Spain. They talked things over for months, feeling a strong urge to do something, but knowing that once they had started down that track, they would be unable to stop. After much soul searching, they finally made the life-changing decision. In August 1987, they formed FAACE – Fight Against Animal Cruelty in Europe, as a platform from which to work. First, they had to obtain clear photographic evidence and make accurate reports on what they saw. They dreaded the idea, but knew that this evidence gathering would be vital.

The newly founded charity hit the headlines right away. As early as July 1987, the British and Spanish had been fed with news of a bull fiesta in the town of Segorbe, 50km inland from Valencia. Vicki had been asked by ADDA to highlight the plight of the 'toros embolados'. These fighting bulls were released into the streets with balls of fire attached to their horns and then tormented by young men. On the first day of September, Vicki flew to Spain for her 'second solo mission', as the media put it. "Bull Burning Señors Sicken Vicki", wrote the *Liverpool Echo*. It was hard to believe that this could be legal, even in Spain. Yet, according to official statistics, there were approximately 2,400 'traditional' fiestas involving cattle in the area of Valencia, Alicante and Castellón alone. The *Southport Visiter* spoke of "an underground sport that sets live bulls on fire for fun".

Vicki was unsure of what to expect. As in Villanueva de la Vera she hoped to be able to talk some sense into Segorbe's Mayor, Miguel Angel González. This was naïve, because on the day prior to her trip, *The People*, in an effort to help, had published a fierce attack on the fiesta. Strong quotes were put into Vicki's mouth: "Time to expose savage señors … They can call me a crank or whatever, but I intend to embarrass them until they stop … I plan to shame every mayor, in every village, into stopping these cruel practices."

News of the article had travelled to Segorbe, which explained her rather frosty reception by the mayor. Although incredulous that people in Britain should care so much about animals, it was obvious that he and the council had been greatly disturbed by the international attention focused on them. He diversified into all sorts of irrelevancies, "Why do you care about mere animals when there are so many other problems? And the way you've treated your colonies ..." Vicki reminded him that the Spanish colonial record wasn't too healthy either. He was also aware of her call for a tourism boycott and had received a massive pile of letters from Great Britain which he had shown to the townspeople and the council. Some of them were very strong; the 'may-you-burn-in-hell' variety, but Vicki was thinking, great! Well done everybody!

With ill-concealed annoyance, he explained to her and Bob Mayer, the Dutch animal rights man who acted as translator in the meeting, that a 'protective cup' would be used underneath the balls of tar to prevent the animal's eyes and skin from being burnt by molten substances. He also promised that the 'wild element' in the population would be prevented from attacking the animals.

On leaving the meeting, she was approached by American journalist Larry Mangino, who asked whether he could accompany her during her stay. With her previous experiences of journalists fresh in her mind, she saw this as a complication in which she was not particularly interested. A photojournalist, she had spoken to him on the phone a couple of times after being given his number, but there had been no arrangement for him to meet her, but since he was already here, she agreed, hoping a little publicity might help her cause.

The fire bull was not the main event in Segorbe, which is principally known for its cattle drive from horseback. The fire bull had only been integrated into the fiesta in 1981. Fiestas meant crowds, and crowds meant a lack of control on behalf of the authorities, which is why many fiestas all over Spain had been banned during the Franco era. Since this year's fire bull would only take place two nights later, Vicki decided to travel incognito to two other villages in the Valencia area to try and find out about their fiestas. The first of these was Farnals, where she was shocked to see a small herd of calves being run through the streets by children. Firecrackers were thrown at them, they were beaten and had dust kicked in their eyes. The little animals huddled together in terror. Their bowels turned to water with fear and they lost all control of them. Eventually, they were driven, shaking and distressed, into a cattle wagon. She could not understand that while all this was happening, bars and restaurants and squares were full of people having a good time. Could nobody see that this was wrong?

Shortly before midnight preparations for the fire bull started. The bull was in a small box-like crate. Youths from two local 'peñas taurinas' (bullfighting clubs) sat on top of the crate. From all sides men kicked and banged the crate, apparently warming up for this part of the fiesta. Finally, the animal was dragged out and tied to a pole, which took quite a while with the bull trying to resist the crowd. The ball contraption was attached to his head, then lit and the bull cut loose – the signal for the crowds to run for shelter. The animal was driven through the dark streets by sticks and firecrackers.

Armed with a cheap compact camera, Vicki, who was terrified of cattle, suddenly found herself running after a bull on the loose in the narrow streets. She inched closer and closer, until she was within two or three yards of him. She regretted her technical limitations and those of her camera with its weak localised flash, but it was all they could afford. She observed the villagers using poles studded with nails. They considered it great fun to goad the animal into charging against walls and barriers, thus injuring himself even more. "Suddenly goaded into movement by a spiked pole thrust into his anus, the bull, with a contraction of pain, rushed forward. I was swept along with the men. The street was narrow, the houses crowded in on either side. The animal was very close on our heels. I and several men round me looked in vain for a safe perch, nothing. Suddenly, a large door into a storeroom lobby was opened to admit us. We piled in. Before the door was closed the bull thrust his shoulders through. The bare whitewashed entrance was illuminated by the flames springing from his head. He too had thought he could escape from his suffering on the streets. The men, who numbered some half a dozen, were straining every muscle as they somehow managed to push him out with the door and then closed and barred it against him. It was a heart-stopping struggle … In those seconds I visualised the carnage there would be if the animal got into this confined space. Maddened by pain and terror as he was, some of us could die."

When it was clear the bull had left, the men opened the door and ran after it. Except for one, a heavy older man, who tried to prevent Vicki from leaving the room and started to grope her. She reacted quickly, kneeing him in the groin and breaking free. "Shaking a bit from this episode, I left the main street of the baiting and turned into a little side alley. There I rested my back against the wall of a house and shut my eyes. Suddenly I smelt smoke and within a second or so the bull was in the alley – he and I, face to face. What should I do? I thought, don't make any sudden movement, pressing back against the wall hardly breathing, I tried to direct my thoughts to him, not to think of me as an obstacle, or a cause of pain, I was his friend and my heart twisted with pain that I could not help him. The poor animal ran past me as though he had not noticed I was there, shortly followed by his pursuers. They say that if you are in such a predicament the best thing is to lie on your stomach and protect your head. If there are such beings as guardian angels I think mine was on duty. The young bull did not have such luck."

After nearly four hours the bull was no longer good sport. The attacks grew in savagery by the minute; burning shirts and cloths were draped over his head to augment the dying flames of the tar balls that were billowing vast clouds of acrid smoke … and the crowd started to stone him. Large chunks of concrete were hurled from balconies and roofs, in addition to missiles from the streets. The animal could barely stand. To drive the bull back to the crate a thin steer was used, a typical strategy when the bull is not killed on the spot, and which exploits the herd instinct. The bull tends to follow the steer, which seems to know exactly where to go. This 'knowledge' is usually acquired by a huge amount of beating.

Anyone who has spent a night like Vicki, running with the crowd in a dark and unknown village, knows how exhausting it is. It is difficult to assess who is more dangerous, the animal or the crowds. They drove in virtual silence back to Valencia, her American companion for once short of a wisecrack. In her hot and stuffy little hotel room, she slumped on to the bed and sat for a long time with her head in her hands, feeling degraded and mentally raped by what she had seen.

The next morning Tony called her at the hotel and was shocked by what he heard. It was unbelievable, unimaginable, really. And he was worried for her safety.

With time to kill until the evening's fiesta in the village of Canet, Vicki decided she had to get out of her hotel. She strolled around Valencia for quite a while, but time dragged in the suffocating heat, so she decided to head for the coast. She took a train to Sagunto, a short train ride north of Valencia. "Getting out at the bare little station at Sagunto, I was glad I had decided to spend some time seeing other things and directing my mind away from the miserable hours the night would bring. In a small plaza near the station stood a few trees bearing dusty out-of-season oranges. To a Spaniard they would be poor things out of time and condition, but I found them delightful. To this day for me there is always something intensely wonderful about seeing oranges and figs, lemons and olives growing on trees, instead of being neatly set in rows or jars, or tissue-wrapped in shops."

However, Vicki could not simply switch off her conscience and just enjoy the impressive surroundings. It was siesta time, when Spain goes dead in the stupefying heat. Nobody was on the street, the shops all closed and shuttered. An all too familiar sound broke the silence; a miserable 'meow' sounded two or three times from across the street. A cat in distress! In no time Vicki located the little cat, high up on a balcony, locked out of the house, with no shade from the blazing sun. The house looked deserted, the shutters all drawn. Vicki rang the doorbell. No answer. She knocked. No answer. She rang the doorbells of the neighbouring houses. No answer. She assumed the cat's owners had just gone out for the afternoon. She would return later to make sure it was all right.

Vicki resumed her sightseeing, but could not get the little cat out of her head and when she checked on the animal again, it was still there. Now there were people in the streets, but neither the owners nor the neighbours had returned. It dawned on Vicki that there might not be anyone around until the next day, when shops would open regularly. Speaking virtually no Spanish, she knew she would not get anywhere here, so she decided to go back to Valencia where she had arranged to meet the animal rights people for the evening's fire bull fiesta. They would have to come back with her for the little cat.

When they returned to Sagunto, daylight was already fading. Vicki, who was terrified of heights, tried to borrow a ladder from a nearby construction site but it was too short. They went to the police who agreed to assist by writing a report for the fire brigade, but not until the next day, adding a warning that their ladders must not be used for such a 'trivial purpose' anyway. He knew about the owner and his whereabouts but chose not to be of further assistance.

Saddened and frustrated, she worked out a way to at least leave some liquid for the cat by throwing a cup of ice-cream on to the balcony, which would melt in the heat. She was determined to come back the next day.

The fire bull fiesta in Canet was equally as appalling as the previous night's, the only difference being the strange decorations. Dummies resembling humans but bearing animal heads were suspended along the streets, controlled by ropes from houses on either side. "As he [the bull] ran through the streets, the dummies were lowered on to his back. The animal went frantic trying to dislodge them to the uproarious amusement of the crowd.' His life ended in a shed amid the sound of firecrackers, shouting and laughter from inside.

Vicki spent another sad and sleepless night. The little cat in Sagunto was on her mind too. Her stamina would be seriously tested in this case. "It took another two days of phone calls to Madrid, and England, a couple of more trips to Sagunto, and finally calls to the Spanish Embassy in London by a British national newspaper before the cat was rescued by the fire brigade from the balcony. Being ever the doubting Thomas, I went back to check. The cat was no longer incarcerated up there."

Back in Segorbe she was met by the mayor, who fidgeted nervously. The townspeople were aware of the presence of animal rights observers and the hostility was palpable. Vicki and her companions Pilar Alvarez from ADDA and Marisa Martínez from ALA, were denied free movement in the village, and forced to observe from a stand. The mayor never left their side, which was passed off as a measure to guarantee her safety, but of course she did not buy that. Unbeknown to the mayor, they had secretly positioned their people in different locations.

At thirty minutes before midnight, the bull arrived in a trailer. A rocket was shot into the sky and the animal was dragged out. A heavy collar bedecked with bells and colourful ribbons had already been attached to his neck. It took quite a while to tie the bull to the post and secure the tar ball contraption and the mayor conceded that the animal might suffer a little at this point. Vicki scrutinised the protective cups, which she deemed inadequate.

The two hours the bull endured on the streets were gruelling, despite being given water and people being prevented from abusing him with blow darts. When he was finally locked back in his pen, Vicki reminded the mayor of his promise to let her inspect the animal. He was hesitant, this was not a good idea, the crowd seemed too hostile. "I persisted and insisted, and reminded him that he had given his word. He stood up and led the way down. We clambered down as unceremoniously as we had climbed up and were very much aware of the quietly seething hostility. My heart was beating fast when I confronted the bull from behind a callejón-type screen … I felt ashamed of my species, how dare we treat this noble and innocent creature as a living candelabra, to play bogeyman in an aberrant game for adult children. The sight of his short stocky legs and dusty worn hooves further moved my heart to pity. I asked his pardon in my heart and turned away."

Evaluating the three fire bull fiestas she had witnessed, Vicki came to the conclusion that international pressure and the official monitoring of the fiesta in Segorbe had made a difference. Although the animal had suffered because of the burning flames attached to his head, he was otherwise unharmed, but she felt very much betrayed when she learnt that there had been another fire bull in Segorbe the night before that had been killed. To get rid of her, the mayor had claimed they would have only one fire bull. She had fallen into the trap and gone to other places. She would never be that trustful again.

The American journalist managed to sell his article to Spain's magazine *Interviu*. Preceded by a lengthy article on Che Guevara, they dedicated several pages to Vicki and her work. Despite being several pages long, it was not a friendly piece, but rather cynical.

*Her first encounter with a fire bull took place in the village of Farnals (Valencia). The Farnalese don't quite know what to make of this lady in white, camera at the ready with a frightened expression on her face. She wanted to pass herself off as a tourist but Vicki Moore doesn't know how to pretend.*

Vicki was furious at this, because Larry Mangino actually blew her cover several times, trailing her in the villages and popping up in front of her taking pictures with his bright flash, trying, he said, to get candid shots. He did. His unflattering pictures show Vicki's face distorted with horror and disgust, her complexion as white as her dress.

Vicki took a living souvenir home from Segorbe. She told Red Rose Radio: "I was driving with a young woman from one of the Spanish animal welfare societies … through countryside not far from a town called Sagunto and we came across a group of youths. They had a little six-week-old kitten in their midst. They were throwing it from one to the other. They'd cut its tail in half and they were burning its little face with cigarettes. All its whiskers were gone and it had several nasty burns. We pitched in good style and got the kitten from them."

She got hold of the tortoise-shell kitten and put it down. It ran over to her handbag, which was on the ground and managed to crawl inside. Since the animal apparently had made the decision to stay with Vicki, they took her to the car.

Vicki christened her 'Alita', the diminutive of ALA, her friend's animal rights organisation. It also means 'little wing' and within a few weeks, Alita would take wing and travel to England. The *Liverpool Echo* celebrated her rescue with an article entitled "Saved from the Sadists".

Tony met Vicki at Manchester airport, very relieved to have her back. She was happy to be back home too, but she "was a puzzle of conflicting emotions. There was so much to learn, so much to try to analyse, we had so much work ahead and so much research to do."

Tony had her pictures developed. They were grainy and dark, but clearly showed what the animals had suffered. Meanwhile, Vicki opened her mail. There was a letter from Segorbe, "You speak of our bulls, but what about the ravens artificially maintained at the Tower of London?" And there was another letter from Spain. "Come at once, something important is going to happen at Tordesillas, it is vital you are there." She looked at the date. She would have to leave within three days. She looked at Tony, who took the letter and read it fully, "Well I suppose I'd better see if there is a cheap ticket at the travel agents."

# Run for Your Life

Tony somehow managed to scrape the money together for the trip. He had mixed feelings about it but felt a strong moral obligation. It was obvious that Vicki would not be welcomed with open arms in Tordesillas, so he argued that maybe he should go this time, but she would not be held back; her higher media profile would make it easier for her to expose the village.

On 14 September, she teamed up with some Spanish animal rights people in Madrid. They had to leave at 6.45am the next morning for the three-hour drive to Tordesillas, in the Valladolid province, north west of Madrid and they were there by 10 o'clock. There was little time to sightsee, or appreciate the town's historic significance. It was in Tordesillas that Queen Joan 'The Mad' (Reina Juana La Loca) of Castile and León spent the years after her husband, King Philip 'The Handsome's' sudden death, until her own death in 1555. The famous Treaty of Tordesillas was negotiated in 1494, settling a dispute about the possession of newly discovered and uncharted territories between Portugal and Spain. Prior to this, Spanish Pope Alexander VI's bull on navigation and conquest had divided the new territories, much to the advantage of Spain.

Had she come for any other reason, Vicki would have loved the town with its picturesque narrow streets and impressive bridge, over which the bull would be chased out of town. The fiesta is in honour of the Virgen de la Peña, and several bullfights and bull runs were scheduled to take place. The 'Toro de la Vega' is the main event and attracts huge crowds. By the time they arrived, thousands of people had already taken up positions, hoping to catch a glimpse of the bull. Being short, she had the advantage of being able to squeeze to the front, without blocking anyone's view. Her aim was to get photographic evidence. She had also taken a tape recorder, as FAACE did not yet have a video camera.

Back in her hotel room, with no one to talk to, she taped the following testimony of the event: "Already the streets through the town had been barricaded off. In a field on the left as one drove into the town on the main road there were the familiar barriers erected and people already beginning to trickle into the enclosure. Horses were brought out of boxes and groomed ... We endeavoured to liaise with the Italian and British journalists who were supposedly in town. Not to a very great effect. We decided the most important priority was to be in a good position to watch the fiesta itself. So we arranged ourselves in the field at about a quarter past ten, the fiesta being due to start at eleven ... Already people were rapidly filing in, with many peñas, the bullfighter clubs, taking a predominant position ... We saw many, many spears ... One group even had the sick idea of having a large teddy bear mascot, which they carried on their shoulders, and this was dressed in the same uniform [white and red] and even had a tinfoil covered spear.

"At ten past ten there were quite a lot of horses; I counted, at that point twenty, but this would double later on. And they were being ridden in, admittedly, a very elegant and easy style by the many caballeros, all, of course, armed with lances. The horses were beautifully cared for and seemed fit, very well groomed and I sincerely hoped that the pictures that I had seen on sale in town of a severely gored horse ... would not be re-enacted on this occasion. The number of people crowding into the field was well beyond what we had imagined. Farm trailers arrived, lorries, in fact any type of conveyance that could be pressed into carrying dozens and dozens and dozens of people and before long, the field was quite black with the crowd.

"Announcements on the tannoy were made, including one that warned the population to have some respect for the bull and not to bring dishonour on the brilliance of their tourney and fiesta. We heard very little of the bull and, in fact, 11 o'clock came and apart from petardos [rockets] being fired and the inevitable tannoy announcement, there didn't seem to be very much under way. People were by now climbing trees and finding places wherever they could for when the bull charged. I couldn't understand the delay, because normally these events seem to be reasonably punctual. Patricia came into the field and told us the delay had been caused by the fact that the bull had started to run through the town and had in some way – and she doesn't quite know how, but it must have been very, very tormented, or pushed into an awkward position – broken its leg, which is quite unusual for a bull, but nevertheless it had and it lay in the road in great agony. But they still goaded it and tried to get it to stand up and charge forward. They even attached ropes to its horns and tried to pull it. Many, many men were pulling on the ropes, but the bull kept falling back on its broken leg and screaming in agony. This went on for quite a few minutes until the order came to kill the bull and this was done without further ado by slitting its throat in the street.

"A second bull was driven through the streets in an encierro [bull run], by about forty horsemen, followed by maybe two thousand peña members, the youngest and fittest running with their spears. I caught a very good glimpse of the poor bull as he surged by in a choking cloud of dust, even though the whole atmosphere was so dense and dusty that for a few moments it was almost impossible to see more than a few yards. And the great fight at this moment was to try and keep up with the hordes of hooligans and the bull and also to keep your footing, because there seemed to be no constraints to this charge and people's safety was not taken into any form of consideration. Also, I had already caused some suspicion and was being pointed out as an 'ecologist', and I seemed to be being purposely jostled and tripped, making it very difficult to try and keep my tape going. I endeavoured to take the odd picture, although unfortunately I only had very few exposures on my camera and no extra film at this point and also needed to see what was happening to the bull.

"This was, of course, the main object of my whole mission, because I feel that I must see what happens in these things in order to give some form of testimony ... And this necessitated running and running and running. The terrain was very, very hard. They surged forward like Attila and his Huns and we tried, tried, tried to keep up with them over sand hills and scrubland, through pine woods and all the time the dreadful screaming and waiving spears ahead of us ... We kept up as well as we could. And all the time the crowd rushing towards the bull was growing. There was every type of weapon available on that field, from spears to lances and each with blades some eight or nine inches long and very broad. And in addition to these, there was every type of motley kitchen utensil, sharpened and honed, and tridents and even cut-throat razors on sticks and, of course, sharpened sticks and everybody had a few pockets full of stones and all manner of knotted and knarled clubs, walking sticks and canes. Everybody out of those thousands and thousands of people, including women, carried some form of weapon, but all the men were armed with things that were particularly lethal.

"Eventually, the bull was cornered two fields away and the end came pretty quickly for it, because no creature could survive being engulfed by thousands of men. They speared it first as far as I could tell, it is very difficult to tell, because they always form a protective barrier around the kill. The same old tactics; a great big rugby scrum around the action, that is, the killing. Men rushed in with various weapons to ensure that the animal was really cut into shreds. Before long there were dozens and dozens of weapons caked and oozing with blood. The animal must have received myriad and myriad wounds. The body, even before they had pulled themselves together after the kill, was immediately removed into a lorry – a trailer with built-up sides – of course the leading members of the peñas climbed in and appeared to be sitting and jumping and dancing about on the corpse of the poor bull. Blood was running from the tailboard of the lorry and of course blood soaked everywhere in the field ...'

On her way back to the town Vicki noted "a strange feeling of anti-climax about everything. Bloody weapons, spears, sticks, all dripping blood and at the killing place large red smears in the grass. Does it really benefit them in anyway? Sand – blood – and a dead animal. Their idea of a fiesta."

They had planned to go to the slaugtherhouse, but no longer dared after having witnessed the extremely violent behaviour of those involved. At the hotel Vicki sighed when she spoke into her tape recorder, "It always seems so exceedingly pointless and left a very sordid and unpleasant taste in my mouth. I think it really is a tragedy, not only for the bull, but for his opponents and protagonists, because the animal has no chance whatsoever. The bull is so disorientated and terrified and just overwhelmed by the extraordinary number of people that attack it. It's not hundreds, it's thousands! And, of course, the accompanying noise and disturbance. The animal is really just looking for a way out, any way out. Once the animal is killed and loaded up on to the lorry, it's taken through the town and its testicles paraded.

"Then there is the corrida in the afternoon, in which six or more bulls will die and then perhaps at the end of it all, as the moon rides high in the sky, Tordesillas will go to sleep. I don't suppose they even have nightmares. Those are probably reserved for people like me. It's a very sad and sordid tacky sort of business, to see people treating the death of an animal in such a light and unconcerned manner. It is not just the death of an animal, it's the death of their own decency, really.

"It is very difficult to get anything going with the press at this end, as they all seem to be intimidated by the small hierarchy of bullfighting mafiosos. I laughed when I first heard them called that, but I think it's an exceedingly appropriate name." But her trip did capture the interest of the media back home. BBC Radio Merseyside reported all day long, and the *Daily Star* ran the story under the headline "And They Call This Fun". Thousands of their readers jammed their switchboard, expressing their disgust. So they decided to run another piece for which they contacted Euro MP Madron Seligman, who was hopeful that the exposure would lead to a change in the law. "Thanks to the *Daily Star*, I think we'll soon see the end of this barbarism."

She was wrong. In September 2002, fifteen years later, Tony, his friend Billy Johnson who ran his own video production company in Southport, and myself, attended the same fiesta. It was exactly as Vicki had described it. Fifty thousand people baying for blood and the same open hostility to strangers. There is no protection from the special police unit, the Seprona, either. Even though the agents told the Spanish television that they think what happens is barbaric and disgusting, they don't get involved in any way but merely monitor the event.

I was prevented from taking video footage of the actual killing, because, "It was not dignified to film the dead bull", as the president of the Patronato de la Vega, the club that promotes and runs the event, told me on the field, blood stains all over his white outfit. One does not argue with a man with a deadly lance in his hand, closely surrounded by fifty equally armed men on foot or on horseback. Billy, who is in good shape and not easily frightened, described his experience, "I was genuinely worried that I'd be lynched ... There was a hostile atmosphere about the town and I kept getting told to move from a vantage point I'd taken up for the filming ... I was sickened when I witnessed the locals kill the bull and then mutilate it. They chopped off his testicles and towed his body away like rubbish."

Apart from getting into trouble with the crowd, Billy nearly got into trouble with Morenito, the bull. Since he did not speak Spanish, we thought it safer for him to stay behind in town, rather than enter the field, because, surprisingly, even people who are actively involved in sadistic animal abuse warn members of their own species, when they think one of them might get into trouble. Billy would have been unable to understand those warnings. However, once the bull was through, Billy followed the crowd on to the field. He did not run after the bull to get good pictures, but was taking his time, when, suddenly, something crashed into the small pine tree just a few inches in front of him. It was Morenito with the end of a broken spear sticking out of his body. Terrified and disorientated, he was seeking shelter. He was in mortal danger, but the wounded animal seemed to sense that he meant no harm. Staying calm, he continued filming with his huge television camera. The mere thought of what might have happened to him was shocking when we saw his footage.

Tony, as usual, was close to the action too. Being quite tall, he held his camera up high and clicked away, getting the much desired pictures, while I was singled out as a foreigner by a reporter of a regional radio station. He wanted to know what I thought about the fiesta. Bearing in mind that the interview was going out live and we still had to get away safely with our footage, I spoke in neutral terms, even though I felt like hurling insult after insult at the participants and bystanders. Back at home, Tony and Billy's people created a video about the fiesta, in which Vicki still plays a part. The impressive opening shot of the bloodstained spearheads up in the air is a picture taken by her.

Considering it her duty to get the story out, Vicki continued to give interviews. When she spoke on Red Rose Radio, the presenter observed that she was still haunted by her memories of Tordesillas, "I can see the pictures going through your mind as you're talking to me. I mean, you've obviously come back very angry. Depressed as well?"

"Yes, depressed to an extent but very, very angry and very disgusted …"

"So, what's your next step? I bet everybody asks you that, don't they? When you're going back? What you're going to do next?" From the tone of his voice it was obvious he was desperate for her to tell a cheerful story for a change. Vicki obliged.

"I may be due back in Spain in a couple of weeks, but on a more personal note, to do with a little kitten I rescued while I was over there, which had a very nasty beginning. Obviously you could collect kittens, puppies, dogs and cats in a terrible state on the streets of Spain any minute. Domestic animal problems over there are horrific as well, even throwing stray dogs into the grinding machines of dust carts; a sort of municipal policy for cleaning up stray dogs. But I knew this little kitten was a bit different. I couldn't leave her. She was tiny, she could hardly get around at all. So she's had veterinary treatment in Madrid and she's being looked after there by animal welfare people. But unfortunately they can't keep her indefinitely, so she's going into quarantine in Chester and I'm hoping to get her back shortly."

On 7 October 1987 Alita arrived in London. Vicki had insisted that she be transported by British Airways, even though it meant a higher fare, because rumour had it that the Spanish airline Iberia had lost pets during travel. A day later, the kitten arrived at Chester, where she would spend the following six months. At that time, Great Britain still had severe regulations for importing pets. They had to go into quarantine until it was clear they carried no contagious disease; rabies being the biggest fear. That meant that once a week, for half a year, the couple made the journey to Chester to visit Alita. When Tony met her for the first time, he forgot all the expense of bringing her into the country, as she put her little paws in his beard and looked him directly in the eyes. She pulled his head down and pushed her face into his.

Meanwhile, the Spanish animal rights people asked for Vicki's support once again. On 20 November, despite death threats, she participated in a three-day conference on bullfighting in Mallorca, organised by ADDA, which excited media interest. Roger Phillips, of BBC Radio Merseyside, questioned her on the phone, "There may be some people who might say, why don't you spend your time campaigning against the cruelties and tortures that go on against people rather than animals?"

Vicki, by now used to that question, replied, "You could also say why do people fight for trees and the environment, why do they fight for ideologies and philosophy and art. Animals are a very important part of our planet and we've abused them for far too long and it is time that we all now try to rectify our past mistakes."

Did she think there was some truth in the argument, that if one can be cruel to animals, it makes it that much easier to be cruel to people? Vicki was prepared for that question too, "Normally cruelty to animals and cruelty to children and people are interrelated. Cruelty has no boundaries. Somebody who will be cruel to an animal will continue this attitude to people. So really, promoting a humanitarian and caring attitude to all creatures is very important."

Another common question which Vicki was asked back home, was what the Spanish government felt about her going over there and interfering with their traditions and some of their ancient ceremonies. Should she be doing that? She did not have to think long, "Well, they're not really such ancient ceremonies, the fiestas. These are just modern exploits of hooliganism. The authorities are exceedingly embarrassed that their skeletons are coming out of the cupboard and their dirty secrets, you know, are discovered. I think that it was very necessary that we interfered, just as it was to help the children in Ethiopia that were starving and I wished to heavens that perhaps we had interfered to help the Jews in Germany prior to the last war and then we wouldn't have had the Holocaust. No, I think the world's a global village now and we've got to help each other."

After such a fast-paced year, that had changed their lives so drastically and which had demanded so much physical and psychological effort, Vicki and Tony looked forward to a quiet Christmas with their large feline and canine family and a quiet transition into 1988, but it would not remain quiet for long.

# Spanish Lessons

The bad publicity that Blackie the donkey had brought to Villanueva de la Vera, had failed to impress the villagers, who were determined to use another donkey in the festivity of 1988. So Vicki decided to start the campaign early. On 12 January, about a month before the actual fiesta, she flew to Madrid and teamed up with Pilar Alvarez from ADDA. They went to see the Governor of the province of Cáceres, Angel Hernandez Craqui. In the hour-long meeting they were surprised to learn that Spain's President, Felipe Gonzalez, and the Minister of the Interior, in a telephone call to the governor, had expressed their concern about the fiesta. They had also mentioned two other fiestas in the area, those of Coria and Cuacos, which later would play an important part in Vicki and Tony's life. The governor said that he could not ban the fiesta, but assured his two visitors that he would take all necessary steps to protect the donkey, including sending in extra Civil Guard to ensure public order. He also thanked them for their work in endeavouring to reform the people's attitudes.

The next day they had an appointment with the new Mayor, Felix Perez Gonzalez. "A British woman is in Cáceres to protect the Pero Palo donkey," wrote the local newspaper *Hoy*. Pointing out that Vicki was thirty-three years old, the article went on disparagingly, "… she has not yet found enough time to have children and lives with two dogs and thirteen cats …" The journalist tried to convince Vicki that it was still common in Spain to use donkeys as beasts of burden and that the donkey in the fiesta would actually suffer less than many others. Vicki was quick to ask, "Do the people of Extremadura kill the donkey every year when working with them? Besides, the animal is led by its owner during work and not surrounded by all the villagers. It's a shame that those people have to prove that they are enjoying themselves by hitting the animal."

In the village they met with the deputy Mayor, Antonio Martin, who told them the town hall had been inundated with protest letters from all over the world. They would make every effort to return the fiesta to the way it had originally before the 'hooligan element' had taken over, which had resulted in terrible 'accidents' for the respective donkeys. He then took them to that year's fiesta organiser, Felix Mayoral Hernandez. He had bought Beauty, the donkey to be used in the fiesta, only two months before. "We eventually persuaded him to take us to meet Beauty and were taken into the mountains. When the track became impassible for our vehicle, we waited for Beauty to be brought down from her secret place. She is fifteen years old, brown coated, very similar to

Blackie in appearance and very gentle and sad ... She has a fallen crest which a veterinary surgeon assured me is caused by a sudden deterioration in condition at some point in her life, and this can happen in a few weeks."

Vicki took pictures of the animal and Hernandez. The atmosphere was cordial; they were asked into his home, took food and drink with the family and were officially invited to monitor the fiesta. Vicki left the village with the feeling of having made some progress. She wrote in her report, "This year there is to be an attempt to change the emphasis from the donkey part of the fiesta to a newly arranged song contest. If the interests of the participants can be nurtured along this new path, it will be a very great achievement for all concerned ... for me, it would be a wonderful culmination to a year of work which has fluctuated between hope and despair ... I will not be fully reassured until I have witnessed the fiesta take place and seen Beauty emerge unharmed."

Intending to make the most of her expenditures, Vicki wanted to check on the village of Cantalapiedra in the Salamanca province. She had heard that on 15 January cockerels would be used in a festivity. Due to a last minute change in schedule by the village, she missed the actual fiesta but described what she found: "The open field where this took place has a desolate and miserable appearance ... with churned up earth from the hoofs of the horses, and piles of bloodstained white feathers drifting in the wind."

A Civil Guard whose duty it was to monitor the fiesta, told her that seventeen live cockerels were suspended on a rope, while young men on horseback ripped off their heads. It had been horrible for him to watch and he called the villagers 'savages'. Since such activities were due to take place all over the area over the next few weeks, and Vicki realised it was urgent to apply pressure for an animal protection law.

The weeks prior to her return to Villanueva de la Vera were spent doing interviews, thus increasing the pressure on the village to keep their promise and behave themselves in the fiesta. There was also a forum on the problem of animal welfare throughout Europe to be organised. Euro MP Andrew Pearce and the RSPCA's international liaison officer, Ian Ferguson, were invited as guest speakers. Fund raising also needed to be addressed. Apart from Vicki giving a speech at a local Rotary Club, a fair for FAACE took place at the beginning of February. Vicki was pleased when the mayoress of the Borough of Sefton, Gwen Storey, gave a civic lunch in her honour. She supported Vicki's campaign with a letter to the Mayor of Villanueva de la Vera, in which she thanked him for any assistance he could give to Vicki.

Meanwhile, the Spanish Embassy in London was again flooded with letters from angry protesters. Those letters really hit home, as one can see from their standardised answer:

*In exactly the same way as letters addressed by Spaniards, or by Spanish Animal Protection Societies, to the British Embassy in Madrid would make little difference to British fox hunting, deer stalking, badger-baiting, hare coursing, organised dog fights, and other so-called sports, so, equally, letters sent to this embassy cannot eradicate age-old customs, particularly in remote country areas in Spain, where it may not even occur to the locals that cruelty to animals is involved, or that it is reprehensible in itself ... Furthermore, there, as here, pressure from abroad is resented, particularly where statistics show that the cruelty record of the country of the protester is, if anything, worse than that of the country protested against ... Again, many claims are ill-founded, simply invented by certain sections of the media, which make no retraction when shown to be wrong. Apparently, the sale of newspapers is a justified end in itself ... Furthermore, the wording of the greater number of protests is so crude and offensive against Spain and the Spanish people (which is counter-productive in itself), that again doubts are raised as to whether love of the animal may not be tainted with national, historical, or religious prejudice ...*

On 13 February Vicki was back in Villanueva de la Vera. By now her face was well known and, on the whole, she was treated in a friendly way. Early in the morning of the fiesta, however, she had a hunch that something was wrong. In a radio interview from her hotel she said, "... there is always the factor of the drunken youths in the village. And they have been drinking now for two days solidly. They were getting very, very tanked up last night and the whole atmosphere was winding up very drastically. So it only takes a little aggravation, something just flares up and then, you know, things could be very bad indeed. The atmosphere was not as co-operative yesterday as it has been up to that date. Whether the fact that there are a lot of the British media there and they have been in and out a lot ... certainly the attitude has changed. Yesterday it was verging on hostile, in fact, one man who spoke a little English came up to me and said: 'You must be very careful tomorrow, it's better people don't know who you are. Some people here don't like you.'"

She described Beauty as, "a nice old donkey, a very sad old thing." She also mentioned that if it was up to her and ADDA, Beauty would find sanctuary within Spain, should she be in trouble but she feared another British newspaper feud over the animal. What she did not know then, was that some troublemaker had circulated a copy of *The Daily Star* in the village the day before the fiesta. The newspaper, in order to keep up sales, had tried to create a situation. It published a scurrilous article containing a very unflattering picture of the donkey's owner, Felix Hernandez. "Beast Who Wants to Flog Beauty – When He's Dead", proclaimed the huge letters next to it. "Smirking señor, Felix Hernandez, is the beast masterminding a horrible death for Beauty the donkey ... 'Ees good fun, no?' grinned frightful Felix yesterday, as he swigged sweet Spanish wine, as sickly as his conscience … 'Perhaps,' he slobbered, a stream of wine dribbling down his chin, 'you buy Beauty from me after the carnival.'" But the paper assured its readers that it would continue to work towards a happy ending, "Many of the dirty dagoes are still furious with The *Star* for spoiling their fun last year with Blackie. Some of the local youths carry wooden clubs and have vowed revenge on the 'interfering Ingleesh gringos'. But despite the threats, rest assured that we will continue to do everything in our power to save Beauty from a grisly end." The villagers did not take such a personal and racist attack on Señor Hernandez lightly. When I met him in 2003, I found he was nowhere near the caricature the *Daily Star* had depicted. Instead, he accepted Tony's reason for being in the village and he and his wife remembered Vicki fondly, saying they were sorry about her death.

Vicki was furious about the newspaper literally putting her life at risk: "By printing some absolute rubbish about what the villagers intended to do to this year's donkey, and adding my photograph at the bottom to make it look like I'd said all this, they destroyed, in a matter of a few moments, the trust and goodwill that I'd built up in a year of visiting the village. But what sickened me most of all, was the fact that enough copies of those papers arrived in the village the day before the fiesta for certain people to see them and want their revenge."

Around lunchtime, British radio stations reported that Vicki had been attacked by angry villagers. The mayor had invited several animal rights people from the UK and other countries, however, Vicki was best known to the villagers. She was lifted off her feet and manhandled by a group of men. Several times someone tried to club her on the head and youths tried to entangle her and her friend Pilar with the rope and throw her into the fountain. Back in her hotel she told a radio station, "We were taking pictures of the donkey from the upstairs balcony and shots were fired directly at my face. They were screaming to push me out, 'We want her out! We want her out! We want to give her a souvenir of the village!' Their idea was to burn my face off."

Luckily, she had three guardian angels – young villagers, who saw what was about to happen and threw her backwards out of the way on to a bed. They had followed her around the village from the beginning of Beauty's rough ride and fended off several attacks. As shocked as Vicki was about what had happened to herself and Pilar, she was also glad, that even though Beauty was frightened and stressed out, she was not visibly injured. She took a moving picture of Beauty's former owner. The woman, with tears in her eyes, hugs the animal and is visibly relieved that Beauty had survived the ordeal relatively unharmed.

The next day the *Daily Star* claimed victory: "We Save Beauty from the Beasts. Cruel Señors Keep Pact with The *Star*." Other newspapers announced their victory too. "We Stop Señors Killing Donkey", wrote the Sun, still not reconciled to losing the previous year's battle, "The *Sun* rescued last year's victim Blackie".

The local papers joined in too: "Saved! Your Caring *Echo* Comes to the Rescue", wrote the *Liverpool Echo*. Tony was quoted: "They [the villagers] have given in to the pressure and it is thanks to the *Echo* ... Spaniards have been greeting her, saying 'You are Vicki. You are from land of the Beatles and we see your *Echo*'." All news to Tony, who is able to laugh about it.

Unfortunately, one victim did not escape death. Two nights prior to the fiesta, *Daily Star* reporter John Mahoney and photographer Tim Cornall visited the Tangara discotheque in Aldenueva de la Vera, another village in the Gredos region. At 2 o'clock in the morning, some youths brought a week old baby lamb, dressed up as Bo Peep, into the disco and started kicking it around like a football and beating it with a walking stick. "After witnessing the stomach-churning blood-lust, I snatched the stunned creature and dashed for the exit. In the uproar, *Star* photographer Tim Cornall had a camera knocked from his hand," wrote Mahoney. The youths managed to get hold of the lamb again and sped off in a car with the by now apparently dead animal.

Vicki flew home to England on Wednesday, 17 February, the same day the Catalonian Parliament passed the animal protection law, as she noted in her diary. Just three days later she was back on a plane again, this time to Rome, invited by the organisation, LIDA. During what she called the 'European Campaign', she met Italian animal rights people and was impressed by their activities at home and abroad. In the *Nino D'Amato Show*, on Italy's state television RAI, she spoke about her crusade against bullfighting and blood fiestas. She also did an interview for a documentary.

Back at home, in letters to newspapers, she was criticised by people who seemed to envy her sudden fame. Instead of travelling abroad, she should concentrate on British animal cruelty. Her response was: "If one were to impose physical boundaries on the work of helping animals, where would we draw the line? The next country, town, street, or back garden? I wonder where M Victoria de Lara [the sender of the complaint] was on 1 March. I was carrying the FAACE anti-coursing banner at the Waterloo cup at Altcar."

Indeed, barely back home, Vicki joined the preparations for the anti-hare coursing demo. While the Brits are famous, or infamous, around the globe for fox hunting, relatively little is known abroad about another British pastime involving the killing of animals: hare coursing. This might be because the image of a hare being ripped to pieces by two dogs is sickening to the majority of the British people. Not even the fox hunters seem comfortable being associated with the coursers and farmers do not want them on their land. When Vicki and Tony moved to Southport, it became an integral part of their lives, whether they liked it not.

Each year, in February or March, the biggest hare coursing event, the Waterloo Cup, took place on Lord Leverhulme's estate at Altcar, a few miles from Southport. They were alarmed by the rise in the number of spectators and the heavy betting that was going on at the event. West Merseyside Euro MP Ken Stewart echoed the attitude of the general public on Merseyside. "Here in my own constituency the barbaric custom of hare coursing still survives and apparently thrives. If a group of people were to gather in a public park and allow their pets to behave as the owners of these greyhounds encourage their animals to do, the RSPCA and the police would crack down on them with the full force of the law ... The British Government seems reluctant to act in these cases, I hope that my motion to the European Parliament in Strasbourg might embarrass them into action."

In 1985, a protester had suffered a fractured skull, so it was hoped that this year's demo would remain peaceful. However, twelve people were arrested when a group of protesters burst through the police cordon separating them from the coursers. Photographer Brian Pearson was beaten up by protesters who mistook him for a coursing fan and a female protester was trampled on by a police horse, needing hospital treatment for her leg. The problem was that the several hundred protesters were not one homogenous group. The plan to swell numbers by inviting sympathetic but autonomous political organisations backfired disastrously, as some were more radical than others, wearing balaclava masks and throwing smoke bombs and rotten eggs.

After approximately half an hour, the protesters were told to leave. About a hundred refused and sat down in the field. A protester, coincidentally also called Vicki, described their mood: "Eventually we were forced to leave before someone was injured. We all walked back to the buses feeling pretty sad, dejected and a bit defeated."

Following the violence, the League Against Cruel Sports issued a 'no more demos' proclamation and launched a tactical rethink on how any future anti-blood sports campaign should be conducted, because the few violent protesters were diverting attention from the cruelty inflicted on the hares.

Vicki, however, perceived the demo as fairly peaceful. "One group just stood there singing 'Bright Eyes', which was a very moving experience when viewed against such a background." The next day she rang into James Whale's phone-in show on Red Rose Radio. He had a lot of pro-hare coursing callers and she wanted to defend the protesters, "I've been rather amazed looking at the media reports in the various papers today. It's almost as if they were dealing with a different demonstration to the one that I witnessed."

The presenter was on the defensive: "I can never understand about people who want to go and demonstrate about anything, not realising what the media will do to somebody ... Someone's gonna hurl abuse at somebody and that's gonna be the bit that will get into the papers."

"I've had some experience with the media over this last year ... so I do understand what the media do," replied Vicki.

"Well, the media, I would've said, helped you no end in that ... I object also to you sort of wanting to fly the flag of being this wonderful crusading person ... I've been to some of these things and seen the gleam in the eye of the so-called demonstrators, who were there purely because that is their hobby. They enjoy it."

He recommended that they should all write letters instead and Vicki asked him if he denied the right to protest and the right of freedom of speech.

"Don't be pathetic. I didn't say that. You wanna twist my words I can twist your words, Daisy! If you wanna be that stupid, you can do it. But it seems to be a little pointless."

Vicki, trying to bring some facts to the discussion, reminded him that eighty per cent of the British population were against hare coursing.

"Well, I don't think eighty per cent of the British population know what hare coursing is. Unfortunately, I think you bring more attention to it and more publicity to it than it deserves."

Tony had warned Vicki to keep her cool, because he knew the presenter would try to provoke her. She managed to stay on for a long time, keeping the conversation focused on her issues and Whale gradually mellowed.

A week later Vicki had her first Spanish lesson. Even though some of the Spaniards she met spoke English, it seemed wise to become independent from interpreters. They could only afford one lesson per week, but she was a fast learner.

In April, Alita's quarantine was finally over and her arrival was celebrated at FAACE's spring fair, where the kitten would make her first public appearance. Pictures taken at the fair show a smiling Tony with the kitten in his arms. What they don't show was his shirt, drenched in Alita's urine. He didn't mind. She could do no wrong: "When we brought her home, she was the underdog. To protect her from the other cats she had to spend the first night in the bathroom." She gradually fitted in, but would always be the lowest in the pecking order. "Except for Topas, who was already very ill by that time. She came up to her and put her paw around her and treated her like her own kitten."

Vicki's next meeting with animal rights people in Madrid in May, gave her a hint of the conflict to come within the international animal rights community. "Very disenchanted by their behaviour and lack of vision. Would seem is signal of cooling of relationships," she wrote in her diary.

# Coria

Tony decided that he should go to Spain to witness a fiesta instead of Vicki. It was unfair that she should always take the risks, besides, Coria, where the fiesta was to be held, was too close for comfort to Villanueva de la Vera, where she was well known. For financial reasons they were unable to travel together. There were also nine cats and two dogs to take care of.

Having managed to buy a new camera, in June 1998 Tony travelled to the small town of Coria in the province of Extremadura near the Portuguese border, intending to investigate the fiesta of St John, which takes place from 23 to 29 June each year. At Madrid airport he met Georges Roos, an Argentine musician and tango singer living in Spain. He spoke good English and they had been in touch for quite a while already. He offered his own car for the trip. With him were two young people from the Spanish animal rights group ALA: Lorenzo, a driver in the Spanish army who spoke some English and his friend Maria. The three of them drove to Plasencia, 260km west of Madrid and arrived at 11 o'clock at night. When parking the car, Lorenzo smashed the gears and from then had to stop the car each time he wanted to change gear.

Plasencia was packed to bursting because the town was in fiesta too but eventually they found a cheap hostal. They went out to eat in a bar and Tony had his first encounter with the Spanish laid-back sense of tidiness. They could hardly make it to the bar because the floor was ankle deep in rubbish. Cigarette-butts, olive seeds, paper waste etc, as if it had not been swept for days. He was also surprised to see huge glasses on the table, holding four litres or more of beer, being passed from person to person.

Tony shared a room with Lorenzo and hardly slept due to anxiety about the fiesta and two clocks which chimed every hour. The clock in the hostal corridor chimed first, followed immediately by the clock on the church tower. At midnight there were twenty-four chimes and Tony heard every one of them. When it was time to get up, he had just dozed off.

After grabbing a quick breakfast, they set off to Coria on the narrow roads punctuated with hairpin bends. It was very quiet when they arrived. They had expected the fiesta to be in full swing, but there was hardly anybody about, except for the odd drunk. One was lying semi-conscious on the pavement with his feet in the road. There were two squares in the medieval part of the town, one by the church, the other by the town hall. The latter was fenced in with metal poles, with seating above, enabling people to sit on all four sides of the square with standing space underneath. The cobbled square, about 40 metres long by about 20 metres wide, was covered with sand. The air was filled with a terrible stench of human as well as animal urine, combined with the sulphuric smell of blood.

All the bars were open and had poles set in the doorways, wide enough for people to run in and out, but too small for a bull's horns. Tony's party stood out as strangers and people eyed them with suspicion. A policeman was scrawling notices, ordering people to move their cars by midday. They went into a bar and were told that the first bull would be out on the streets by 12.30pm and another at 3.30pm. At noon they went to the square and bought tickets. Even though the tickets were not cheap, the place was packed. Tony took a seat on the stand where he overheard two men behind him discussing his telephoto lens, which made him uneasy. To diffuse the situation, he turned round and showed them the camera. They then nodded and smiled.

Shortly before 12.30pm, a man with a tabor walked around the arena followed by a charanga band. An announcement was made requesting those watching to honour the wonderful tradition and not to throw bottles at the bull, because people might cut themselves on the shards. A bell, followed by rockets going off, signalled that the bull had been released into the streets.

Five minutes later, about ten men dressed in white with red scarves came chasing into the plaza, followed by five bullocks and a beautiful sleek black bull, about four years old. It took about ten minutes to separate the animals – the bull leaving the square through one gate and the bullocks through another. A few minutes later he came chasing back in again. The 'divisa', a short barbed harpoon with coloured ribbons attached, indicating the owner, had been thrust into his shoulders. From balconies, people blew darts out of blowpipes at the animal, aiming at his testicles and eyes. Tony saw at least one stuck in his muzzle. Youths on the ground stuck banderillas in him, then tried to pull them out to reuse them.

After a while, the animal's body was peppered with darts. He looked like a porcupine. The Spanish call such a spectacle 'toro acérico' (pin cushion bull). In fact, the points of the darts are large dressmaker's pins and there was a rumour that the local nuns manufactured the darts. That proved to be false, but the nuns were involved. They assembled the banderillas for bullfights for the whole area, assembling the wood, the paper part and the metal points. It was said that an animal rights activist from Madrid had asked the Mother Superior about it on the telephone. "Well, somebody has got to do it," she replied. "Why not us?"

The exhausted bull no longer had the breath in his body to charge. He stood panting, refusing to move. They charged at him from behind and tried to touch the middle of his horns. This was not as dangerous as it might seem, since the bull could not see them coming and they had to be very unlucky for anything to happen to them.

A bull in a fiesta is only any fun as long as he keeps charging and moving. So the youths took a stick, seven or eight metres long and thick enough to hold a spike on one end, and used it to attack the bull repeatedly to make him move. His great mouth hung open, with his tongue lolling out, a sign of complete exhaustion. Saliva was streaming out of his mouth and every now and then he emitted a low moaning bellow. His sides were heaving and he looked utterly bewildered.

At the end of thirty minutes they ran him out on to the streets. and people were climbing off their seats. Having had no experience of fiestas and the extent of the cruelty involved, Tony thought it was all over. He had not appreciated that the whole aim was the prolonged but definite destruction of the animal. It was this particular experience that turned him into a vegetarian.

Tony, Lorenzo and Maria were strolling morosely through the town, when all of a sudden a great cry went up and people came chasing towards them, running as if they were on fire. Anyone else would have run with them automatically, but not Tony, who stood still because he saw no point in running away from nothing. He wanted to see what was coming, confident that he could either jump the barriers, or run through them if necessary.

He soon realised that the commotion was about the bull. He walked towards him in the church square where some villagers were now throwing bricks at him. The bull ran frantically up and down the side of the church, then stood for about ten minutes and moaned and moaned and moaned. Tony had a tape recorder and captured the pitiful sound. Mustering all his strength, the bull then staggered into the shelter in the church doorway and would not be moved. On either side of the doorway there were carvings which served as handholds for his persecutors. One of those who scrambled up was handed a banderilla which he stuck right into the bull's anus, from where it hung from then on. People were trying to pull it out, but to no avail.

Tony was very close, taking pictures, when the villagers suddenly became aware of the foreigner in their midst witnessing their shameless ritual. Some of them approached Tony and started shouting at him. The only word he could make out was "Hombre!" but he heard the threat all too clearly. They tried to shove him towards the bull. He used the universal sign language to make it clear that he was not as 'brave' as them. Eventually they laughed, slapped him on the back and said it was "muy bien", it was all right. Tony felt like a traitor as he nodded and agreed that it was "muy bien".

The bull suffered in that square for a further two agonising hours, moving very little. As they continued to throw stones, or stick objects into his body, Tony could stand it no longer and walked away for a short time. A loud bang stopped him in his tracks – the villagers had shot the bull, who had fallen by the church door. They dragged him up the church steps and stabbed him in the back of his head, before slitting his throat and castrating him. Blood oozed everywhere, masses and masses of it. Kids jumped up and down on the body – there seemed to be as many kids as adults, aged from about eight upwards. The bull seemed to have shrunk after death. He looked so small, so fragile. Tony could see the calf in his face.

A van pulled up and the corpse was unceremoniously winched into it and carted off to the butcher's. As it drove away, Tony could not resist taking a picture of the kids making little canals with sticks in the huge dark puddle of congealing blood.

Suddenly, a shout went up. A group of men was running towards him – it was time to get out. Trying not to break into a run, he left the square as quickly as he could. He assumed they were after his film and was determined not to give it to them. He would give them an empty roll instead. As he opened the back of the camera, he realised that he had forgotten to rewind it. He slammed the camera shut and rewound the film manually, took it out and put it away. He would pretend to take a film out, which was, in fact, unused. He mixed in with the huge crowd and they gave up following.

He eventually found Lorenzo and Maria and they went to a bar to rest and compare notes. Five men came in, filthy with the dead bull's blood, and seemingly very proud of themselves. As they strutted about, Tony told the others what had just happened to him. They all agreed that it would be foolhardy to stay on for the second bull and risk a confrontation. So they left for Madrid in their broken-down car.

During his flight back to Heathrow, Tony began to worry that he might have lost some of his pictures during his escape from the mob, so first thing the next morning he took them to be developed. A few hours later he was relieved to find that he had only lost a few of the ones of the kids playing in the blood. All the really important ones were saved. Vicki burst into tears when she saw the extent of the bloodshed. The pictures have been used extensively by the media over the years, particularly as they showed children involved in the cruelty. It was vital to highlight what was going on in Coria, but Tony struggled to find adequate words to describe his experience. While Vicki spoke freely in public, and was able to control her emotions, Tony found it far more difficult. During a radio interview he broke down and the presenter had to divert the conversation on to a more general level. Both he and Vicki were well used to how the media operated and regarded them as crucial to their campaign, but acknowledged that they did not necessarily share their aims and aspirations and that their reporting was unpredictable at best.

# Bloody September

Tony thought it might make more economic sense for FAACE to fund Spanish animal rights people to monitor fiestas. With less travel involved, more people would be able to go and compile evidence and thus cover a greater number of events. Since FAACE was unable to provide enough decent cameras, however, the results were poor. Also, the membership of the Spanish groups appeared to change constantly, making it hard to keep track and find a diplomatic way of working with groups that seemed to be competing with each other. So, for the time being, they would have to go it alone.

On 1 September Tony arrived in San Sebastian de los Reyes, north of Madrid, also known as 'Pamplona Chica' (the little Pamplona), because of its Pamplona-style bullruns. There he saw a poster of a chimpanzee dressed in a suit of lights sticking a banderilla into a bull, advertising the group 'Toronto y sus Enanitos Toreros' (Toronto and his midget bullfighters). Even though the chimpanzee was not actually taking part in the bullfight, or the killing, it had to smoke a cigar, hold the end of a skipping rope and perform all sorts of stunts. The children seemed to have a good time but Tony was disgusted, describing it as, "lacking in humour, sordid, smutty and lewd" and was glad to leave the place.

'Bloody September' seems to be an appropriate epithet for that month in Spain, since it has the most fiestas. After only two days back home, Tony drove Vicki to Manchester Airport, leaving barely enough time to exchange impressions, or instructions for the tasks to be carried out during her absence.

The Spanish animal rights people had assembled a full programme for Vicki. On 8 September she witnessed her first 'Corrida de Rejones' (bullfight from horseback), in the village of Pozuelo, just west of Madrid. For the first time she had the chance to observe the handling of the bulls in the pen just before being driven into the bullring. To separate the six bulls and the bullocks from the little herd, sharpened wooden sticks were used. One stick even had a steel spike on the end. Thus beaten and stabbed, the terrified animal was then driven through a system of gates. Depending on the size of the bullring, these systems can be more or less elaborate, but all are designed to enable the animals to be handled without any risk to their handlers.

The next day Vicki's acting talents were tested to the extreme. Together with Patricia Pau and Veronica Zabala, she went to the fiesta of Fuente el Saz del Jarama, a village just outside Madrid. All morning she watched the village youths in action. They were obviously hung over and recharged their batteries with more alcohol as they went along. The young bull survived the event, but since barbecues were set up, Vicki assumed the steaks would come from him. Strolling through the village while waiting for the next part of the fiesta, they came upon an old bashed-up blue car with a white top. Slogans and girlfriends' names were sprayed all over the blue parts of the car, which belonged to the Peña el Derribo. This bullfighting fan club had been predominant in the bullring before. Patricia speculated that the club's name might reflect their methods, since it meant 'The Knockdown Club'.

At 1pm a beautiful pale brown cow, almost like a Jersey in appearance, was released into the barricaded streets. The usual cruelties went on for half an hour, then shouts for "el coche!" (the car) were heard. The cow was chased into an area of wasteland and the gate closed, preventing them getting through. "We chased back along the street, and running fast, followed the dirt paths leading in the direction of the back of the walled area. As we turned the corner and came in sight of the high brick wall that enclosed the ground, we heard excited shouts and the unmistakable and sickening sound of some object in collision with a vehicle. On reaching the top of the wall, we watched in horror, as the old blue and white car that we had seen in the village that morning, and now packed full of El Derribo members, deliberately drove into the little cow," she wrote in her report. This happened several times until the animal collapsed. When the youths realised she was unable to get up they became annoyed and tried to kick her back to life. Vicki and her friends moved closer. Although sickened, they did not turn away, "We considered it important to be able to keep taking photographs and observing this savagery, so that it could be recorded and passed to the appropriate authorities."

Her presence was acknowledged in a way she could never have imagined. "One man cut the cow's ear off. He handed the warm bleeding ear to me, with the animal's suffering eyes watching me. I took the ear." Someone took pictures of Vicki with the ear in her hand. She pretended to be delighted by putting on a forced smile but the smile would not have gained her an Oscar, and from behind her huge sunglasses her eyes are not looking at the camera but at the ground. She froze, horrified, not knowing how to handle the situation. When offered a cigarette, she took it, even though she did not smoke.

One older man disapproved of the youths' actions and demanded the vet be called to put the cow out of its torment but the vet was in a bar, drunk. So the villagers proceeded to bleed the animal to death in the clumsiest, most cruel way. Informed about the fiesta by Vicki and Patricia, Rosa Montero, well-known Spanish journalist and writer, in her column in *El Pais* wrote:

*A man bounced his eight-year-old son on the convulsing flank of the cow, an instructive game that teaches children how to become tormentors ... It's infuriating to have to share a country with this brutal and wild Spanishness.*

A dilemma – what to do with the ear. Vicki would not throw it away and near her cheap hotel there was no place to bury it without arousing suspicion. To preserve it, she put it in a cardboard box and packed it full of salt. Luckily, nobody went through her luggage at customs, or she would have had a hard time explaining how she came to be in possession of the ear. Tony buried it later in their small garden.

There was yet another place to visit before Vicki could go home – Navalcarnero – another village near Madrid. The fiesta had been going on for a few days already, apparent from the copious blood stains fouling the streets and the walls of the houses. She was to witness her first 'novillada', a bullfight carried out by inexperienced, would-be toreros, on younger bulls. A kid, whom she reckoned to be only about twelve years of age, was dressed up in a matador's suit. The pictures she took had a surreal quality: a young boy assuming the vain postures of a bullfighter, his face distorted, mimicking their facial expressions, standing opposite a bull coughing up blood with a sword sticking in his back.

Back home, Vicki and Tony discussed the terrible things they had seen over the last two weeks. Enough was enough. It no longer seemed sufficient to highlight these cruelties to the British public and call for a tourism boycott. Strong believers in the European Union, they decided that Euro MPs had to become more involved, so they compiled the 'Catalogue of Cruelty', or 'Vicki's Shock Report', as the *Southport Star* called it. Over the next few weeks, Vicki travelled to Brussels and Strasbourg three times. Their work with animal rights issues left virtually no time for their career as musicians. Events such as the FAACE Christmas fair did not contribute substantially to their expenses, so fundraising was becoming a pressing, though dreaded issue.

# Judas Day

Shrove Tuesday was celebrated early in 1989 and on 7 February Vicki was back in Villanueva de la Vera. Undeterred by the villagers' horrific behaviour the previous year, she wanted to check on this year's donkey, José, so named for the benefit of the British public. Out of fear for her own safety, they decided she should go incognito, no journalist was contacted and only a handful of Spanish animal rights people knew of her intentions. Used to stage outfits, she felt comfortable in her curly blond wig and the disguise seemed convincing. Several European animal rights groups were present, yet nobody recognised her. The ultimate test came when she held the door open for the British Donkey Sanctuary representatives and wished them all "buenas tardes". She preferred not to be seen with them, because the unfortunate term 'British Animal Welfare Task Force' had been circulated and held uncomfortable connotations with the Falklands War.

José had a very rough ride. The villagers venting their anger on him, because they felt deeply insulted by a gift from the Donkey Sanctuary: Blackie II, a life-size toy donkey on wheels that could master the cobbled streets and was said to have cost a thousand pounds, and which could be ridden instead of the real one. When the toy donkey arrived in the village, word spread quickly. Youths approached the trailer, shouting abuse and threatening to destroy it, so it seemed wise to move the toy donkey out of the village. Mayor Felix Gonzalez had his picture taken with Blackie II, but was sceptical about the villagers' response. "It would be better for you to go back to England now. Take your stuffed donkey away and keep it away. We do not want it here. If you bring it into the village square, the men will rip it apart and anyone with it. I cannot control them," he warned *Daily Mail* journalists.

Since it was clear that no pictures could be obtained of the locals riding the toy donkey, Blackie II was taken to another village, which just happened to be in fiesta too. The journalists were lucky, not only did the villagers wear similar festive outfits to those in Villanueva, but willingly rode the donkey up and down the streets. Back in England people wouldn't know the difference and only a few noticed they had got the name wrong, substituting Beauty for José.

Vicki was unaware of this sub-plot and followed the real donkey to the town hall, where three bottles of spirits were forced down his throat. The frail animal collapsed several times in the streets. He was beaten and had insecticide sprayed in his eyes, making them run during the whole ride. All foreigners received the usual treatment. Shouting, "Argentina! Argentina!" and, "English in the fountain", the youths tried to lasso them and shotguns were fired close to them.

The ride took between one and two hours, after which José was visibly shaken and had a nasty cut between his front legs. Vicki inquired about his fate. The current owner, a donkey dealer, had already sold him to a butcher prior to the fiesta, but Vicki was determined that after the hell he had gone through, he wasn't going to land up on somebody's plate. On the way back to Madrid she hatched a plan; one of her Spanish friends would call the donkey dealer claiming a woman and her two children had seen the fiesta on television and fallen in love with José. Even though the dealer had been threatened not to sell the donkey to anyone, the offer of two hundred pounds helped to change his mind.

The people from ADDA journeyed through blizzards to pick up José a few days later. He was taken to his new home near the famous monastery El Escorial outside Madrid. A thorough veterinary check showed that he was eleven years old and in a weak and starved condition. His wound was treated, as were his eyes. Tests also showed that he was suffering from from severe anaemia, so he was put on a serum drip for three weeks. By September, he had made a full recovery and could look forward to a peaceful life with his new friends, Pepino the donkey and Chunga the pony.

Spanish animal rights activists felt the fiesta had been a setback. Georges Roos wrote, "I admire the offer, but the idea to bring a little cardboard donkey to Villanueva de la Vera appears to me a particularly clumsy gesture. They did not have to deal with an African tribe forgotten in the bush, but with Spanish villainous hooligans who did not wish to be underestimated." The following year they would appeal to 'a group of Britons' who supposedly intended to come again with the mock donkey, to reconsider their actions, concerned that the villagers would again use their presence as an excuse to abuse the donkey.

After just two days at home, Vicki found herself en route to the European Parliament in Strasbourg full of expectation. The Committee on the Environment, Public Health and Consumer Protection, had drawn up a report on possible legal action against events involving cruelty to animals. The motion was tabled by German Euro deputy, Gerhard Schmid. The report argued that it was time to regulate cruelty inflicted on animals in entertainment. In July 1985, a group of Euro deputies had stated the need for a resolution concerning bullfighting with a view to the imminent membership of Spain and Portugal in the EU. However, Spain repeatedly managed to evade a ban. In the Spanish *La Vanguardia* newspaper, MEP Javier Elorza boasted that it cost him only a few dinners to have a clause included in protocol No 13 of the Treaty of Amsterdam, dealing with animal welfare, acknowledging that while animals are sentient beings, the Community must also recognise the cultural and religious traditions of its member states. Of course, culture and tradition just served as a pretext to justify blood fiestas and bullfighting.

On 14 February 1989, the Schmid report was introduced into the European Parliament, observed by Vicki from the visitors' area. It failed after only a short discussion, doomed from the beginning. Spanish MEPs managed to have it referred back to committee. In the preparatory stages, Spanish and Portuguese MEPs called for amendments to allow bullfighting to continue and tried to deflect attention from the subject by claiming that priority be given to "rampant racism and xenophobia, child abuse and the manifold violations of human dignity involving migrants, refugees etc" and "to prevent the corruption or brutalisation of young people in Europe, they should also be shielded from works of art whose source of inspiration, theme and artistic expression reflects these subjects: pictures of hunting scenes and still life, works by Goya, Matisse, Renoir, Manet, Picasso, Miro, Bacon, etc, poems by Rilke, Garcia Lorca, Miguel Hernandez, etc, the novels of Hemingway, operas such as Bizet's Carmen etc."

Another problem was that the report also included fox hunting and hare coursing which were non-negotiable for British MEPs. The goal of getting rid of all cruelty to animals in one go was simply too ambitious and the initiative was abandoned.

Back at home, their cat Topas had been very ill for a while. On 3 March Vicki wrote in her diary: "Between 2.10 and 2.20pm my darling Topas put to sleep." However, there was not much time for grief. Squirrels, cats and puppies needed help in Robledo de Chavela. Visitors to Spain will know that Semana Santa celebrations virtually bring the country to a standstill. This village, situated 63km west of Madrid, had a particularly nasty Easter tradition, 'El Dia del Judas', which takes place on Resurrection Day. After Mass, effigies of Christ and the Virgin Mary are paraded through the village in two separate processions. The priest, dressed in a festive gold and white robe, leads one of them. Around noon, they end up on the village square, where an effigy of Judas, prepared by village youths, hangs from a fifty-foot pole. The effigy looks different every year, depending on which personality has been most in the public spotlight over the previous twelve months. Small terracotta containers on the pole are arranged to form a cross. The signal to start the action are the phrases:

"Who killed you?"

"That one." [Judas]

"Stone him!"

The youths then take stones from a huge pile and hurl them at Judas, the main target being the terracotta pots. Inside the pots are not only sweets, but live animals. In 1988, people from ADDA agreed to monitor the fiesta for FAACE and sent them a report. Even though the pictures were poor, they illustrated in shocking detail the death of a full-grown white cat, which hit the ground when its container broke. Squirrels and pigeons were also injured, to a backdrop of the Spanish national anthem.

In order to prevent the same thing from happening in Easter 1989, Vicki made appointments with those people she thought could make a difference: the Directors of the Agriculture and Environment Departments for the Madrid province, the then Governor of Madrid, the second in command to the Bishop of Madrid, Secretario de Vicaria Sona Octava, and the mayor of the village. While the officials appeared sympathetic to her plea, she was very disappointed by the cleric's comment: "When the pots break it is a symbol of the liberation of the animals." The Mayor, José Iglesias Montero, promised that no small mammals would be used in this year's Judas Day celebrations. However, century old-traditions are difficult to eradicate and pigeons would continue to be used – after all, they could fly. Vicki tried to insist that no living creatures be used, but the mayor would not budge. Instead he invited FAACE to monitor the celebrations.

A few days after Vicki's return, Tony flew to Spain, armed with a newly-purchased video camera. Judas turned out to be a big orange and black striped cat. "Obviously a symbol of defiance and fury by the local youths, at being baulked of their living cat victims," said Tony. The pigeons had been in their tight containers for approximately twelve hours, exposed to extreme cold and great heat. Stones varying in size from eggs to oranges left one pigeon dead and the rest in shock. Two doves fell to the ground where they lay fluttering helplessly. The stoning was interrupted momentarily as two boys snatched the injured birds and ran off.

Ten years later, when Vicki and Tony checked up on the festivity again, no less a person than Bill Clinton had caught the villagers' attention. "The crudely made effigy of President Clinton clutched a flag of the stars and stripes, and the top of its head featured a tumescent protuberance ... Youths waylaid passing cars and demanded money for drink. Some were already drunk, swigging beer and anise from bottles. At midday, a sizeable crowd had gathered in the village square, ribbing each other about the Clinton figure and making crude jokes," Vicki wrote. To this day, despite new animal protection laws, the village continues to use doves and pigeons.

# A Dog's Life

The day before the fiesta in Robledo de Chavela, Tony looked into the fate of Spanish hunting dogs, as part of his investigation into what it was to be a dog in Spain. Together with Patricia Pau, he met a woman who ran a shelter for strays, just outside Madrid, on the road to Toledo. It was little more than a house crammed full of dogs and cats. All very well intentioned, but the situation had got out of hand and they could no longer cope. An overpoweringly nauseating smell assailed the visitors' nostrils and there was muck everywhere. A place where disease could spread easily.

This was not a good start but was just the beginning of a catalogue of abuse and neglect. Spanish hunting dogs are used in shooting parties, to run in packs and stir up prey and Tony set off on a journey to learn about their everyday lives. For what seemed an endless time they trundled their way across dirt roads, then went on foot for quite a while, in search of a place where they had been told the dogs were kept. Just when they had determined they were in the wrong place, they came across a compound of sheds, roofed in corrugated plastic. They had been warned not to try and enter the compound, because the hunters did not appreciate visitors. In fact, as it was a Saturday, they were out shooting in the nearby hills, the gunshots clearly audible.

There were no windows, but Tony found a few holes in the walls, through which he could stick his camera lens. The dogs, different breeds and mongrels, were chained to great wooden logs, the chains just long enough for them to stand up, but nothing else. They were crammed together like sardines or, as Tony observed, "like oarsmen in a galley – like galley slaves".
An ancient emaciated greyhound was staggering around the yard, in reality, probably not that old, but he looked it and his feet were in a very poor state. Since most of the hunters went out only at weekends, the dogs must have led a miserable, monotonous life. Hearing a disturbance, the dogs all started yapping at once, so Tony took his pictures and left.

At another shelter he was shown a dog that was blindly stumbling around. "It was obviously a hound that hadn't done his job properly and they had shot both of his eyes out. How bloody callous.' He was told that some owners, rather than waste a bullet, hang their dogs from trees when they are ill, or no longer useful and leave them to die.

On the way back to Madrid Tony took pictures of dead dogs on the side of the road, their bodies grotesquely bloated by the heat. He also took pictures outside the municipal shelter Canto Blanco, surrounding which there were rumours of dogs being sold to laboratories for vivisection and he wanted to get evidence. A new European directive had just come in, prohibiting laboratories from using stray dogs for such purposes. Patricia had done some research and discovered that Madrid's huge hospital Hospital Universitario La Paz carried out experiments on dogs. The complex, in the north of Madrid, consists of general, maternity, traumatology and children's hospitals, the latter with a research centre close by.

Claiming to be journalists representing a British women's magazine, they found their way to the vivisection building and asked an employee whether they could see the lab. He called his supervisor and the answer was no, which led them to conclude that the centre had something to hide. Tony decided on a change of strategy; if it was that complicated, he was no longer interested, he would tell his readers that they would not let them in to see the dogs. Even before Patricia could translate, there was a sudden change in attitude. The supervisor told the employee to let them in, but not to mention the 'salvajes'. Even though Tony spoke little Spanish, he clearly made out the word for 'stray'.

Once inside the laboratory, they confirmed the use of dogs from Canto Blanco and that vivisection was only possible because of this free source. Selecting only the fittest animals, approximately three hundred were used per year. Rabbits were used for traumatology research and rats for digestive surgery, as they resisted pain better and needed less attention than dogs. In the long run, they wanted to switch to Beagles, because stray dogs bore the risk of illnesses and were less docile, but the law allowed them to continue for a further two years. As a diversion from the subject of the dogs, Tony asked, what other work they were doing. They used pigs occasionally for lung, liver and stomach transplants.

When Tony asked to see the animals Alvarez became visibly uneasy but he was allowed to see the place where the dogs were kept and was appalled by what he saw. "The dogs had the tops of their skulls removed and stitched back on with great big black stitches, so they could undo them again to look inside. It was about water on the brain, as far as I could gather." He surreptitiously took photos when Alvarez was out of the room. "There was one very, very thin dog, all his ribs standing out and his skull laid like a hat on top of his head. He looked awful."

On his way out, Tony asked whether there was another hospital in Madrid that did research and was given the name of the Ramón y Cajal hospital. Perhaps they were pushing their luck to go there, but Patricia was sure the two hospitals would not be in touch. A sign outside the vivisection department read, 'No entrance except for authorised personnel'. Ignoring the warning, they walked along a corridor and came to a lift. As they got in the lift, they were joined by some workers wearing white boots and white coats. Two stories below ground level they found themselves in the corridor of the vivisection laboratory. It was lunchtime – perfect – because there were very few people about.

The doors were open into a room with cages round the walls containing rats. They could not go in, as there were people inside, but found a smaller room, with bigger cages and no personnel. Monkeys were locked up in cages. Tony wanted to take pictures, but his camera played tricks on him. The flash would not work properly. He decided to change film and try black and white. However, rewinding the old film would be a problem, because the camera was very noisy and he did not dare to shut the door. He found a door that led to a stairwell. "So I went in there. There was nothing below, it was just a stairwell. I got under the stairs and put my camera underneath my jacket and put the camera on to rewind. It seemed like it was an echoing noise, hammering like a machine gun. It probably wasn't, but to my ears it was, because I was thinking everybody's gonna come running any minute." He changed films, went back to the monkey's room and took pictures. By then the lunch break seemed to be over, and people were working in every room they passed. It was time to get out. "We walked along as if we were supposed to be there. Obviously they didn't know what we were doing, or why, so nobody stopped us."

Tony could hardly wait to see whether his pictures had come out all right. At first they looked badly exposed, but he had them printed by a specialist in Liverpool and they turned out perfectly. Some of them show two marmosets huddled together on a metal perch in their bare concrete and iron cage. They were obviously not being used for research at this point, but what a miserable restricted life for such beautiful, agile creatures.

Tony and Vicki had acquired something of a name in the Basque Country because they had helped to prevent a dog shelter in Bilbao from being closed down. They also became involved in one of the strangest cases of Spanish criminal justice.

On 15 August 1987, a young man was arrested by the Bilbao police. His crime: loitering with intent to commit a burglary. Claiming his innocence, he managed to escape, but his seven-month-old Alsatian pup Sally was not so lucky and was confiscated by the police. Judge Yolanda Domena Nieto sentenced her to prison, until her owner came back for her and confessed. She was put in a small cage which allowed no movement. Due a total lack of exercise, her claws had overgrown and her kidneys had started to fail. The owner's family tried to get her out, but while the young man remained in hiding, the judge refused to budge.

In April 1988 the Basque animal rights people sent a tiny picture of Sally to Vicki, who contacted the press. Her large eyes looking at the viewer from behind bars caused readers of several British newspapers to appeal for her immediate release. Yet still nothing happened. At the beginning of December, an article in *The People* caused confusion: "FREE! – Goodbye Prison: Sally is now in a home". The sad truth was that she had only been transferred from one kind of prison to another, as she was now in the municipal dog's home, in strict solitary confinement. Vicki started another appeal. Johnny Kennedy on Radio City gave her ample space to describe Sally's plight and came up with the idea of involving schools. The response was overwhelming. Vicki sent batch after batch of signatures over to the Bilbao authorities. Finally, the good news arrived, the judge had been replaced and the dog released, the manager of the dog's home keeping her as his pet.

Early in May 1989, they were contacted about another urgent matter. This time by the Society for the Protection of Animals and Plants of Alava. The Armentia refuge for dogs on the outskirts of Vitoria was going to be shut down. Built by the council in the early 1970s, it had been operated since by the society. Their members had worked miracles to keep the shelter going, when the council failed to invest in its upkeep. In January 1987, the council appointed a municipal vet to take charge of the centre and from then on, things really went downhill. The society accused him of neglect and misjudgment, as, rather than treating ill dogs, he chose to put them down. At the beginning of 1989, the drainage system was close to collapse and the sewage diverted into a river, which understandably caused complaints by local residents.

On 27 April 1989, the head of the council put a twenty-four-hour police guard on the building. Despite their best efforts, no members of the society were allowed in to care for the approximately five hundred dogs inside. Hoping international pressure on the council would be enough to solve the problem, Vicki and Tony alerted the British press. However, on Friday 12 May they received a call alerting them to the fact that all five hundred dogs were to be put down around 15 May. Vicki caught the next train to Heathrow and flew to Bilbao. Arriving in Vitoria the next day, she was met by volunteers of the society, among them a British woman named Ruth. They immediately took her to the notorious 'dogs' Belsen', as the shelter was now nicknamed, where she was shocked by the sheer number of animals. There were dogs everywhere, some with broken limbs and skin injuries, and all seriously undernourished, as the society was no longer allowed to feed them.

As she stood, dumbstruck, a tiny dog suddenly began to dig its way out underneath the front gate. Vicki caught hold of it as soon as its black head and most of its white body was through the hole. Under the eyes of the stunned police, she jumped into one of the volunteers' cars and drove off at full speed. The dog had recently given birth, but her pubs had been eaten by other dogs. Vicki chose a name for her – 'Mariposa', which means butterfly.

She had intended to hand over a bag of letters and petitions from British citizens, but Mayor Jose Angel Cuerda refused to meet her, so she gave them to the civil governor of the region instead. She told the local media that Armentia would soon be the centre of world attention. This statement was supported by the presence of the *Daily Star* ("*Star* to Rescue at Spanish Hell-Hole Kennels –

we win a reprieve for 500 dogs facing death"). Indeed, the killing had been miraculously postponed, but Vicki did not leave with a good feeling.

Back home, they decided that Tony should fly over immediately to make a technical report and approach members of the Basque Parliament. By the time he arrived, the police were becoming a bit slack; not waiting for their replacements to arrive at the end of their shifts and sometimes leaving a half hour gap in which the kennels were left unguarded. The dogs were being fed with leftovers from an army barracks. On one particular day three big dustbins full of 'food' arrived. Tony examined the contents of one of the bins and found it full of broken glass and melon skins … So he stood in the way of the council workers who had come to feed the dogs and refused to let them in. Having some extra money with him for emergencies, he went to a chicken processing plant and bought a lot of the waste products, which they cooked for the dogs. They also bought a great pile of dog biscuits.

He also met Hope, a medium-sized, sandy-coloured mongrel whose picture was used by the *Daily Star*; chosen because she was the only dog who had any life left in her. Tony gave her that name, because she always came to the wire first and looked so hopeful.

One of the Vitoria volunteers was a make-up artist and she took Tony into a San Sebastian television studio, to meet four Basque candidates for the European Parliament who had just taken part in a debate. He spoke to three of them through a translator, but Txema Montero, candidate for the Herri Batasuna party, the political branch of the Basque separatist group ETA, spoke English. Tony begged him to talk to the mayor and to pass on another three thousand, five hundred signatures from England. He agreed, only to be ridiculed in the press as being a man who bombed people and saved animals, due to his party's close affiliation with ETA.

Tony returned home cautiously optimistic but soon received a worrying phone call. One morning, when the volunteers had arrived, they found all the dogs were very sleepy. Vicki theorised that the municipal vet might be trying out the correct dosage for killing the animals. He was said to have a favourite poison called anectine, which is administered by intramuscular injection causing all the muscles to relax, leading to a slow death from suffocation and cardiac arrest. Thirteen dogs had been put down in this way in the winter of 1987, but Vicki suspected that this method would be too complicated to kill five hundred dogs. The situation gave them grave cause for concern.

In the meantime, two tons of dog food donated by British manufacturers Gilbertson and Page had been shipped to Vitoria. Iberia airlines carried one ton free of charge and FAACE paid for the other to be transported by land. The food was smuggled into the shelter daily.

On Monday 5 June, the terrible news came: nearly all the dogs had been destroyed. FAACE later paid a detective five hundred pounds to find out exactly what had happened. Apparently, during the night, the dogs were given food containing the drug Dexeutanol 234-G, which should have been administered according to their weight. In any case, it is not a fast-acting drug and takes several hours for death to come. The smallest dogs received a relatively larger dose, so died more quickly, but the larger dogs were only unconscious when they were thrown into the pit and covered with quick lime. Some of them, drugged and disorientated, tried to scramble their way out of the pit and were shot by the police. Vicki and Tony were devastated by this illegal and callous slaughter.

Four days later, Vicki flew to Spain to join the fight for the lives of the remaining one hundred and thirty dogs. Homes had been found and other shelters had offered to take in small groups of dogs. The council, however, had different plans; they would build a new shelter on the same site, in the sole charge of the municipal vet. No more than forty dogs would be allowed at any one time and they would be destroyed if they were not claimed within three days. Surprisingly, the veterinary facilities would be very elaborate, considering that nothing but lethal drugs would be administered to the animals.

On the day of her arrival, Vicki received further shocking news. The Council of San Sebastian had employed the same strategy. The society which ran the Villa Lolita shelter was expelled from the grounds and, in an act of sheer barbarism, the cats' house bulldozed with forty cats and kittens still inside. Several dogs had also been run over by the bulldozers, but approximately one hundred and fifty others were loaded into vans and transported to a provisional compound. It turned out that they were not welcome; only about a third of them were allowed in. About a hundred were loaded up again and a desperate odyssey began. The then president of the organisation, Alberto Cifuentes, said with bitterness, that the search for a home " ... had been like travelling in a boat affected by the plague, not allowed to enter into any port." After two days, during which more than forty dogs had not been able to leave the vehicles at all, the volunteers could see no other possibility than to put the animals down.

Vicki went home discouraged. Meanwhile, the MEP for Stockport, Glyn Ford, had agreed to get involved. He flew over and met with officials and the press. He criticised the 'unnecessary massacre' and threatened to deliver a report to the European Parliament. Vicki, who was back in Spain to represent FAACE in an anti-bullfighting demo in Madrid, travelled up to Vitoria to meet him, which took a whole day. They both left Vitoria with the dogs' fate still in the balance. However, at least one life was saved. When Vicki visited the shelter that day, Hope had finally given up and was lying around despondent. Terrified of heights, Vicki psyched herself up and during the police changeover, which gave her about half an hour's grace, she climbed on top of a car and over the wire. She scooped up Hope, then climbed back up, passing her over to Ruth, who was waiting on the other side. They bundled her into the car and drove off.

After nearly twelve weeks of campaigning, the council no longer threatened another massacre and conceded that new homes could be found. Hope and Mariposa were flown to England, where they passed their quarantine, then went to the same home close to Vicki and Tony. However, the story was not yet over for the dogs left behind. A German organisation was found which could provide homes for twenty-five dogs but every conceivable effort was made to thwart their transfer to Germany. Finally, after having drummed up huge media attention, twenty-three dogs were loaded into a lorry, with beds of straw inside, en route for Malaga and then to Germany.

After this soul-destroying episode, Vicki and Tony decided to avoid getting involved in dogs' homes in the future, because it was just too painful. Although, of course, they did not refuse to help when they were needed in Tenerife in 1998.

# Mother

August 1989 was warm and sunny and people seemed happy and cheerful as they joined friends and family for barbecues and other outdoor activities. But for Vicki, things had a darker aspect. Her mother, Louise, who had lived in a nursing home for some time, was admitted to hospital. The very next day Vicki received news of her aunt Dolly's death and five days after that their cat Shiraz had to be put to sleep because of kidney problems. Louise was in the final stages of cancer and Vicki spent every available minute with her. On 13 August she entered in her diary: "My beloved mother died peacefully with me at her side at 4.20 this morning in Southport hospital, aged 86 years and 8 months." Apart from being devastated by her loss, she was in an awkward position, as she was scheduled to fly to Spain the next day to monitor a fiesta. They could not afford to cancel the ticket and she did not wish to let her Spanish friends down, or the two journalists who were to accompany her. Tony helped her to resolve the dilemma by suggesting the funeral be postponed until after her return. He would take care of all the arrangements.

Feeling deeply depressed, she left for Madrid. The village of Brihuega in the Guadalajara province, 85km north of Madrid, celebrates its local saint, the Virgen de la Peña, in August, the traditional bull runs taking place on the 16th and 17th each year. Unlike the usual Spanish bull runs, in Brihuega, young bulls are not only pursued through the village, but over a vast area of open land. The village further distinguished itself by chasing the animals with jeeps and tractors, running them down and killing them in the process. ADDA had already protested to the authorities, but felt that international protest was needed. August being the 'silly season', with the government being on holiday, anything could make the press, and the *Daily Mirror* and the *Daily Star* found it a welcome opportunity to bash the Spaniards once again, "If Spain is to hold its head up in a civilised Europe, its government must step in and ban barbaric customs such as these at once. Their national image is already too heavily stained with blood."

Brihuega's Mayor, Jesus Simón, assured her that this year all vehicles would be banned from the bull run but there would be about thirty thousand people in the village, three times the size of the population, so it would be hard to control them. Some 'wild men' might ignore the new rules, but extra police would be deployed. Those known from previous years to have hurt the animals had received letters telling them to behave themselves and there were warning posters throughout the village. The mayor and the villagers were well aware that

Vicki had brought the British press with her. "Obviously my presence was not welcomed in the village and shouts and insults accompanied me everywhere. I also received a warning that plots were being hatched to do me mischief."

Vicki awaited the start of the bull run in the village square. The press people had left earlier on, so she sat alone at a table drinking coffee. Suddenly, the mayor approached her with a megaphone and shouted abuse in her ear, accusing her of destroying their fiesta and some youths started throwing cans at her. Anything could happen with emotions running so high but she would not run away and let them declare victory over her. She decided to stare them down and continued to sip her coffee with dignity. This strategy proved successful and after a while the abuse stopped but she must have wondered whether this was a prelude to what was going to happen once darkness descended on the fields.

At 6.30pm, four slender bulls were released from their pens and chased out of town by a crowd armed with sticks. It was still hot and their pitch-black coats glistened in the sunlight. Thousands followed them uphill to the fields and rocks. Among tree stumps in the brown grass, there were trailers packed with people, who encouraged the animals to charge at their vehicles. Others tried to attract the animals' attention by throwing stones at them. A young man literally grabbed one bull by the horns and hung on for quite a while, as the animal tried to shake him off. It was extremely difficult for Vicki and the journalists to follow closely, because the four bulls were driven in different directions and it was soon too dark to see properly. Vicki had to watch out for herself too, "I had to put up with a lot of aggression as I videoed and photographed proceedings, at one point people were screaming at me through loudhailers not to take photographs. Needless to say, I kept taking them."

When the time came for the bulls to be locked up with the bullocks in front of the Church of San Felipe, two were missing. Vicki was told by villagers that they were lost in the country. She saw a tractor with a trailer passing by with bloodstained ropes on view. She hung around in front of the church until 4am and watched as empty cans were thrown at the exhausted animals. There was no attempt to feed or water them.

By lunchtime the next day, the two animals were still suspiciously missing. The other bulls were run to the bullring, together with the bullocks, where youths taunted them for twenty minutes. They would be slaughtered later for a communal feast.

The Spanish state television was in the village too and in the morning an ADDA activist had passed on to them the claims of several villagers, that two bulls had been castrated and killed the night before. The organisers insisted that they were alive and in a safe place awaiting slaughter, but Vicki did not believe them. The television crew interviewed the villagers, the mayor and Vicki for the national news. While some villagers admitted there had been abuse in the past, the mayor denied it flatly. Vicki looked drawn and exhausted. For several days she had not slept properly, having spent many nights at her mother's bedside. Stumbling around in the dark fields for many hours had been draining. She told the reporter that while she acknowledged the effort made on behalf of the council to prevent cruelty, she did not think the animals should be put through such stress and that this kind of behaviour most certainly did not belong in the twentieth century.

Obviously all this happened in pre-internet times. Now there are several pages promoting the fiesta, which has been declared of 'regional interest' by the authorities. However, there are online discussions about the treatment of the bulls too. There are complaints that some people try to reopen the pens in the early hours of the morning, putting others at risk and that the animals are beaten and stoned and when they collapse and people try to get them up by force. It still seems to be the norm that not all four bulls return. There is a call for a ban on four-wheel-drives, motorcycles and quad bikes being used to chase the bulls. Remarkably, interest in the bullfight at the end of the day no longer attracts as many people and some people complain that the council is spending too much money on that part of the festivity. So Vicki's presence in the village may have sparked a new line of thinking.

Even when she had left Brihuega, her ordeal was not yet over. As she waited outside her Madrid hotel for her taxi to the airport, a car drove up, two men jumped out and punched her so hard, that her skirt buttons slashed her stomach. She was then thrown to the ground and kicked. The men then jumped back into the car, taking the video camera and all her footage of the fiesta with them.

She arrived in England utterly dejected. "I was bruised and shaken, and the theft of the video camera was a tragic loss. It took a tremendous effort to buy such a vital piece of equipment, and owing to the circumstances in which we are working and the risks we have to take, it is very difficult to get our equipment insured, so it has been a total loss. We are struggling to replace it but we don't know if we will be able to do so in the near future."

Tony was disappointed that there was no footage to show the British media, but it mattered much more to him to have Vicki back relatively unharmed.

Louise's funeral took place three days later in Southport's St Philip's Church. Since Louise did not have many friends in the end, there was a reception for the small group of mourners at their home in Stanley Street. Next, the room in the nursing home had to be cleared out. Only then could Vicki catch up with some sleep and begin to come to terms with her mother's death.

# Travelling Companions

Shortly after the funeral, Tony left for Spain, having replaced the video camera by persuading a local dealer to accept payment in three installments. Two fiestas in the area around Madrid, a children's bullfighting event in Alcalá de Henares, and a bull run across the countryside in Tortola in the Guardalajara province, were on his agenda. Their lives had become a rollercoaster ride of trips to and from Spain, often with little respite in between, and so, two weeks after this trip, he was back in Spain again, this time with Vicki. For the first time they had been able to raise sufficient money to travel together, while their friend and FAACE volunteer Nora Fee looked after their many dogs and cats.

Travelling together added a further complication, as they were soon to discover when they videoed in the streets of Fuenlabrada, just 20km south east of Madrid. What Tony described as 'a hellhole' bore the unofficial title of 'Europe's youngest town' for many years, due to its large number of school-age children. Due to relentless promotion by the authorities, its rural charm had disappeared completely; the small, white-painted houses giving way to high-rise buildings. Today it looks like a suburb of Madrid.

During fiesta time, in 1989, its young population did not welcome outsiders, at least not whilst committing atrocities in public, so the atmosphere was hostile when two foreigners arrived in town. Both used to working independently, they now worried that the other might take too great a risk and checked up on each other constantly.

The villagers' thirst for excitement resulted in having four head of cattle out on the street at the same time. The animals were attacked from behind barriers, leaving pools of blood wherever they ran. There were people on roofs and in open doorways, ready to shut them with a bang the moment one of the animals should mistake the opening for a safe haven. Vicki noted a strong police presence, with a police helicopter circling overhead.

After more than two hours, and four dead animals, they walked around the village before returning to their hotel. "In a bunting-decked adjoining street there were many stalls selling sweetmeats and fiesta novelties. One stall was selling day-old chicks, alongside sticks of liquorice and toys. The chicks, dyed different colours, were bought by children as toys, and carried away in plastic bags, they cost one hundred pesetas each." Vicki could not bear to inquire what the children did with the live toys.

The next days were spent at third-rate bullfights in San Pablo de los Montes in the Toledo province and a fiesta in Chiloeches in the Guardalajara area. Since the place was very remote, they could not use public transport, so were driven around by a Spanish animal rights activist, who unfortunately did not speak any English. Chiloeches consisted of twenty houses at most and when they arrived, all heads turned. About fifty men hung around a makeshift bullring. A bull and a small cow, both in very poor condition, were being tormented by the men. They were all in their forties and fifties and had a sort of dead look in their faces. It was so sordid. A dirty farmyard, the buildings all ramshackle. One cow so thin it was pathetic. Someone had a hessian sack on the end of a long pole, which he tried to flip over the cow's head to make it move. But the animal kept its head down.

Vicki noted that there was a smashed up car by the plaza, daubed with peña slogans, which, in her experience, had a very ominous significance. For the first time during their travels, they decided that it was too dangerous to take out their cameras and if they couldn't expose what happened by proving it on film, that would have turned them into spectators, or even accomplices. There was no point in staying, so they attended yet another bullfight for small children in a place called Cifuentes instead.

They had heard about a town on the Costa Brava which was about to be declared 'ciudad antitaurina' (anti-bullfighting town). The Costa Brava being an important area for tourism, this was a very important signal. They wanted to meet the man responsible to see if this could be achieved in other places. They travelled by train all the way up to Barcelona and Tossa de Mar – a resort of which they would always have fond memories and to which they would return several times over the years. According to its tourism leaflets, 'the flower of the sea' was a place of ten superlatives. Not only was it the first village to obtain the European flag, it had the first municipal animal refuge, the first beach with an area reserved for sunbathers and their pets and, of course, it was first to declare itself anti-bullfighting. Local animal rights people had managed to convince Mayor Telm Zaragoza, that foreign tourists avoided Spain because of its bad animal rights record. What good were a beautiful beach, marked footpaths in the mountains and a new sewage system, if people felt uncomfortable about the animals?

This argument made sense to the mayor, who revealed that he and the council had refused permission to build a bullring the previous year, despite heated opposition but he seemed uncertain as to when to actually implement the ban. Local animal rights people were worried that in the end nothing might come of it. Also, a Catalan animal protection law from 1988 was repeatedly ignored in places around Tossa. At that point, Vicki and Tony came into the picture. Tony acknowledged the mayor's courage but pressed for a date for the ban and asked if he would also ban bullfighting paraphernalia, such as advertisements for bullfights in the area. The answer was vague – maybe next season. It needed pushing, or it would just have fizzled out.

Since the national and international media had yet to show any interest in the story, Tony offered to spread the good news to a huge audience. Together with local people, FAACE invited supporters from all over the world to congratulate the mayor on his wise decision. The English media picked up the story and Tossa suddenly became the emblem of a guilt-free Spanish holiday. Whenever Vicki or Tony appeared on the radio talking about Spanish blood fiestas, callers mentioned Tossa as a positive example. Everybody suddenly claimed that they personally had convinced him to ban bullfighting, but it had been a group effort. From then on, Tossa's tourism brochures were stamped with the slogan 'The first village in Spain against bullfights'.

Over the years, Tossa would host international conferences on the protection of animals and the environment, in which Vicki and Tony would give talks. On one occasion, as they left the conference after showing a particularly nasty video, they were approached by a woman. Tony thought there would be some kind of trouble but instead, she invited them to dinner. Rosa Monraba, who together with her husband owns the Castell Vell restaurant in the beautiful medieval Vila Vella, claims that Vicki and Tony turned her love of animals into more active involvement. She agrees that the mayor had already taken a stand against bullfighting but that he was under pressure from many sides. Vicki and Tony's support was vital to strengthen his resolve. Rosa is one of the few people who got to know Vicki on a more personal level and confirmed the huge difference in her public and private image, "She wanted to appear very professional in front of the media ... and had to study her facts thoroughly. Any weakness would have made her an easy target. But once the cameras were off, she was a warm and caring human being and later on, her accident gave her supernatural strength ... Ella tenia el corazon a flor de piel," she said, which means Vicki had a big heart.

Pilar Taberner, a strong woman herself, says, "She was very determined in what she was doing. I believe in destiny and her destiny was this, hard work. I'm amazed that she risked so much, but you have to risk something if you are convinced."

Not only was Tossa put on the map by the mayor's decision, but also the man himself. Telm Zaragoza became an animal rights hero, even catching Brigitte Bardot's attention, who became involved in Tossa's local elections in spring 1991. Coinciding with the international conference on animal rights hosted by the town hall, leaflets bearing the letterhead of her foundation were distributed, encouraging voters to re-elect Zaragoza. But the local animal rights movement did not appreciate her involvement. They rejected the introduction of politics into animal rights issues and in an open letter to her, pointed out that the positive developments in Tossa had been achieved by many people, not just one particular person.

The small seaside resort led by example, with many other places declaring themselves anti-bullfighting, Barcelona being the most prominent. Sceptics point out that most of these are in independent-minded Catalonia, where bullfighting is regarded as a symbol of Spain's dominance. But Tony, proud of being involved in what he considers the beginning of the end of bullfighting, is optimistic that this trend will eventually become mainstream.

# The Leaping Goat

News of the campaign had spread beyond Europe and in 1989 Vicki was invited to New York by the Argus Archives for a series of speeches and interviews, as guest of millionaire Dr Dallas Pratt.

Then, in 1990, the year of the British Poll Tax and the violent riots against it, she was catapulted into the middle of two strange fiestas, one of which, involving the throwing of a nanny goat from a church tower, would haunt Spain's image abroad forever, even long after it had been stopped.

On 17 January 1990, the day of St Vincent, she was back in Tordesillas hoping she would not be recognised from her earlier visit on the occasion of the 'Toro de la Vega' festivity, after which she had created such bad publicity for the village. However, she need not have worried, because this time the crowd was different and much smaller, mostly made up of women and small children, all of them covered up against the cold grey late afternoon. The Brotherhood of San Vincente honoured its saint, not only by a procession, but also with the gift of five chickens. Maybe the creator of the event considered that the simple slaughtering of the birds would not be worthy of the saint. Instead, they had to die at the hands of young women from the village, supposedly virgins.

The five white chickens were brought to the Ermita San Vicente dangling from a pole supported by two men, their legs tied up. Four chickens were put on the ground while the crowd waited for the first participant to be blindfolded. Her task was not an easy one. One chicken was left dangling from a rope waiting for her to kill it with a sword. Small children watched with wide eyes and open mouths, while she hacked away at the bird, which flapped its wings in panic. Soon the dark bare ground in front of the saint's effigy was littered with white feathers. Probably to spare the bird endless suffering, it was eventually untied and killed by a man stamping on its head with his heel, as if it were a cigarette stub. Vicki and her companion continued to video and take pictures until all the girls had completed their grisly task. Apparently, the chickens would later be eaten by the members of the brotherhood. In former times they were donated to a nursing home, which now no longer existed. There was no need for further enquiries – the grisly spectacle spoke for itself – so they headed back to Madrid, before being asked too many questions.

It took a while to sort out public transport to Vicki's next destination, Manganeses de la Polvorosa in the Zamora province, north-west of Madrid. It was a long trip. The main event of the St Vincent's Day festivities was the throwing of a nanny goat from the church tower. An article Vicki had read in the *Norte de Castilla*, showed a picture of a goat on a rope dangling from an opening in the church tower. In the aperture, in front of the bell, were five smiling youths, the Quintos. The article said that the goat was not killed in the fall, because it was caught in a canvas sheet held out by people on the ground. Later, the animal was raffled to raise funds for the Quintos.

Since tradition was invariably used to justify the use of animals in festivities, the newspaper had questioned Francisco Rodriguez Pascual, Professor of Anthropology, about the origins of the practice. He had great difficulty in establishing the tradition of the fiesta with even a minimum of reliability. There were no written accounts and the testimonies of the elders only agreed that the term 'salto de la cabra' (the leap of the she-goat), did indeed applied to the use of a live goat. However, traditionally, the goat was not thrown from the church tower, but paraded around the village and, in one version, made to jump a ditch from a steep rock. If the goat survived, 'el baile de la cabra' (the dance of the she-goat), took place.

The 'tradition' of the goat being thrown from the belfry could hardly qualify as such, since it had only taken place for eight years. Neither did it always take the same form, with a straw puppet being used instead in one year. However, for three years running, the goat had been thrown without any safety rope.

A fancy dress parade was just about to start when Vicki arrived in the village. A band was playing and women were dressed up as sailors and nuns. There was even an imitation of the Pope Mobile. Vicki calculated that one hundred and fifty people took part in the parade – and a goat. Various signs were painted on her coat and she was led around the village on a piece of string. At some point a group of village youths disappeared with her into the church tower and everybody stared upwards to catch the next part of the proceedings. Vicki followed their gaze and saw the goat appear in an opening, which she reckoned was about fifty feet from the ground. From behind the goat, the youths started to throw sweets to the crowd, who were cheering and shouting, "La cabra, la cabra, la puta de la cabra" (the she-goat, the she-goat, the whore of a she-goat). For quite a while the goat stood precariously on the window ledge. To further increase the excitement, one boy started to milk the goat, squirting the milk all over crowd, while the animal seemed totally paralysed with fear.

Vicki was filming all this. However, at the moment the goat was thrown from the window, she was so shocked that she pressed the pause button by mistake. The men who were supposed to hold out the canvas sheet, dropped it to the ground when the goat was thrown, so the animal crashed on to the cobbles. Vicki pressed the record button again when they tried to make her stand, but she kept collapsing, so they dragged her to a door next to the village disco. Vicki tried to follow to check on the goat, but they shouted at her threateningly and locked the door. She decided not to stay on until the raffle later that evening. There was nothing further she could do on her own, so she set off back to Madrid contemplating the despicable sights she had just witnessed; by far the most unbelievable fiesta so far.

Back at home, she tried to attract the media's attention with her shocking footage but, for some reason, the British press did not consider it newsworthy. Nevertheless, she and Tony would continue to highlight this fiesta until it was banned.

Meanwhile, preparations for the annual demo against the Waterloo Cup had got under way. This year the date coincided with the donkey fiesta in Villanueva de la Vera. Spanish groups had called upon all foreign groups to stay away from the fiesta, arguing that their presence – especially that of the so-called British Animal Welfare Task Force – would inflame and antagonise the villagers even further. Respecting the Spaniards' wishes, FAACE stayed away. After the fiesta they received reports that the donkey had had a very rough ride and had collapsed right after leaving the town hall. Photographers were prevented from taking pictures and journalists and animal rights people from Italy and Belgium were physically threatened. The mayor failed to keep his promise to allow the donkey to be inspected prior to and immediately after the fiesta by the vet brought to the village by the Spanish activists.

Vicki and Tony concentrated on the hare coursing event. FAACE had come up with the idea of an open forum on coursing and Vicki appealed on radio for people who could not demonstrate at the actual event, to attend the forum. They were rewarded with a full house and people standing at the back. Lord Ronnie Fern, then Liberal Democrat MP for Southport and Ken Stuart, Labour MEP, were present. Tony managed to get hold of Ricky Tomlinson, who urged people to protest and show their disgust at what these people were doing.

Joseph Durkin, a local bookseller and former hare coursing enthusiast turned animal-rights protagonist, made an emotional appearance, "I've been coming for thirty years: twenty-five that side, five on this," he confessed. "I used to be a great supporter, then I saw a hare beat the dogs and it was limping away from the field when a beater took a pole and beat it to death. You've got to protest against something like that. They say hares can escape into the bushes – so they can – but they'll be driven out again in the afternoon. Eventually, they'll kill them. It's death deferred, if you like. The ones that are killed first are the luckiest." The forum received good media coverage and on the day of the demo, despite snowstorms, the media turned up in great numbers.

Undeterred by the incompetence and seeming indifference of the European Parliament on animal protection issues, Vicki again travelled to Strasburg to lobby Euro MPs. Upon her return, sad news came from Spain: donkey José had died unexpectedly.

Spring brought a trip to London. On 20 April, an international demo against bullfights scheduled to take place in Moscow in the middle of June, was due to take place outside Russian embassies in several European countries. Early in December 1989, Vicki had been received at the Soviet Embassy in London and had spoken to a representative of the cultural attaché. She had handed over a video on bullfighting entitled *Bloodbath*, filmed by Tony and herself, to be passed on to President Gorbachev. She protested energetically against this export of bullfighting to Eastern Europe.

For the Russian corrida, thirty-six bulls would be transported from Spain to Moscow. There would be three corridas on foot, one bullfight from horseback and even two comic bullfighting spectacles. Even though her protest was duly noted, the bullfights were still due to go ahead by the spring of 1990. So an international demonstration was planned. FAACE had chartered a bus to transport the protesters from the North West to London, leaving very early, because the demo would start at 9.30am, in order to synchronise the protest with those in the rest of Europe. It was felt that if the Kremlin received reports from all its embassies simultaneously, the protest would have most effect.

Just before leaving home, they received news that the bullfights had been called off. Referring to the bullfighters, the Russian authorities stated that they already had enough criminals of their own, without importing more. As the bus was already paid for, Vicki and Tony decided to go anyway. They stopped at a florist and bought a huge bouquet of red roses and handed it over with a letter of thanks. They were very graciously thanked for their campaign by the permanent member of the embassy diplomatic staff, Alexander Korsik, the Soviet spokesman. Since the Spanish Embassy was very close, they decided to pay them a visit too. They had a person dressed in a matador outfit made by Vicki with a skull mask. They had also made a big black fighting bull's head with huge horns. And there were four people in white robes with pointed hoods like the Ku Klux Klan with bloodstained robes in imitation of the Semana Santa parades in Spain.

A letter was handed over protesting about children's attendance at bullfights. Unfortunately, the defeat of the Spanish bullfighting industry was only temporary. In years to come there would be several more attempts to introduce bullfighting into Russia. Luckily, the brave Russian animal rights movement had gained strength, and with support from animal rights groups from all over the world, these events have been prevented.

The fiesta of San Juan was coming up in June and it was decided that Vicki should go to Coria to get some video footage. Coincidentally, an Italian animal rights group approached them about Coria and Vicki agreed to take two people with her, one of them a photojournalist. They met in Madrid, hired a car and drove to Moraleja, near Coria. Vicki wore a black curly wig to escape recognition. The Italian girl's room was next to Vicki's and all night long she could hear her sobbing, apparently, dreading what she was about to see. Vicki went on her own to film the first bull at 4 o'clock in the morning, not an easy task, since it was still dark and the streets poorly lit. As a stranger, unfamiliar with the area, it is difficult to guess what will happen and where to run for shelter. Also, people have been up drinking all night and don't have normal reactions. The wig made little difference because she was still recognised as an outsider and as such, an object of suspicion.

The Italian girl was in a very distressed state when Vicki met her later that morning. As the square in Coria started to fill up, she suddenly rushed out, shouting, "Stop! Stop! Killers! Assassins!" in Italian. People did not know what to make of her. Vicki hustled her out of the limelight and urged her to be quiet, or they would not get any footage. If you are going to make a stand like this, you have to do it at the right time. It's no good going into the middle of the square before it all starts. You need to go in as the bull comes in and carry a large sign. Vicki and the photojournalist quietened her down, but the incident caused a lot of problems when they returned to the hotel, because word had got around. The girl probably thought Vicki was very hard but nothing could have been further to the truth.

Vicki went back to the village square and mistakenly sat down in the seat of the man who makes the darts. They tried to push her out, but she made it very clear that she would not move. So they all bunched up and she shot some very useful footage. In the video you can see the darts flying from beside her and after a short while the bull was like a pincushion. Three or four darts were sticking in his horns, proving that they had gone in with some force. The bull kicked his foot when one hit him in the back of the leg and there were darts all over the back of his legs. He was totally smothered in them.

There was a also French television crew in town who had not been able to get decent pictures, so they contacted Vicki. She had bribed someone to let them into the town hall, where they were led into a room overlooking the square, from where she managed to get some good video footage.

She befriended the leader of a peña who lived in Barcelona, but always returned home to Coria for the fiesta. Even though there was a bull out on the streets, they sat in a bar drinking. There was not much point in going out, they explained, because it was not their bull and they were not allowed to do very much to him. The bulls for Spanish fiestas are generally bought by the town hall, or the local peñas. Vicki's questions gradually became more daring, "What about the bulls, are they tampered with in any way?"

"You see the size of them," he answered hesitantly. "Well, you don't think we'd go on to the streets without a bull being drugged, do you?"

They invited her to join them at midnight, when their own bull would be out on the streets. They would show her some real fun. Vicki did not go, because she felt that if she did, they would be showing off the sadistic things they could do, just because of her. Both she and Tony recognised that there was a line which must not be crossed. It is acceptable to record, but definitely not to take part. It is fine to observe what is happening, but certainly not to instigate anything.

# Water Bulls

Tony and Vicki were frequently asked about the involvement of the Catholic Church in blood fiestas and bullfighting. Pope Pius V's Bullarum Romanorum Pontificum, of November 1567, forbade clerics to attend, or take part in, bullfighting spectacles, threatening them with excommunication and denying them an ecclesiastical burial should they involve themselves in activities in which animals are used for entertainment. This being largely ignored, Pope Pius IX, in 1846, reiterated the ban. By and large, it seemed to depend on the attitude of the individual Pope whether or not he socialised with the bullfighting industry. While Pope Pius XII, in 1940, refused to meet with a delegation of the union of bullfighters, his various successors saw nothing wrong in accepting the cape. In response to sending their video material to Pope John II, Vicki received an ambivalent statement from the Vatican:

*'... The Holy Father appreciates the efforts being made to secure proper treatment of animals, and as you know, he has himself on various occasions urged such respect. The defence of all living creatures, of course, has to be seen in the context of the principal duty of protecting human beings, created in the image and likeness of God, from the crimes of abortion, euthanasia and sexual abuse and from other attacks on their dignity and worth ...'*

In 1982, in Madrid's Santiago Bernabue Stadium, he was presented with his first matador's cape, which he accepted. In 1988, Spanish bullfighter Dámasco González gave him a luxurious specimen during a general audience in the Vatican and was blessed for it. It is said that over the years John Paul II accumulated quite a collection of capes.

Vicki and Tony came upon a priest who had raised money for the renovation of his church, in the Alicante area, by organising two bullfights. His taste was exquisite; only marble walls and floors would do. His clerical status did not prevent him from flaunting the fact that he was an 'aficionado' (bullfighting fan). So-called 'beneficial bullfights' are not uncommon in Spain. The bullfighting industry is quick to get its foot in whenever there is a natural disaster, or a high profile incident like the 2004 Madrid bombing. A series of bullfights raised funds for the victims' relatives. Famous bullfighters had their expenses paid and thus their participation was not quite as charitable as the public was led to believe. For a time, there were so many beneficial bullfighting events, for the Red Cross, or cancer charities, that the participants in second or third rate bullrings complained that they could no longer make a living. The bullfighting priest used to enter the ring dressed in the outfit of a 'rejoneador' (a bullfighter on horseback), and performed all sorts of chores like presenting the cut-off ears to the bullfighter. One eye-witness claimed that he was actually involved in the killing of one young bull.

In August, Vicki and Tony met Father Eduardo Martinez in his parish in San Fulgencio. Naïvely they hoped they could talk some sense into him and point out that his activities were not appropriate for a priest. However, the church was obviously not yet finished; the upper part of the altar was covered in plastic and the rear of the church looked like a construction site. Though courteous, he did not relent. The Bishop of Alicante had forbidden him either to organise, or take part in, further bullfights, yet he managed the former through a friend, convinced he was doing the right thing. He needed to make money and thoroughly enjoyed this method of doing it.

Having failed in this mission but having some time to fill until their next assignment, they tried to investigate some fire bull fiestas in the Valencia area. In Chiva, Tony learnt that there was never an ideal position for filming. He had climbed up a wall thinking he had found the ideal spot but just as the bull was about to be released in the dark streets, someone climbed up a palm tree, which due to his weight bent down, blocking his view completely.

Their American contacts Ron Scott and David Finkbeiner wanted to get a feel for the Spanish fiestas themselves and had arranged to meet the Moores and Pilar Alvarez in Castellón. Tony was surprised and pleased that Ron Scott turned out to be about two metres tall, a distinct advantage where filming is concerned. They agreed to drive to the town of Morella, in the northern part of the province of Castellón. The Americans would follow in their car. The town was visible from a long distance away; enclosed by two kilometres of ancient walls, the town wraps itself around the ruins of a fortress perched on a rock. The obligatory bullring is semi-embedded in the rock. Tony was impatient; there was no time to marvel at the towns's medieval character and, dumping his luggage on the bed, took out his cameras. Having lost two hours already, due to the late meeting with the Americans, he was anxious to dive straight into the fiesta crowds. Also, he was restless, as they had had to stay at their friend's house in Alfaz del Pí, near Benidorm, for three days – very pleasant, but not what they were there for. So when the others suggested refreshments before setting off, he snapped at them, "I've come here to film a fiesta." Reluctantly they trailed after him.

A tractor passed them on their way to the town centre. Blood spilled out of the back of the trailer and they could see part of an animal's body. It was a cow that had smashed her head against a barrier and broken her back. Internal injuries had turned the meat black and inedible. Disappointed, the crowd had a whip-round to buy another cow but luck was not on their side. The new cow died too quickly and they had to buy yet another. After a couple of hours, the exhausted animal was dragged to a drain in the street then held over the drain while they slashed its throat. Simultaneously, in an adjacent street, the bodies of the animals killed the night before, were being skinned and hacked to pieces by men soaked in blood and sold to the general public. Within a few days, fourteen animals had met their deaths.

For the evening's fire bull Tony carefully checked out the area. He was especially keen on getting good footage of the preparation of the animal, because he wanted to prove that its suffering did not only start when the flames were set ablaze, but right from the beginning. He located the post where the bull would be tied up, opposite which there was a spot where Ron could get excellent shots over the spectators' heads. When the time came, they took up their positions. Tony and Vicki stood on a balcony and filmed how the bull was dragged out of its container and tied to the post. Two separate contraptions were screwed to the horns, each equipped with a ball of hemp bound with wire and soaked in wax and paraffin. A wide leather belt with bells on was secured around his neck. When the hemp was lit the bull was cut loose and, panicking, ran frantically up and down the streets. Trying to rid the fire from his head, he charged at the barriers, desperately trying to get out. He was even more frantic when the fireworks which had been incorporated into the contraction ignited, showering him with sparks. At this point, Tony went down into the street and followed the animal closely. Gradually, the fire petered out. He was roped and subdued then, to Tony's surprise, shot in the head instead of being stabbed.

Meanwhile, the American had lost his cool and tried to let the crowd know what he thought of them. Tony quickly realised what was happening and managed to calm him down and thus prevent the situation from escalating, putting them all at risk.

In those days, vegetarians were still viewed with suspicion in Spain, so eyebrows must have been raised when all five of them ordered vegetarian meals during their stay in that bloodthirsty place. No wonder that Ron felt under observation after a while. Since they had had their fill of the fiesta, the Americans decided to spend a day visiting local tourist attractions, while the others continued to follow the proceedings. They watched as grown men ran away from a three-month-old calf whose horns had only just started to come through and which posed absolutely no threat. After an hour in the street, the terrified and sweating creature was bundled into a van. They were told that a woman who ran a pastry shop had fallen in love with the animal but Tony was not convinced. He was right to be sceptical; she had bought the calf to make meat pies out of it.

Gothic arcades line the narrow streets leading up to the fortress, and barriers had been erected between the arcade's pillars in which spectators could stand. Vicki was there one evening while Tony was taking stills of a gaunt young cow being taunted by youths who fled at the slightest movement. Tony tended to stand his ground a little longer and the cow would usually then stop. "I was taking pictures and I suddenly realised it was charging on. I ran behind a telephone box and it chased round after me. Luckily it couldn't get at me, but it was bashing at the telephone box. It rocked and smashed the box and I thought, oh God, that was a bit stupid. But you have to take pictures."

The crowd was so impressed with his performance that they offered him a glass of their fiesta brew. Tony suspected it was spirits and wine mixed together. He was not willing to make himself sick, but did not want to offend the people and accepted the glass. "I pretended it was far too strong for me, splattered and coughed that it was too much for me. I couldn't handle it like you brave boys." They laughed and thought he was good fun. He decided not to take too great a risk in future, a resolution he seems to have forgotten fast.

The next day Vicki also earned the respect of the aficionados. A great help if you want to move cattle is the herd instinct, frequently used in fiestas, or in the bullring, when an animal is to be put away. Trained bullocks or 'mansos' are brought out. They walk up to the bull or cow, which usually joins them and follows them. That particular evening, something must have gone wrong, because the two mansos and the two cows were split up. The cows bolted down the inside of the arcades, while the bullocks thundered down the narrow street. "I saw them coming and didn't know which way to go. Vicki tried to run out of the cows' way and ran right into the way of the mansos. They were huge animals. They could have done her a lot of damage."

Meanwhile, Tony had found refuge between the pillars of the arcade. "I swung out and hit her on the shoulder sending her flying out of the way. I held myself back and they hurtled past me and the cows went by on the other side. If I hadn't pushed her, she'd have been killed, or seriously injured. It would have been like being hit by a bus. She managed to regain her balance, got up and ran screaming in terror. She was in a total panic. Something that people never knew about Vicki was that she was absolutely terrified of cattle." Once, on a dairy farm near Southport, she did not dare to enter the byre, even though the Friesian cows were tied up. She stood trembling at the entrance. So you can imagine it took quite a lot of guts to actually be among them like that. In that fiesta, when she was hysterical with fear, two men got hold of her and said, "It's okay", but all the crowd around was shouting out, "Torera! Torera!" because they thought she had run in front of the mansos deliberately. So she was a heroine – a torera.

Having had two close encounters and escaped without harm, they judged it was time to leave. Tony has a theory that if you spend more than two days in a village, the locals start to wonder why you're always taking pictures of the bad things, even though you pretend to take pictures of the good things too. Besides, they had had enough of the daily spilling of blood: two cows and a bull killed each day. One of the villagers admitted, "We only had one cow a week in the past. We couldn't afford any more. But since we joined the European Union, we have so much money from them, we get all these animals now."

Tony read in one of the newspapers that there was to be a cattle exhibition on the coast and had a hunch that it would not be like cattle shows in England, where they are walked around on halters, given marks and awarded prizes. The Americans were only too delighted to decamp to the seaside and Pilar needed to get back to work.

Situated about a 140km north of Valencia, the small town of Benicarló indulges in several fiestas each year. The 'Fiestas Patronales', during which several patron saints are honoured, take place around 24 August and last for about a week. The main event is the 'Bous a la mar', which is widely advertised. The colourful official poster for 2005 shows a bull on the beach, sand flying, as he charges at someone who jumps into the clear blue sea.

Having found a hotel on the main road, they headed straight for the docks. The fiesta was about to start, so all five of them took up positions amongst the spectators on a wall above the dock. A collection of pathetic-looking cattle was held in a pen. Emaciated, their ribs standing out, they all had diarrhoea and were squirting everywhere. They were a pitiful sight.

In a space between the dock and the harbour wall, about a hundred metres long and thirty metres wide, were two makeshift shelters made from oil drums and wood, in which people could seek shelter. Tony climbed over the wall and dropped down on to the dock, because you really have to be down amongst the action to obtain the best pictures.

One cow at a time was let out and chased around the dockside; the idea being to tempt the animals into the sea and soon a brown cow fell in. They approached her with a rowing boat and put a rope round her neck, then towed her back to a wooden ramp and back on to the dock, one man pulling hard on her tail all the time. Tony was only a few feet away from the animal and saw that she was shaking from exhaustion and fear and coughing up water.

Another cow was released and the procedure repeated several times. Vicki took notes of what she witnessed, "During the animals' towing by the boat they were submerged totally several times and dragged along under the surface for many yards. Totally exhausted and suffering from the ingestion of great quantities of oil polluted seawater, some lay virtually unconscious on the ramp. They had no respite but were brutally dragged into the centre of the arena where the rope was loosened and they were made to run again."

This so-called cattle exhibition took place twice a day, over four days; the same animals being used all over again. The seawater got into their stomachs, making them sick and causing diarrhoea. They were housed in a cattle wagon, the floors thick with ordure. They didn't survive for very long, but every time one died they would just buy another to take its place. The cattle are taken up and down the coast and the sickening spectacle repeated. This kind of event is very common in the area of Valencia and Castellón. Animals repeatedly die, either from drowning, or from exhaustion after being dragged out of the water. In the summer of 2005, one bull died in Denia and one in Moraira. Animals rights groups like ANPBA file complaints against these spectacles but little ever changes.

The following morning at breakfast, Tony wanted to discuss the plan for the day. Since they had a full day before their departure to Barcelona, he wanted to film from a different angle to capture the cows falling into the sea and there would be a fire bull at night. Suddenly, Ron declared that they were leaving, they had had enough of Spain and were off to Italy. They must have been unaware that Italy, as of today, still has fiestas in which animals are abused. Apart from the infamous Siena horse race, the 'Festa della Palombella' in Orvieto and the brutal oxen race in the village of Chieuti, continue to attract criticism from around the world. Tony was shocked and wondered what the Americans had expected of their trip to Spain. Even Vicki could not convince them to stay.

So, with their lift to Barcelona gone, they had to find other means of transport to cover the 220 kilometres. There was a train, but they could not guarantee that it would be on time to make the airport connection. Disappointed, they went back to the docks. Despite filming all day, Tony did not get the shots he wanted, just a heavy dose of sunburn but they had more luck with the fire bull. The wooden barriers erected on the harbour leaned backwards at a 60 degree angle and were full of gaps and difficult to climb. Tony had just taken up position when the bull ran straight at him. Vicki tried to pull him back but he kept on filming. He got some very good pictures, including one where the spectators actually hit the bull in the eye with a can of Coke. Since this particular shot was used on NBC television, he is convinced it was worth the risk. They slowed it down, so that you could actually see the can spinning across and hitting him in the eye. It was used to great effect and people were really shocked by it.

At the train station the next morning, they were not allowed to buy a ticket until the train came in and there was a long queue of people ahead of them. Queuing patiently would not have been a problem under normal circumstances, but Tony was determined to board that train. "As it was coming in I barged to the front. People were implying, 'There's a queue. Go to the back!' But I said, 'No entiendo. I don't understand,' and carried on. I couldn't afford to miss the flight. There was no money to buy another ticket."

In the last weeks of 1990, an almost forgotten project was finally realised. In the spring of 1988, Georges Roos, their main contact in Madrid, had approached them with what seemed to be a very good idea. As a musician, he wanted to produce an animal rights record; a concept album touching all forms of animal cruelty. The songs would be interspersed with short spoken pieces. French,

English and Spanish versions would be professionally produced and marketed all over the world to open people's eyes and educate them about the creatures with whom they shared the planet.

Vicki agreed to do the English version and with Dave Gartside accompanying her on the electric piano and Tony on the guitar, she recorded three songs on a cheap tape recorder in the FAACE office to give the record company an idea about her vocal range. Tony made a copy of the tape and sent it to Georges in Madrid; the record company was impressed by her voice but funding was still a problem. Georges went to a lot of trouble approaching French and American animal rights organisations and there were times when it seemed that the project was doomed to failure.

He sent the music and the English lyrics to Tony, who suggested minor changes to make it appear more modern and to fit better with Vicki's voice. Unfortunately, this dented Georges' Argentinian pride and led to a rift in their friendship. Eventually, however, Vicki flew to Madrid, followed a while later by Chris Mason, the drummer in the Tony Moore Band, who sang in the chorus of the record, to record their songs. Apart from the title song 'Animal Eyes', Vicki sang 'Platero', 'The Man from Assisi', 'The Dawn of the Bull' and 'Mr Matthew's Lighthouse', a lovely duet about dolphins and whales. She also gave a spoken introducion to the song 'Pegasus'. American jazz singer Donna Hightower recorded the last song on the album, 'My Brothers'.

Two years had passed and Vicki and Tony had given up on the record ever coming out. However, in autumn 1990, Georges suddenly informed them that he was busy completing the record cover for printing. Entiltled *Animal Eyes*, the cover would feature his beloved dog Karina's eyes. A few weeks later, the album was released in Spain by Solera Records, as a proper long playing record, whereas the French and English versions were only released as promotional tapes with the sad eyes of a chimpanzee on their covers.

With no proper marketing, the record was largely ignored and even those sympathetic to the cause found it too depressing. Tony's efforts to get it released on the British market came to nothing and they soon forgot about it. In researching this book the master tape was unearthed by Pilar Taberner and Tony had it made into audio CDs at a studio in Southport.

# Pepa and Magdalena

Vicki kept her promise to the goats in Manganeses de la Polvorosa and flew to Spain on 22 January 1991. Prior to the fiesta she was to meet fellow animal rights people in Madrid and do some research. On her second day there she received sad news from home. She wrote in her diary, "On Thursday 24th, at 5 o'clock in England, Trigger, our dear old boy was put to sleep, lovable teddy bear cat. We'll miss his little ginger presence greatly."

On the day of the goat fiesta she teamed up with a young man from Alcalá de Henares near Madrid, who would serve as a driver, and Regina Davis, whom she knew from the disaster of the San Sebastian dogs' home. She hired the cheapest car possible and they set off for Zamora province. The atmosphere in the car was not too tense. It was only when they went to see the Civil Governor in Zamora and it was clear to them that promises to stop the fiesta might not be kept, that their mood changed.

Prior to the fiesta, Vicki and many others had sent letters to Governor Angel Gavilán asking him to ban the fiesta and she also had a letter from the Spanish Ministry of the Interior stating that no animal would be abused in the fiesta. The government indeed suspended the throwing of the goat by sending a letter to Mayor José Manuel Gil Barrio at rather short notice. The prohibition was based on guidelines for the policing of public spectacles and recreational activities drawn up in 1982. The guidelines enabled the police to suspend events in which minors could be exposed to danger, or in which animals might be harmed. The letter said that, according to the information received, the fiesta had degenerated over recent years and the throwing of the goat represented "A severe attack on the sensitivity of the spectators." However, on the day of the fiesta the local paper *La Opinión de Zamora* published a front page picture of a goat and a quote from the villagers, "The ban will not prevent the Leap of the She-Goat".

Thus the three of them felt a short meeting with the governor was vital. The governor had come to an agreement with the mayor and councillors to allow their fiesta to go ahead if – and this order was exact and categorical – the goat was to be lowered from the tower to the ground on a secure rope and no maltreatment of the animal should take place. Vicki felt this compromise contained too many risks for the animal and, expecting the worst, she went to the Guardia Civil headquarters in Benavente, in whose area Manganeses is situated. Two officers had been detailed to the fiesta. After a lengthy conversation, the police chief decided to attend the fiesta himself in the company of four officers.

The village was more crowded this year, bad publicity having served as a magnet for outside spectators. However, the collective mood was tense rather than festive. Vicki had taken up a position on the steps leading into the church tower and when the drunken youths approached with the goat, she stood in their path and warned them of the consequences of any injury to the goat. Ignoring her pleas, they thrust her to one side and dragged the animal up into the bell tower. There was nothing she could do to save the animal, so she positioned herself by the canvas to ensure they attempted to catch the goat. To everyone's amazement they now had two goats in the tower. The animals were dangled out of the window. The larger goat, dressed up in tinsel, ribbons and a large pair of frilly knickers, was undressed in a degrading mock striptease. Then to shouts of "Throw her! Throw her!" from the crowd, she was flung out of the tower without a rope. She was caught in the canvas, shortly followed by the smaller goat, who bounced off the edge of the canvas and then hit the ground.

Vicki had only a split second to examine the animals, before the larger goat was dragged away through the crowd. Reacting quickly, she got hold of the small goat, Magdalena, and offered to buy her. Twenty thousand pesetas was a great deal of money for a common goat and the villagers accepted. Vicki then said she also wanted to buy Pepa, the older goat, but she wanted to pay only fifteen thousand pesetas for her. After an argument amongst themselves, the Quintos accepted, before joking that next year there would be six goats. Vicki quickly wrote a receipt for each goat and had them signed by the respective owners. From that moment things started to get very unpleasant – she had effectively bought their prizes – the goats having been destined for a raffle in the village disco, then slaughtered and eaten. Things got so ugly, that the Guardia Civil had to intervene and help Vicki prepare the goats for transport. Regina had brought the tranquilliser Combelén. Had the goat been badly injured, Vicki had planned to put it out of its misery immediately. This not being necessary, both goats were injected with a small dose to keep them calm. The trip to Madrid would last at least five hours and Pepa, who was eighteen months old, was already visibly distressed.

British journalist Bill Bond had just snapped a radiant Vicki kneeling between her two goats before putting them in the car, when an angry local shouted that the animals were his and Vicki could not have them. Upon which, she produced the receipts; the goats were hers and she would not return them; he should seek redress from the two youths. Strong words in Spanish and English were exchanged, until the Guardia Civil put an end to the dispute, making sure they got out of the village safely.

A young man drove and Vicki sat in the back of the cramped little car with the two goats. Magdalena mostly slept with her head either on Vicki's knee or tucked under her arm, but Pepa was more frisky, and as the traffic came to a halt in an underpass in Madrid, she suddenly decided that she had to get out of the car and scrambled towards the rear window, her large horns scraping the roof. Vicki had to smile when she turned round and saw the shocked expression of the driver in the car behind. Unfortunately, both goats also emptied their bowels in the rental car.

Late at night they arrived in Alcalá de Henares. There the goats would find temporary accommodation while Vicki and Tony sought a permanent home for them. Discussing the matter back in England, they came up with the idea of moving the goats to Tossa de Mar. Chari Cruz, who looked after the animals in Tossa's shelter, agreed to take them. Once preparations were finalised, Tony called Georges Roos in Madrid with the good news. Their relationship had gone a bit sour over the album but there had been no open animosity, so Tony was shocked to find him fuming over the goats. "He told me that I had no right to have them, they were not my goats and the woman who ran the shelter would not give them up. I said they *were* our goats, that we had bought them and saved their lives and that I would definitely be taking them." Their argument went on for a while, until Georges called Tony "an arrogant fool".

Chari and Salvador arrived in Alcalá two days later and teamed up with Vicki's friend Pilar. The young man who had driven Vicki and the goats began to show hostility towards her and then announced that Pepa and Magdelena had been stolen. They should leave immediately and not come back. Unsure what to do, Pilar called Tony, who dismissed the idea of the goats being stolen as ridiculous. They should enquire at the police station to see if they had been reported missing. It turned out that the report was made just two hours after his phone conversation with Georges Roos and two days after they were supposedly stolen. Tony did not believe it was mere coincidence and asked the girls to speak to the police again.

As they waited to speak to a police officer, they leafed through the newspaper on the table which contained a picture of the two goats. The article said that they were rescued in Manganeses by the woman who ran the shelter. The police officer recognised the house where the picture had been taken and gave them the address and directions. Bearing in mind the threats that had been made against them, Pilar and Chari did not want to go alone.

When they arrived at the house the young driver was there and tried to threaten them into leaving but at that moment the police arrived on the scene and made it clear that legal action could be taken for making a false report. Pilar presented a power of attorney signed by Tony and a copy of the receipts for the goats, upon which they were handed over to them without any further trouble. Vicki wrote later, "Both Tony and I were absolutely stunned and appalled at the trickery and lying over the goats ..."

However, Magdalena was not well and had to be put down a few months later. Pepa, the older goat, lived in Tossa until she died of old age.

# Fame

"L'Europe rendra-t-elle l'Espagne moins cruelle?" (Will Europe make Spain less cruel) asked the Brussels *Le Soir*. The day before, 10 April 1991, Vicki had presented a shocking video on blood fiestas in the European Parliament, together with a Belgian animal rights group. As the meeting was about to start, Tony received a frantic phone call from Vicki. She did not know how to operate the video cassette recorder and there was nobody available to assist her. They had to start on time, because the room and the interpreters were only available for so long. Not knowing the make of the VCR, Tony tried to explain the process. Despite this setback, the presentation was a success, receiving good media coverage and securing many pledges of support from MEPs.

Next on their agenda was another trip to Tossa, where Vicki spoke about bullbaiting in England at the annual conference on animal rights. She had put a lot of work into research and impressed the audience with her in-depth knowledge. In former times, the English had taken similar pleasure to their Spanish counterparts in bullfighting, though the English bulls had been killed by dogs rather than matadors. In many places there were actual bullrings, or yards. Bull running, accompanied by all sorts of atrocities, had also been very popular and even continued until 1839 in the town of Stamford. She also traced the use of birds to countries like Belgium and Germany. Of course, they could not leave Tossa without paying Pepa a visit.

Earlier in April, she had been invited by the Director of the Madrid Complutense University to be a guest lecturer in the summer classes. She accepted the invitation with enthusiasm and in mid-July flew over to Madrid. She was picked up at the airport in a limousine and driven to a smart hotel, which the university had booked for the duration of her stay. Her club class airline ticket and all further expenses were paid by the university and she enjoyed not having to count her money every day. The course "La actitud del hombre antes los animales" (Man's attitude towards animals) lasted a week and was directed by Professor of Philosophy, Priscilla Cohn, of the Pennsylvania State University. She had invited a panel of international philosophers, veterinary scientists, legal experts and theologists. Among them were American philosopher and animal rights writer Tom Regan and Reverend Andrew Linzey of the University of Essex. Vicki enjoyed being among these like-minded, educated people, though feelings ran high when differing opinions clashed. She even had to act as peacemaker when one of the participants threw a glass of wine in his counterpart's face.

She gave her own lecture on the second day entitled "Animals in Entertainment: A Special Look at Spain" and was pleased to have the chance to hand a FAACE video on blood fiestas and bullfighting to Queen Sofía of Spain, who attended part of the summer course. The Queen had assumed that it was about Blackie the donkey, but as soon as Vicki revealed that it was about bullfighting and bulls and cows in fiestas, the Queen's security guards rushed over. It is a well-known fact that, while King Carlos is an adamant aficionado, Queen Sofía is criticised by the media for not attending bullfights. Queen Sofía remembered Vicki and in 2006, in a letter to Tony, had one of her aides write, "Her Majesty remembers your late wife well and asks me to thank you on Her behalf for your continuing concern for the welfare of animals, and to convey Her best regards."

One morning, as the group of lecturers left the hotel, a kitten ran across the street and hid underneath a parked car and started to climb up using the tyre as support, before disappearing inside the wheel arch. Vicki was concerned, because any moment the driver could come back and move the car but her fellow animal rights lecturers thought the animal would be fine and urged her to move on. They were told in no uncertain terms that it was not enough to give educated speeches on the treatment of animals. To the embarrassment, as well as the amusement, of her colleagues, she stripped off her blouse and in only her bra, got underneath the car and searched for the kitten. She retrieved it carefully and put it in a safe place – a story that somehow made it into the British tabloids.

In 1990, journalist Rob Moore had approached Vicki and Tony with the idea of doing a documentary on Spanish blood fiestas, focusing on the involvement of the Church and the impact on children. He had been running with the bulls in Pamplona and had contacted ADDA, who in turn put him in touch with FAACE, as they had so much more material about animal abuse in Spain.

At first, Tony and Vicki were not sure whether to get involved, but they were assured that the programme would expose and not promote the cruelty inherent in Spanish blood fiestas. So they chose to highlight three fiestas: the chicken fiesta in Nalda, the bull fiesta in Cuacos and, of course, Coria. The documentary would be called *Blood Lust*. They were asked to keep a low profile with the press until filming had been completed. However, it would take almost a year before they set off for Spain, because it was not easy to find a producer to take it on. Eventually, Paul Woolwich, the executive producer of Thames TV's *This Week* programme, agreed to do it. He believed in the cause and thought it would create a stir. Tony and Vicki were asked to meet the team in London. Rob Moore cheekily suggested a tapas bar, but Tony thought this was a bit over the top and they met elsewhere.

On 12 August 1991, after nearly a year of preparation, Tony and Vicki left for Spain. Their dogs Susi and Fritz were put into a shelter and their good friend

Nora Fee looked after their nine cats. In Madrid they met their friend Pilar and Rob Moore and his interpreter. The associate producer had travelled to Spain earlier to check out the locations and prepare the filming. Their first location was Coria. As it was August, the town was not in fiesta but the television crew wanted to interview Mayor Antonio Lisero. In the town hall he explained that the purpose of the darts was to make the bull look 'pretty' and did no harm. The driving instructor who made the darts demonstrated on camera how they were made. First he took a square of paper and rolled it into a tight cone to fit into a blowpipe, which was just a piece of aluminium piping. Next he pushed a large dressmaker's pin in, so that it protruded from the pointed end, followed by a piece of lead shot. Finally, hot wax was dripped in to hold everything in place. He then shot a dart from his blowpipe at the door, which was made from hard dark oak. Even though the mayor claimed the bulls would not feel the darts, this clearly proved the opposite. They could not get the dart out by hand and had to send for a pair of pliers.

Tony had been waiting outside while all this was going on. Suddenly, Rob came out and said, "They want us to turn the cars round, so we can get straight out of the village."

"What for?"

"They're going to introduce Vicki to them and see what they say. And we might have to make a quick get-away. But I don't really see what the problem is. The place is full of police. So nothing's going to happen."

"But don't you understand? The police are the *local* police. They belong to the village. They are paid by the village. If the mayor says, 'Stop these people', they won't help you."

Vicki was introduced as somebody who had actually been to their fiesta two or three times. In response to the mayor's claims that the darts did not hurt the bulls but were purely for decoration, Vicki asked him to stand against the wall. She would take a blowpipe and a couple of darts and would it be all right if she aimed for his eyes and his testicles, if she could find them? This created animosity and one of the villagers called her a mad woman but they got out of Coria without problems.

The next stop was Cuacos del Yuste, which is also situated in Extremadura. The main fiesta in honour of the Virgin of the Ascension takes place in the middle of August. Wooden scaffolding and stands had been erected on the main plaza, where the bullfighting events took place. The crew was allowed on to a balcony, while Vicki and Tony sat among the crowd expecting the worst, because some youths had boasted they had hundreds of banderillas. It turned out that they also had metal spiked poles and homemade spears. They watched in horror, as one bull's body was punctured and lacerated all over, blood pouring from dozens of wounds. Desperate for water, he tried to drink from a fountain but was prevented by one youth stabbing him repeatedly in the head and eyes. Some time later, the dead animal was carted away by a front loading tractor, its head dangling over one side. Children pulled back the bull's lips, "to make it smile".

When it was all over, Tony asked producer Clive Edwards for his thoughts about what he had seen. He said he thought he was going to be sick and had to go back inside the house for a minute. This beautiful animal had come out in all innocence and they had done that to it; reduced it to a bloody mess. Until that point, Tony had been preoccupied by the trustworthiness of the media people. "They were on your side, but you are never sure, are you? They might turn it around."

Now he was sure that this report would come out all right, but it took reporter Margaret Gilmore a little longer to realise the full extent of the villagers' cruelty. A small cow, with a broken spear stuck in her chest, who had been running around, was soon was spirited away by her tormentors. Vicki was convinced they were going to kill the cow, or even bring her out again and then kill her, but at this point Margaret Gilmore was not prepared to believe in such an outcome; the animal would be fine, because she had been told so. Her opinion shifted abruptly when the next animal to come out was killed right in front of them, its blood spattering Tony's shoes. She took a picture of Vicki and Tony next to a huge puddle of congealing blood, which provoked the anger of the local people.

There was no time for grief, because the schedule was so tight. They drove all the way up to Logroño in the Rioja region, where they were to stay for the next few days. As they were eating in a restaurant, Rob Moore, in the ultimate gesture of bad taste, entered dressed in the outfit of a bullfighting fan club. It went down like a lead balloon and he later apologised for his bad joke. They met an animal rights person who had organised protests against the chicken fiesta but he was too frightened to accompany them to Nalda, fearing for his life; graffiti had already been scrawled all over his shop front. Since there was graffiti all over the area, Tony suspected that it probably had nothing to do with the fiesta but the man would not be convinced. Nevertheless, he gave them some very useful advice.

The next morning they left early for Nalda. Understandably, Tony and Vicki were nervous; one never knew what to expect in a fiesta. On arrival in the village they split up from the film crew, it having been agreed that it was safer for Vicki, Tony and Pilar not to be seen to be connected to them. It was still early, so they had a coffee in the village square, whilst the film crew collected background footage and managed to find a girl willing to speak out against the fiesta and a fan keen to provide an opposite view.

When the fiesta was about to start, they positioned themselves on a high grassy bank. Rob Moore stood out in his blue and white fiesta outfit with a blue neckerchief. Someone must have given him the wrong advice – the area's colours were red and white.

When the fiesta started, Tony and Vicki climbed to the top of the bank and started filming and were filmed in turn by the television crew. On a flat area at the bottom of the bank two poles were set up, with a washing line strung between them, on to which chickens were tied by their feet. Some village youths gathered at one end of the flat ground and mounted their horses without saddles. Soon the first of the riders was galloping towards the washing line in a billowing cloud of red dust. When he came within range, he reached out and tried to rip a chicken's head off. The other youths each took their turns. Much of the time they failed; often ripping the skin so that it pulled down over the head, leaving the chicken still alive with the neck exposed. The poor creatures flapped their wings in agony and terror until each of them had been decapitated. The heads were then thrown into the crowd as macabre trophies, or discarded like rubbish. By the time all the birds were dead it was almost dark. Young girls gathered up the mutilated headless bodies and waved them around like cheerleaders' pompoms. A truly sordid little affair.

Mayor Juan Garcia brazenly maintained that the chickens did not suffer and dismissed the protest letters as irrelevant. The village priest, Father Luis Canillas, also made it clear that the animals' suffering was not a priority on his list. Margaret Gilmore later questioned an official from the Interior Ministry, who claimed that a memo had been sent to the village requesting them not to abuse animals, but added that they really did not wish to interfere in the matter. He had no explanation as to why the village had used two batches of ten chickens this year, instead of just one batch, as in previous years.

In a rare and brief interlude between changing locations, they had the chance to spend a few hours in Segovia, just an hour's drive from Madrid. Declared a World Heritage Site by UNESCO in 1985, the town is packed with churches and monuments, the most outstanding of which is the Roman aqueduct, with its one hundred and sixty-six arches. Since 2003, the town has featured a witchcraft museum, cementing its esoteric reputation. Mysterious legends surround the various monuments, particularly the Iglesia de la Vera Cruz. This church, located outside the town walls, is built in a unique shape. People tend to think it is octagonal, but in fact, it has twelve sides. Knight templars built it at the beginning of the thirteenth century to celebrate the matyrdom of Christ. It boasts a splinter of what is claimed to be his authentic cross.

Legend has it that shortly after the inauguration of the church, a brother of the order died. By an unfortunate omission, his body was left unprotected in the building overnight. When the brothers returned the next morning, rooks had got into the church and destroyed the body. The prior put a curse on the rooks, which from then on have never been seen on the church roof.

Vicki was more intrigued by another curiosity. Apparently, visitors sometimes experienced an odd sensation and perceived a strange glow inside the church. So Vicki went in … nothing … Pilar went in … nothing, but when Tony stepped in, his hair shot up on end, as if he were wired to an electric current. "Weird. Of course, they didn't believe me but my hair really did stand up at the back of my neck ... I got out fast. It was such a funny feeling." The church was sited at a point where two ley lines cross, which for believers means there is a very strong energy present but legend offers a very different explanation for the phenomenon. Supposedly, some templars are still hiding in the crypt from the massacre of 1312, when their order was suppressed. They watch over their treasures and emit lethal radiation if anybody tries to open the crypt.

From the top of the tower the view was extraordinary and Tony took a stunning photograph of Vicki standing against an opening in the tower wall. She looks happy and carefree and her face is shining with a light suntan and her long dark hair is tousled by the breeze. He chose this photograph for her memorial service.

On 21 August they flew home. This time they did not have to seek out the media to get their pictures published, it was the other way round. The *News of the World* was given an advance copy of the programme. Under the headline, "Sick Slaughter in the Sun", they dedicated more than a full page to Spain's gory blood fiestas. Producer Clive Edwards had to cut some of the most horrific cruelty to make the film suitable for general viewing, but the impact was still deeply disturbing. Tory MEP Madron Seligman, who had been interviewed in the programme, demanded a Europe-wide ban of bloodsports, which obviously would have to include fox hunting in the United Kingdom.

Many newspapers recommended the programme – renamed *Fiestas of Blood* – to their readers. Even before it went on the air at 8.30pm on 12 September, the station received calls from concerned members of the public. "We have enough mindless morons in this country. This may encourage others to do these cruel things, specifically because of the time it goes out," said one caller. Another complained that it was advertised without a warning. Even within the station there had been discussions, as to whether it was wise to show the programme before the 9 o'clock watershed.

Vicki and Tony had not dared to hope for the amount of attention the programme attracted for their work – it really put FAACE on the map. Nor were they prepared for the power of television to thrust people into the spotlight. Total strangers were staring at them and coming up to them to express sympathy for their cause. At times they had to hide to avoid all the attention but it was wonderful to hear people discussing the programme wherever they went. Over the next few weeks, piles of letters poured in. One was from the editor of the *Radio Times*, "... The courage of the English couple who filmed these atrocities was the only shining light in a modern-day horror story."

However, not all the reviews were so complimentary, such as this one from the *Evening Standard*:

*The evidence was undeniable and gruesome ... What was more questionable was the way in which the Moores presented their case ... Although their passionate concern is admirable, a blindness to deep human emotions, like attachment to tradition, is unlikely to help in these notoriously difficult clashes of culture.*

One person who questioned his own culture, due to the programme, was Spain's Ambassador to London, Don Felipe de la Morena. He sent a copy of *Fiestas of Blood* to his government in Madrid, concerned that this kind of behaviour was damaging Spain's image abroad. He felt that the disturbing scenes should be shown on Spanish television too, because the cruel reality of these fiestas had not yet been documented over there.

Foreign reporters in the UK watched the programme too. The Swedish newspaper *Expressen* visited Vicki and Tony and published a long piece accompanied by a coupon directed to the Spanish authorities. Tony recalls that, due to popular demand, the paper, with a circulation of six hundred thousand copies per day, had to reprint the coupon. Within a few days they had the Swedish television on their doorstep. After the programme was shown, a massive outcry followed. Forty thousand people from all over Sweden signed a protest, which was handed over to the Spanish Embassy in Stockholm. Creator of the famous Pippi Longstocking, Astrid Lindgren was reported as having sent protest letters to King Juan Carlos and President Felipe Gonzales. The programme was shown twice in one week due to popular request.

While some of the atrocities shown in the documentary still continue to this day, some fiestas have been modified and the cruelty ameliorated. In the case of Nalda, due to continued protests and the introduction of a new animal welfare law, the fiesta was finally banned in 1995. In 2000, it was revived using dummies and the villagers appear to enjoy it just as much.

# Riots

News came of a bloodless bullfight in Torrevieja. Three days before Tony left to investigate, Vicki wrote in her diary, "Fritz Moore, 'Old Heidelberg' our beloved faithful dog and dearest friend, put to sleep at 11.30am aged seventeen, or eighteen years." He had been blind and deaf for some time, could no longer walk and had become incontinent. With heavy heart, Tony flew to Alicante and teamed up with Pilar. Unlike Vicki, who had steadily continued to improve her Spanish, he had not had the chance to take proper lessons and still needed an interpreter. Only about three hundred people turned up for the première. Nothing seemed to be happening. Only when the crowd grew impatient, did someone announce that the corrida was cancelled due to strong winds.

Tony hung around and met bullfighter Mariano Villaescusa, who had retired in 1985 after fifteen years and allegedly six hundred dead bulls. During his last ever bullfight he looked the wounded bull in the eyes and saw the pain. "I began to hear the bull cry and became aware of his suffering. I felt a great sorrow for this courageous beast. He had an exceptional nobility." He realised that they were both victims: the animal for being hurt and killed and he for risking his life. So he came up with the idea of mock bullfights, which would eliminate blood-spilling, torture, and the death of the bull.

He was very much against the 'afeitado' (the shaving off of the horns). From horseback he had seen bulls being prepared for a bullfight, where the horns had been cut off so close to the head that they bled extensively. A piece of wood had to be nailed to the end of the horn and the horns rebuilt using resin. He did not want any of this for the two bulls he had just bought. They would only be played with and teased using a red cloth. His bulls were due to be delivered twenty-four hours prior to the event but only arrived on the day and were obviously not the ones he had selected, but wilder animals. Apart from that, his suit of lights had been stolen and at the last minute his cuadrilla, his crew, left. Tony was convinced it was a fix; why should they help him put themselves out of a job? Also, they were not prepared to face an unweakened bull. "Traditional matadors take me to be public enemy number one," Villaescusa confided and would soon be forced into hiding for a while. His claims that he had the backing of international animal rights groups were not correct. So-called bloodless bullfights take place in the USA regularly in Portuguese communities over there. The bulls are made to wear a strip of Velcro on which the banderillas are stuck. It may be a step in the right direction, but it is still unacceptable for bulls to used in entertainment. People think it's okay because there is no blood but it still serves to perpetuate bullfighting.

Vicki once more travelled to New York alone in November, for a week of meetings and lectures, while Tony saved up for a trip to the goat fiesta in January 1992; last year's stunt having made it difficult for Vicki to go. Shortly before his departure, the *Daily Star* rang, wanting to send a team to Manganeses de la Polvorosa. Tony agreed to meet them in a restaurant in Madrid, where he gave them a map and as much information as he could. He warned them to be careful, because it could be very dangerous but felt that they did not believe him and that he was exaggerating.

The following morning he hired a car and met with José Luis Barceló from ADDA Madrid and Ken Sewell from ADDA Barcelona. Since the chicken fiesta in Tordesillas would take place on the same day, they dropped Ken off in the village on their way to Manganeses. Tony supplied him with many rolls of films and urged him to take as many pictures as possible. They would pick him up on their way back to Madrid.

When they arrived in Manganeses, there was hardly anything going on in the streets and no one about except for a Spanish television crew, who started following Tony, demanding an interview – the last thing he wanted, as he was supposed to be travelling incognito.

Before his departure to Spain he was told that there would be a human chain formed by animal rights people around the church tower, to prevent the throwing of the animal. However, not enough people had shown up and the plan had to be abandoned.

Gradually the streets filled up, until approximately four thousand people – more than three times the number of inhabitants – were jostling for position and he spotted the team from the *Daily Star*. Despite the carnival atmosphere, with singing, banging of drums and a local band, one could sense an undercurrent of trouble. Since Governor Gavilán was responsible for banning the throwing of the animal this year, he arrived in person accompanied by riot police, one of whom went inside the tower and held the door shut from the inside. The villagers, who had been driving the goat around the square in a vehicle, interpreted this as a provocation. "I was directly at the bottom of the tower filming the release of doves, throwing of sweets, the rolling out of a tarpaulin and the singing of the fiesta song. The first inkling I had that there was going to be trouble was when a big cry went up from the side of the tower where the goat is taken in. I struggled up the steps through the crush of people to see enraged villagers banging on the church tower door. I started to film and was accosted by a crowd of men."

The men flung him down the steps but he managed to escape relatively unharmed. Anyone with a camera was a target. The crew of the Spanish national television station TVE had their cameras smashed. Photographer Bernado Díaz sustained severe head injuries and was taken to hospital. His paper, *El Sol*, on the day prior to the festivities had published a particularly critical article. The men even threatened the mayor and the priest; they would encounter the same fate if they sided with the animal.

The whole village was seething with pent-up rage. *Daily Star* photographer Anthony Upton came up to Tony as he was trying to film the villagers trying to rock the Guardia Civil jeep off the bridge into the river, and told him that one of his cameras had been stolen and the other smashed on the ground. He was not a small man, yet, as he was trying to take pictures of the attack on the Guardia, he was punched in the head, kicked on the ground and was lucky to get out.

The Guardia tried to disperse the crowd with tear gas but by now there was another problem – reporter Sue Crawford had disappeared. She had last been seen in the centre of the riot. Tony agreed to help find her but as a precautionary measure put his cameras in the boot of Upton's car. As he did this two teenage girls came up to him and asked if he was the husband of Vicki Moore. "I thought for a second and decided that if they were asking me this, they must already know. So I said 'yes', thinking this is it, if the girls tell the villagers. But they apologised for the behaviour of their village."

They moved the car to a quieter spot where the photographer would wait for Tony to return with the reporter and pick up his cameras. Having ventured once more into the agitated crowd, he began to search for the lost reporter but with no success. After a while, he returned to the car. He had a hunch they would still try and throw the goat and he needed his cameras. At first, he thought he must have gone to the wrong spot, because the car was no longer there. Frustrated, he went looking for his Spanish companion José, who also had a camera, but which proved useless from that distance in the winter late afternoon light. The crowd started to get excited again and it was obvious they were going to throw the goat. They started to lower her by means of a harness around her stomach, using a wheel on the end of a metal pole. The goat struggled and the harness slipped until it was up around her neck and then again, until she was dangling by a horn. They hauled her back in and then just threw her out.

The animal was caught in the canvas and bounced up and down a few times. Tony forced his way through the crowd and saw that the goat appeared to be physically unharmed but in shock. He decided to look for the *Daily Star* team again. After walking through the village for a while he found the photographer in his car. At the same time, Sue Crawford reappeared in a car driven by a French couple. She had been forced to take refuge in a house after being grabbed and chased down a back street by a jeering gang. Tony agreed to meet the journalists later after first picking up Ken Sewell from the chicken fiesta in Tordesillas. In contrast to them, Ken had taken lots of pictures, which Tony offered to Upton, who had got nothing at all.

Back in England, he was disappointed when he saw that the newspaper had somehow been able to obtain pictures of the goat throwing but only mentioned the fate of the beheaded chickens in a very small piece without any pictures. They had also put a silly and inaccurate quote in his mouth: "It's a common way of killing animals in this part of the world. They tie them to a tree with a rope around their neck – and then pull hard."

Once again he seriously questioned whether they should be more selective when working with the press. He was pleased, however, when the paper got in touch with Labour MP Tony Banks, who was so outraged by the report that he put down an Early Day Motion in the House of Commons calling for a tourism boycott. He also said to the *Liverpool Echo*: "The only consolation is that I am sure we have now seen the end of this bloody fiesta in this village."

He was wrong ...

# Friction

After their successful experience with television producers, Vicki and Tony were happy to co-operate with another documentary, this time for the BBC, focusing on animal rights groups and their lobbying of the European Parliament. As they had a presentation scheduled for mid-February in Strasbourg, they agreed. Time was short because the next Waterloo Cup loomed on the horizon. In September 1991, councillors had failed in their application for a by-law making hare coursing illegal throughout West Lancashire. They felt that coursing brought nothing but problems for the district in the form of violence between protesters and coursers. The Home Office had demanded proof that dogs chasing and killing hares caused a public nuisance in itself. In February 1992, West Lancashire council was forced to withdraw an injunction at the last minute to stop the Waterloo Cup, after Lancashire police declined to back it. So once more FAACE had to drum up support to demonstrate on 25 February.

A few days later, they met the BBC crew again in Villanueva de la Vera for the donkey fiesta. They boasted that the mayor had given them a special place to film from a balcony in the square. He had – right at the far end, where they would get no decent pictures! Tony was not known to the villagers and hoped to be able to move more freely in the fiesta and stay close to the donkey. He was surprised when Vicki, who was obviously recognised, was invited on to a balcony, underneath which the donkey would pass. This year's donkey, 'Nieblo', or 'Misty' in English, was the same as before, except that he seemed to fall even more than usual. The crush around him was so ferocious, that he was on the ground more than he was on his feet.

Vicki joined Tony on the streets after the donkey had passed her balcony, by which time the television crew had realised that they had been conned and had left their post. Vicki was filming and Tony taking stills, when the crowd surrounding the donkey suddenly charged at the crew and themselves, squashing them against a wall. They deliberately engineered it so that by the time they were free, Misty had passed by. Nevertheless, they already had some very useful footage and the programme used some of Vicki's, taken from the balcony, showing Misty collapsing in the centre of a chanting mob, and being roughly manhandled back to his feet. When the ordeal was over, the donkey was put in a barn, where, after thirty minutes, they were they allowed to check on him. He was still covered in sweat and stressed out, but there were no obvious injuries.

Back in the village square, they were watching the Pero Palo puppet being put back on his pole, when Tony became aware that Vicki was no longer beside him.

After a few anxious minutes he spotted her in a bar. He was just about to go to her, when a couple of villagers called out, "Vicki! Your husband's looking for you." So much for not being recognised!

The documentary, *Blood Relations – Close Encounters of the European Kind*, broadcast in April, was rather disappointing. Even though Vicki and Tony had gone to great lengths to assist the project, it chose to promote rich charities such as BUAV, IFAW and the Donkey Sanctuary. In addition, the message was watered down somewhat; the film meandering between bullfighting, vivisection for cosmetics and the donkey fiesta. Tony's complaint to the producer elicited a letter of apology.

One interesting aspect of the documentary was how it highlighted the way in which events in Spain were misleadingly presented to the British public by the media. They focused on the *Star* "... whose reporter Sue Crawford continues to massage the *Star* readers' outrage." She was filmed taking notes from the Donkey Sanctuary's vet after his short examination of Misty, "No physical wounds, I am happy to see that." Spiced up, this then became the headline, "Sick Señors Beat Misty Within an Inch of his Life". The article continued, "In the end, nearly blinded Misty was locked in a garage." Such sensationalism does nothing to help the cause.

Accompanying Vicki and Tony in the village was their friend Pilar. When they returned to Madrid they asked her to take a back road and stop in Rozas de la Puerta Real, where the village fiesta was imminent. They inquired about the correct date and were told it would take place in two weeks. So, a fortnight later, Vicki was back in the tiny village. Rumour had it that three goats, dressed up in women's clothes, were run through the village by local youths, the Quintos, for a whole day and exposed to all sorts of abuse, such as alcohol being forced down their throats and their horns torn off, before being stabbed repeatedly until they died. As soon as Vicki arrived she knew she was too late. "There were signs of the fiesta having taken place about a week ago. Lots of dirty streamers in the gutters, plenty of broken glass from beer and wine bottles, used fireworks, the odd spent blank cartridge ... the younger people were not in evidence at all, only the old, pottering round the village."

The mayoress explained that the date was movable and claimed to have made herself personally responsible to the governor over the issue of the fiesta; a misunderstanding about the celebrations had led to a prohibition order but when she had made it clear that the goats would walk and not be run through the village, and would be killed by the slaughterman, opposition was dropped and the affair fizzled out. However, others told a different tale, of blood on the walls and the people. The mayoress herself admitted that the goats had drunk more than the Quintos.

Vicki was not fooled and wrote, "It is more than probable this annual event has been the scene of terrible abuse of the animals involved. It will need to be very discreetly monitored next year. Video evidence is vital, because I think the whole issue is clouded with the usual tissue of lies and evasions." A dog, sick and emaciated and bearing a new and bloody wound on one flank, wandered round the village ignored by all, illustrating, once again, a complete lack of concern for animal welfare. With nothing more to be gained in the village, she and Pilar drove on to Villanueva de la Vera to check on Misty, who had fully recovered from his ordeal and was fit and well. Over the following years, Vicki persevered in her attempt to get evidence on the goat fiesta but due to the villagers' shrewdness, she kept missing it.

A meeting with Brigitte Bardot, who had formed her own animal charity, was scheduled for mid-April at an international press conference in Brussels. Vicki was supposed to show two short fiesta compilations but was denied the chance. Instead, Bardot commandeered the microphone and began a commentary on one of FAACE's videos that she had managed to get hold of. Without a microphone, Vicki had to let it go, even though she felt the actress did not know what she was talking about. But later on, when Bardot was leaving in a crush of reporters, Vicki snatched the video from the recorder, determined she would not use it again. Her impression of the ex-film star's appearance was rather unflattering; she was tall, and still had a good figure but her face was deeply lined. Nonetheless, the men buzzed around her like flies and she would only talk to men, ignoring women completely.

Through their Belgian contacts, Tony was made aware of a goose riding festival in the Antwerp region, about an hour's drive from the headquarters of the European Parliament. He wanted to expose what was happening right on their doorstep. As in the Spanish chicken fiestas, the geese were strung up on a gallows and men on horseback rode underneath to try and tear off the animals' heads. Their research revealed that the use of chickens and geese was quite common in several European countries. Each year, a highly controversial event took place in several German villages in the area around the River Ruhr, involving dead cockerels or geese. In the Belgian Zamdvliet they used dead geese.

Tony also visited a place called Harchies, near the French- Belgian border, to witness a bizarre event in which a dead goose was decapitated. The goose was first killed by inserting a needle into its skull, before being buried in the ground up to its neck. A cord was then threaded through the nostrils and manipulated to make the blindfolded man, who was trying to cut the head off, miss his target. Even though the birds were dead, it was a gruesome sight. At one point an eye flew out, and to much jubilation, one of the men poked his finger into the empty socket. Another seized the bird's eyeball and to further hilarity dropped it into his neighbour's pocket. The whole grisly spectacle was degrading to both participants and animals alike.

In 1992 the eyes of the world were on Spain: Expo' 92 took place in Seville, Madrid was named the European Capital of Culture, and the Olympic Games were held in Barcelona, all of which provided a welcome opportunity to highlight the plight of animals in the country. On the last day of April, Vicki met with top officials in the Spanish Embassy in London and handed over a twenty thousand signature petition to ban bullfighting in Barcelona during the Olympic Games. At the same time, a colourful demo was taking place outside. Tony spoke to the media with the intention of sending a clear message to Barcelona that bullfighting was sickening and cruel and had no place alongside a sporting event which is all about high ideals. "Spain's Olympsick Games" was *The Sun's* headline.

*The Olympics are a symbol of sportsmanship, fair play and man's pursuit of excellence. But as the Spaniards proudly host the two-week spectacular, there are sick rituals being acted out in their own back yards. Far from the TV cameras and the world's press in Barcelona, dumb animals are being taunted, tortured and killed ... all in the name of sport.*

The article highlighted several fiestas exposed by FAACE and all seven pictures used were taken by either Vicki or Tony, yet not a single reference to them was made. Disappointed but undeterred, they gladly provided their pictures for Channel Four's *Stab in the Dark* programme. Comedian David Baddiel asked tourists and locals in Barcelona, whether they would watch goat throwing and donkey crushing events if included in the Olympics. The supposedly funny events were explained to the television audience with pictures of the terrified goat in Manganeses de la Polvorosa and the sweating donkey surrounded by the so-called guards with chamber pots on their heads in Villanueva de la Vera. Shockingly enough, some people said they would go and watch if the animals were not killed. Baddiel also put the same question to members of the bullfighting industry. "The Olympics is a sporting event. What we do is art," responded the director of the Catalonian Bullfighting Association. "Bullfighters never compete against each other. Their real enemy is the bull," explained a torero. Tony felt the programme was weak but had no regrets, "... because it brought it all to light ... and they were mocking the people, not the animals."

Ironically, even the traditional fiestas were movable, once the Olympics actually started. At the end of July 1992, Vicki returned to Spain to attend various fiestas. First on her list was another goose riding fiesta in Carpio del Tajo, west of Toledo, which promised an early finish, so as not to miss the live transmission of the Olympic opening ceremony. Vicki had a hunch that dead geese would be used because there had been rumours that animal rights people would attend. She was right, but whoever killed the twelve birds in the town hall beforehand, was no expert butcher.

Unfortunately, continuous media exposure did not equate to a continuous stream of donations. The Tony Moore Band no longer existed; not a conscious decision, marked by an official farewell concert, but rather a gradual development. Their commitment to the animals had completely taken over their lives. Fund raising should have been properly addressed, yet, driven by their mission to highlight the plight of animals in Europe, they felt compelled to answer every call to attend a fiesta. The FAACE shop, staffed mainly by volunteers, did not generate sufficient income and no one offered their services to create a database and regularly send out letters of appeal. Consequently, these tasks had to be fitted in between trips and while it was important to them that their reports reached their supporters, it was not in their characters to ask for money. They could no longer afford their favourite pastimes, such as going to the theatre, and Vicki now bought her clothes secondhand and her make-up in sales. Emergency funds were always used up in vet's fees.

The demands on their time were relentless and they were soon off again. Alerted by animal rights people from the Basque country, they found themselves in yet another chicken fiesta in the villages of Amasa and Aduna. However, one village had accidentally been tipped off about their arrival and instead of biting off the birds' heads, as was the custom, the villagers chopped them off instead. Only when Tony had put his camera away, did he see from the corner of his eye one man who could not help himself and reverted to the 'old' tradition. Their exposure of this barbarity eventually led to a law being passed in the Basque country, banning such fiestas. But with the law not being enforced, they continued in some places even until 2004, when an international outcry led to the use of mock chickens.

Since the Basque country is also famous for testing horses to the limit by making them pull up to one thousand five hundred pounds, they attended such an event in Zikurkil and also filmed a weight-pulling contest using donkeys. They then travelled to a small village further south, where the local matadors allegedly used dogs instead of calves in the bullring. They did not know whether to be disappointed or relieved when this information proved false.

It had become a habit to travel to Spain on an almost monthly basis. Unlike tourists, they did not travel in a relaxed or comfortable way and dreaded the next assault on their sensibilities. Yet they felt obligated to reveal the whole gruesome spectrum of human creativity where the infliction of pain was concerned. Mostoles, in the community of Madrid, had its very own specialty. After having been run in the streets, the bulls were roped back into their pens by tying them to a tractor on a long rope attached to their horns. Of course, the rope repeatedly got caught up in the wheels and it took a lot of time to free the exhausted and frightened animals; one bull even snapping off one of its horns in the process. "The good councillors in the city hall decided to uplift and enlighten their townspeople and voters, to open the eyes of the babies to their culture and let them imbibe the blood with their mothers' milk. So adult tickets were cheap, the price of a couple of coffees, a pack of cigarettes and perhaps a little something to eat. For the little ones, entrance was free."

Vicki described the beginning of a bullfight in which the tired and hung over, if not drunk, local youths tested themselves as bullfighters in the sunny autumn afternoon. Ignoring the rules of bullfighting, "the lumbering participants harried the animal, swung it by the tail, grappled with its impotent horns, thrust banderillas into its flesh and laughed at the animal's shock and pain. Now with sword passing from hand to hand, they try to kill their victim … They argue amongst themselves how to find the thrust to the rear aorta, or for any thrust to fell the disobliging animal. A boy of about thirteen gives advice, "No! Hold the sword this way, now!" The blade plunges in, the animal still stands, the blade is drawn out, thrust again, the animal cries and shuffles sadly from side to side, blood is beginning to gout from his mouth. The youth who has wielded the sword the most and who considers himself the matador, his moon face puckering with annoyance, decides the animal must be kicked, before he further pierces its head with the sword … Choking, coughing, he [the bull] needs to draw into a little corner of peace to face death, but there is no peace, as he is harried until he falls back against the wall of the ring, a final kick from the young hero's boot sends him to the ground."

Scenes like this can regularly be observed in bullfighting schools and even during corridas with proper bullfighters. However, few people hang around long enough to observe what happens after the presumably dead body has been dragged out of the ring by mules. "A lorry with a small hydraulic crane has been waiting, a chain is looped round the animal's horns then attached to the hook of the crane, and the bull is slowly hoisted into the air, its tortured head with the red wounds from the slashed off ears is rasped in the chain's brutal diadem, causing fresh trickles of blood to flow as the animal's full weight is suspended from the iron claw. The lungs are stretched and opened afresh, as the terrible ascent into the air is accomplished. Swinging silhouetted, only the sun touches the animal with gentleness, as it dapples the bloodied silken limbs with its last beneficent kiss. The crowd curiously gather around the strange scaffold, faces upturn, jocularity ceases, chattering voices fade as in the bull's head so taut and statue-like, the eyes slowly open, the tongue passes over his parched and sand-choked muzzle, seeking to salve his lips. A moan comes forth from his body, low but terrible, a moan of suffering as though wrenched from the bowels of the earth itself. The air seems to grow stiller and thicker as though to breathe were to inhale spider's webs. To some of those watching, time itself seems suspended and the simplest action turgid and laboured, as though in slow motion. Transfixed, the people stare at the animal as he paws the air seeking; his tongue tastes the air, his lips murmur, his eyes … who can hold the gaze of those eyes?

"He is lowered into the trailer of another lorry, still suspended from the crane, until he sits with his back erect and head and shoulders raised, his poor mouth constantly moving. Those who watched surely felt the dryness of that swollen parched tongue, the suffocation and abrasion of the sand in his nostrils and lips, could sense the unimaginable agony from the obscene wounds inflicted by barb, sword and dagger, the nerve-tearing, bone-wracking suffering of his torture now, and see themselves mirrored in his eyes, as he watched them, it seemed in pity, giving pity and seeking pity … The watchers are silent. As in a dream, a man with a camera moves quietly to fix this strange happening lest it pass as a nightmare. A woman crosses herself and an old man trembles. In the stillness, with the soft gaze of the bull, the rivulets of blood trickling from his head, nature itself seems for a few moments stilled."

The man mechanically clicking away with his camera was Tony; his way of dealing with extreme feelings when confronted with suffering, wanting to relieve it yet unable to do so. Only afterwards, alone in the hotel room, or relating to others what he had just witnessed, does he allow himself to become emotional. And this was one of the worst moments, "The poor thing sitting up like a dog in the trailer, with holes where his ears had been. I was shocked. I think everybody was shocked."

Finally, someone had pity on the animal. A man with a long knife climbed into the trailer and stabbed the bull in the neck. However, the animal neither died quickly nor silently, Vicki observed, "On the eighth deep trust, and the last deep cry, he ceases. The bull shudders softly, his bedewed eyes contract in the death agony, then with an expression soft and innocent as a new born calf, he looks upon the earth for the last seconds of his life."

Vicki's way of dealing with the horrors of their work was to write it down, first as minutely scribbled notes in a small notebook, then converted into a report for FAACE supporters and into another version for the media. Sometimes she also wrote pieces for other groups' magazines. Things that touched her deeply she gave even more attention and converted them into more literary and poetic pieces, as with this account, entitled 'A Calvary'.

"It might be imagined or sensed that in those minutes in the vast reaches of the universe and beyond, an account was entered in a great record, something was noted, something that will be judged. An irrevocable shadow fell and an irreparable flaw was traced in the finely tuned atoms of existence."

# The Colombian Connection

Over the years, Tony and Vicki had exposed another specialty of Spanish entertainment: bullfights carried out by midgets, the so-called 'espectáculo cómico taurino'; supposedly funny events put on as children's entertainment. The Spanish *Diario de León* put it like this: "How many aficionados have made their first steps as spectators in a comic bullfight?" In 1988, while Tony was in San Sebastian de los Reyes, he had first come across the group Toronto and his midget bullfighters and was appalled by the show. Again in San Sebastian de los Reyes, in another year, Tony went to a show by the 'Torero Bombero', the comic bullfight ending, like the previous one, with the killing of the little bulls in the ring.

In the village of Cabezarrubias del Puerto, about 60km south of Ciudad Real, Vicki and her Spanish friend Patricia came across a makeshift bullring and posters announcing that 'Superman' was coming to town, along with seven midget bullfighters. Vicki befriended the English dancer who toured with the troupe and was taken behind the scenes. Superman and the midgets were Columbian, touring Spain during the European summer and Latin America during the winter. They all came from impoverished backgrounds and money earned in Spain was sent home to support their families. The owner seemed to live quite a good life, while the midgets were poorly paid.

The show can only be described as pathetic. A brass band marched into the ring to 'When the Saints Go Marching in', the English dancer, dressed in a tight gold top and skirt, posing as their conductor. Three Latino women appeared and danced the samba. The midgets, dressed in fancy-dress outfits, re-enacted several scenes. In one, a boat hinting at Christopher Columbus's travels, was brought on with a midget angling from it. A big rubber fish dangled at the end of his line and served as the capote, the pink-yellow cape, to attract a black bull calf's attention. Later on, to the sound of 'La Cucaracha' the midgets taunted the young bull, two of them holding a capote up together. They took turns sticking banderillas, which were adapted to their size, into the young animal. However, only the sticks were shorter, the metal hooks were of normal size. Since they could not reach the back of the animal, they stuck the weapons in his side and he tried in vain to shake them off. As in a real bullfight, the red cape and sword were used to make the animal perform certain moves. The bull calf stood panting and frothing in the heat. The crowd of very young children and their parents or grandparents enjoyed themselves, repeatedly asking for 'música'.

The little bull was pressed down to the ground, where, like a huge and patient dog, he remained while a rope was tied around his horns. The midgets, who took turns jumping the rope, held the other end. Then one jumped the bull from the front and sat on his neck, while the others grabbed his tail. A small ladder was put on his back and a bride mounted him. They played ring o'roses with the calf. Superman was on hand to rescue the midgets, should they get into trouble, but his services were not needed with this tame animal, whom the crowd dubbed 'Pussycat'.

Pussycat soon had to make room for the next act and so was dragged and beaten out of the ring. In the open door he was repeatedly stabbed in the neck until he was dead, while the dancers stepped over him into the ring. Meanwhile, the midgets had dressed up as North American natives and danced around a fire between some teepees. Superman led a black and white bull calf into the ring, where two men wearing costumes with a hobbyhorse's head and tail attached, taunted the animal. Colourful ribbons with metal hooks were stuck into his body and cymbals were clashed together repeatedly next to the terrified animal's ears. He was punched with boxing gloves and a clown put huge sunglasses and a hat on his head, then, using the bull's tail as a rope, did pirouettes. His entertainment value over, the exhausted animal was dragged unceremoniously like a piece of rubbish out of the ring, then killed in the open doorway.

Vicki described his final moments to the Scottish *Daily Record*, "At the end of the show, I saw the bull's ears and tail sliced off while it was still alive. Then its throat was slit, and Superman jumped up and down on its back to make the blood flow from its body until it died. It was a brutal and obscene sight." A tractor with a front-end loader, a vital ingredient of bullfighting and blood fiestas, arrived and the animal was thrown on to it, while kids paddled in the pool of blood as if they were at the seaside.

Not only was it obscene, but also illegal. In February that year a new national bullfighting law, the Real Decreto 176/1992, had come out, stipulating that animals must be killed out of the view of the audience in comic bullfighting spectacles.

The headlines in the *Daily Record* were uncompromisingly derogatory, "Sickest Show on Earth – Scots tourists warned over evil midget matadors and their sadistic blood rituals." They not only showed pictures of the bullfights, but also of a midget matador showing off his scars. "Dwarf Gored by a Young Bull" ran the sensational headline, but in reality, with its tiny horns, a calf is only capable of inflicting a superficial injury. Vicki was quoted, "Parents living in poverty send dwarf children to circuses, bullfighting troupes and travelling fairs. The dwarfs send money home to Colombia to feed their starving families. In these respects, they are to be pitied. But they show absolutely no mercy to the bulls. They put on a diabolical freak show, and they should be stopped."

The next time Vicki flew over to Spain she read in *El País* that a young bullfighter, calling himself Curro Valencia, and eleven others, had been arrested for drug trafficking. Among them were Superman and one of the midget matadors. In fact, Superman turned out to be Valencia's brother. They had used the show as a cover to distribute drugs. A police raid found more than 6kg of cocaine, three cars, an enormous quantity of jewellery and the tools necessary for the handling of the drug. What an ingenious way to distribute drugs! Travelling from village to village, town to town, city to city, they would have found a ready market and, of course, anyone connected with bullfighting in Spain would be regarded as legitimate by the authorities.

But the story does not end here. What happens when a bunch of bullfighters are sent to a Spanish prison? They put on a bullfight for the inmates, of course. In May 1993, *The European* dedicated half a page to a bullfight in Madrid's Carabanchel prison. Superman and his brother had managed to convince the prison governor, José Antonio Moreta, that they could have a bullfight on the occasion of the San Isidro festivities in Madrid. San Isidro is the patron saint of Spain's capital and every year aficionados from all over the world flock to the Las Ventas bullring. Since the prison did not have a bullring, Madrid's bullfighting school, which some years later was exposed for extreme cruelty by the Spanish animal rights group ANPBA, delivered a portable ring and the animals.

The four-day-event saw several animals killed by the bullfighters-to-be. Inmates were also invited to take up the cape, but could only wear jeans and trainers. According to the newspaper, they had been allowed to practise beforehand with wooden bulls in the prison's own bullfighting school. In the evening, the inmates were allowed to take part in the 'vaquillas', where young bulls and cows are taunted and chased around the ring. A spokeswoman explained that the event served to generate a community spirit and gave the inmates a break from routine.

# Searching for John Major

Being famous comes at a price. Privacy no longer exists and everybody expects a well-known person to be a role model. So when a celebrity participates in an event where animals might be harmed or killed, or simply socialises with people who act cruelly to animals, they tread dangerous territory. On the one hand their presence might be used as an advertisement for animal abuse by the organisers, on the other, animal lovers use them as a vehicle to campaign against animal abuse. This happened to Prince Harry when he attended a rodeo in Australia in October 2003 and was heavily critised by Tony. It also happened to David Beckham, who, after his move to *Real Madrid*, frequently hung out with playboy and bullfighter Fran Rivera. Tony warned him not to go and see a bullfight, since his mere presence could incite his fans to flock into the bullring. This made headlines both in the UK and in Spain and had an effect on other footballers. When asked whether he had been to see a corrida, Michael Owen, also playing for Real Madrid, denied it, saying, "For starters, I'd probably get mortified back home".

When travelling to the donkey fiesta in Villanueva de la Vera, Vicki and Tony had passed through Candeleda, a small town at the foot of the Gredos mountains 180km west of Madrid, having looked it up in their registry of Spanish fiestas. Candeleda celebrates its local saint, the Virgin de la Chilla, in September, immediately followed by the Fiesta de la Vela. Both involve cattle. Vicki decided to attend the August fiestas, since she had learned that John Major, then British Prime Minister, would spend his holidays there. Since money was tight, Tony had to stay behind and look after their pets.

She left on a sad note. On the third anniversary of her mother's death, twelve-year-old cat Fenny died. "Now the first evening without her, a desolate loneliness creeps," she wrote in her diary.

On 20 August she flew to Madrid and caught a bus for Candeleda the next morning. She had only managed to book a place in El Raso, a nearby village, since the town was completely booked. This proved to be a problem, as she could not get any transport into town and had to take a long walk. This meant she could only take the stills camera with her. Video cameras were much bigger and more cumbersome then and she did not want to carry too much weight.

She was surprised how popular John Major was in the town. He and his wife Norma had spent their holidays in Candeleda for the last three or four years and people spoke highly of him and his family. His picture hung in several places. Not only did he give autographs to local people, but donated money for their cancer fund too. *El País* wrote: "John Major is much more admired in Candeleda than in his own country."

Vicki was told he was in town, but she did not bump into him or his bodyguards. 'On the evening I arrived I spoke to the proprietors of the Hotel Pedro, who enthused about John Major's several visits to Candeleda. They said that he had stayed at the Pedro with his wife and eaten in the Mesón Pedro restaurant. I asked if this was in former years and she quite frantically said, "No, no, this year too, he is staying here." "As the Hostal Pedro is a modest establishment and the standard of cuisine in the Meson Pedro basic to poor, I thought it unlikely, but cynically reflected that maybe Mr Major was putting his classless society doctrine into practice. If he had stayed in the Pedro he would have been not much more than fifty yards or so from the bullring and facing a wall plastered with posters for bullfights in Arenas de San Pedro. I was unable to ascertain for certain whether members of John Major's entourage were in residence at the Hostal Pedro."

She took her detective work seriously. "I had a meal at the Meson Pedro in order to see if I could discern any use by English people. I did not see anyone who could have been a fellow countryman of mine. In the bar of the Pedro a signed official photograph of John Major was given pride of place. It had been framed with a flowery statement of his presence in the Pedro."

There was nothing to be gained from hanging around the hotel, so, after having taken a picture of John Major's shrine, she mingled with the crowd in the streets. "Various people I questioned in the village said he was often seen in their midst and 'Majorism' was something of a passion with them. They felt that he came to Candeleda because he liked everything about it. John Major was almost like a mascot, or good luck charm, to the village."

Walking around the town she observed, "Candeleda is a very ordinary village, with little to set it apart from hundreds of others. The old part has dwindled and most of the construction is relatively modern. There is a square on the upper part of the village with a statue grown around with shrubs, of a Spanish mountain goat, La Cabra Hispanica. This now fairly rare breed is to be found in the surrounding mountains. This 'Plaza de la Cabra', as it is called colloquially, is probably the only outstanding feature of an otherwise very unremarkable village although the surrounding countryside is lovely; green and leafy, even in August."

A taxi driver (a much rarer breed in this area than the Cabra Hispanica) scoffed at the idea that John Major might stay at the Hostal Pedro, saying they always stayed with a friend of John Major's in a very elegant mansion about 5km from Candeleda, down in the valley. The mansion had every luxury, including a big swimming pool. The security in preparation for the visit had been immense and anyone approaching the house would be shot on sight! The people of the Hostal Pedro were playing on the fact that John Major had been in there for a meal, and implied that they had got above themselves and now everything was John Major, John Major, John Major. Throughout her time in the village, she saw no sign of any such occupation, even by members of the Majors' entourage.

The fiesta programme announced two bullfights and two 'Capeas' – quite frequent in Spain – where young cows and sometimes young bulls are let loose in a bullring and the village youths can pretend to be matadors. Depending on the law of the respective province, the animals come out dead or alive. In Candeleda they have to die.

The Plaza Mayor was clearly in fiesta, having been blocked off with barriers and stands. Sand had been brought into the square, just below the level of the pavement. Like a spiders web, strings with hundreds of small Spanish and European Union flags covered the square and created a pattern on the sand which danced in the morning sunlight. Even though it was only 10 o'clock, the plaza was packed. Vicki was about to witness events which she later judged to be amongst the worst in Spain. She watched in horror as several young cows, clearly in a very poor condition, were chased around by youths and soon started to tremble from stress and exhaustion. They stumbled and collapsed on top of each other. But the fun had to go on, so people pulled at their tails and horns and poked them in the eyes to make them get up. One cow had her horn broken off when she was chased into the plaza from the streets. The other horn broke off a few minutes later, when she charged the metal gate again and again. A black cow had an open flesh wound from being stabbed repeatedly and many had nosebleeds. Miraculously, Vicki got away with taking picture after picture over a period of four hours. Luckily, she had brought enough film, because there was still the evening's bullfight and Sunday's capea and bullfight to cover. Nineteen animals were killed during the two days and went to their deaths at the slaughterhouse injured, terrified and gasping with thirst.

The evening's bullfight was no less gruesome. The young bulls were not stabbed from horseback this time, because the expense of hiring a picador and horse would have been too high. It took the overweight female French matador quite a while to kill one bull on the pavement. "The suffering of the young bulls during the bullfights was extreme, stabbed multiple times with swords and daggers, the animals for the most part were still alive, when they were mutilated. No effort or attempt was made to ensure they were dead before the removal of ears, tail or the embedded banderillas which were wrenched from their bodies with lumps of flesh attached, causing the stricken animal to futilely attempt to flail its limbs and roll its head in agony ...

"Children watched with glee, and after the final bullfight each evening, they rushed into the ring to grab souvenirs, handfuls of animals' hair, the discarded ears and tails, bloody paper from the banderillas etc.' Vicki spent two days documenting atrocity after atrocity. While the townspeople feasted on the dead

111

bulls' meat, she seemed to be the only one mourning the animals. With nobody to talk to about what she had just witnessed and still no sign of John Major, she longed to return to England.

Her many rolls of film graphically documented the horrific events and she included some of them in a letter to John Major in the fervent hope that he would use his popularity in the town to prevent further massacres. Several British papers published the pictures. "Cruel Spaniards are torturing animals to death for fun," wrote the *Daily Star,* "in Prime Minister John Major's favourite holiday village."

John Major did not bother to answer. Instead, Vicki received a non-committal letter from Tristan Garel-Jones. In his column in *The Mirror* Paul Foot pointed out the irony of this. Major had passed on the letter to the man in whose holiday home he had been staying. "Every effort is being made by the government to combat cruelty throughout Europe," wrote Garel-Jones.

Nothing much seemed to have come out of Vicki's trip. However, the following year, the Majors holidayed in the Douro valley, near the Portuguese town of Porto, instead. Perhaps his advisors were not aware of, or did not care about, Portugal's bad record for the treatment of animals.

When researching for this book I came upon a website which offers holiday properties in Candeleda. It points out that John Major used to spend his holidays there and that the house he stayed in is still for rent. So the village is still benefiting from his patronage.

The animals still suffer in the same fashion. When Tony and I passed through Candeleda during Carnival 2003, our car was stopped by drunken youths; members of the local bullfighting fan club collecting money for their next fiesta. On the town's website I found a comment on the August 2003 fiesta. People who declared themselves as fans of the fiesta openly discussed the animal abuse, as well as the severe breach of hygiene regulations. The capeas were described as 'pathetic'. One person wrote, "The cows broke down and fell to the ground … because they were undernourished and did not have any strength. They appeared to me more like undernourished greyhounds than cows. Nobody has the right to do this to an animal."

Vicki aged eight with her mother Louise.

Vicki as a child sitting on a stuffed lion on Brighton pier.

Publicity shot for cabaret of Vicki, aged 22.

Vicki with donkey friend.

Vicki in 1987 with reporter Don MacKay of the "Star" leading Blackie out of the village of Villanueva de la Vera.

Trying to persuade the mayor of Segorbe not to have a firebull, 1987.

Vicki in Farnals after just having witnessed the killing of a firebull, in 1987.

Pepa, one of two goats thrown from the church bell tower in 1991.

Pepa and Magdalena in Manganeses de la Polvorosa saved by Vicki and taken to safety.
© Bill Bond, Madrid.

Goat dropped from church tower and seriously injured in 1993 in Manganeses de la Polvorosa.

Tony and Vicki in 1988.

Tony's favourite picture of Vicki, in the tower of the church, Iglesia de la Vera Cruz, Segovia.

Vicki in 1992.

Vicki relaxing at a friends house in Spain, between fiestas.

Vicki checking on the health of a dolphin in Malta.

Geese having their heads pulled off by horsemen in Carpio de Tajo.

Vicki filming (bottom left) the decapitation of chickens in Nalda in 1991.

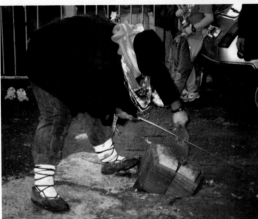

Live chickens in a box being decapitated by blindfolded youth in the Basque country.

Live chickens tied to a rope and hacked at by blindfolded girls in Tordesillas.

Pigeons and doves in clay pots suspended overnight at the top of a pole and then stoned, in Robledo de Chavela on Shrove Tuesday.

Benicarlo, cows chased into the sea again and again.

Harchies, Belgium. A goose that has been killed by sticking a sharp point into its head is carried in procession through the village, buried with its head sticking out with a rope through its beak. It is jerked up and down as a joke so that the blindfolded villagers take a long time to hack its head off.

Mostoles a bull has been dragged out of the bullring, suspended over a trailer. His ears and tail have been cut of but he is still alive.

The bull is
finally killed.

Candeleda, where
John Major holidayed.

A pony roundabout
in Oropesa.

A stray dog used for vivisection in La Paz children's hospital Madrid, 1989.

Coria, a bull has darts blown into him from blowpipes and banderillas stuck into him in the town square. He is then tormented for a further two hours before being killed.

A picture of the Bull 'Argentino' taken by Vicki just before she was gored by him on the streets in Coria June 1995.

Coria 1995, Vicki
being gored by the
bull Argentino.

Tony with Vicki in intensive care when she was beginning to regain consciousness.
Photo Francis Villegas

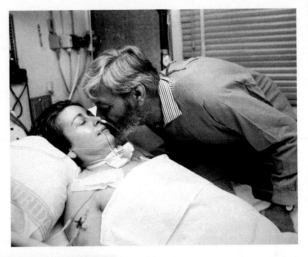

Vicki with two of her nurses Fleur and Pepé.

Vicki in a wheelchair, and Tony, on the "This Morning" show in with Richard and Judy.

Tony and Vicki after she recovered a little in 1995.

Vicki in a wheelchair leading the demonstration against the Waterloo Cup hare coursing at Altcar in 1996.

Live quail chicks in an adapted clay pigeon machine before being shot into the sky as living targets.

Vicki, in blond wig, filming her first bull fiesta after the accident, a firebull in Medinaceli, 1998.

The bull Vicki was filming in Medinaceli.

The little calf Sparky being tormented in the village square in Morater de Jalón before Vicki and Tony saved him.

Vicki taking a break on her way to see Sparky after his rescue.

Tony and Matilda in 2003.

# Thirty Pieces of Silver

Their next destination was the small town Guardarama, northwest of Madrid, close to the monastery of El Escorial and only a few minutes from El Valle de los Caídos – the memorial to soldiers who fell in Spain's Civil War, and where Franco is also buried. The regular bus service from Madrid left them well short of their destination and they had to wheel their suitcases quite a distance. Their filthy hostal was infested with cockroaches and dead flies littered every surface. Even worse, all the bullfighters stayed there. Being the only strangers in town, they could not both risk ordering vegetarian food and there was no other place to eat. Disgusted, Tony ordered a meat dish, considering it more acceptable for a woman to be vegetarian than a man in this machismo society. Even worse, they had to eat their meal in the company of the perpetrators of the cruelty they had come to document, flaunting the tools of their shameful trade.

What brought them to Guardarama was the involvement of the Cofradía de San Francisco de Asís (the Brotherhood of St Francis of Asisi) in the local bullfighting events. Somehow, the brothers did not perceive any contradiction in the fact that St Francis is the patron saint of animals. His picture appeared on official posters announcing a series of bullfights from horseback and cattle events to celebrate his saint's day.

On the morning of 4 October Vicki and Tony left their hostal and strolled around the village. On either side of the road to the temporary bullring, saplings had been planted. That morning all of them had been snapped in half by youths leaving the bullring. Perhaps the youths were annoyed when their fire bull, due to have taken place in the early morning hours, was banned. Notices around town stated:

*By Government order (Superior Department of the Madrid Police) and against the will of the Peña El Capote and the festivities committee, the fire bull announced for Saturday 3rd, for 3am, will not take place. The so-called fire bull spectacle is not authorised because it is not considered as having a tradition in this place and mistreatment and unjustified suffering is suspected. This is according to article 93 of the Rules for Bullfighting Spectacles, Royal Decree 176/92, dated 28 February.*

The villagers came out of the church carrying the effigy of St Francis, as a brass band played and firecrackers exploded everywhere. St Francis was carried aloft by four men on two poles, surrounded by a huge bouquet of red, orange and white flowers, from which several red ribbons were hanging down. The priest, with thinning dyed black hair, walked behind. On reaching a certain square, an auction took place; the villagers bidding for the ribbons. Tony had a hard time preventing Vicki from shouting out, "Thirty pieces of silver!" in Spanish as they filmed.

The afternoon's bullfights involved third-rate bullfighters and cattle in very poor condition. One evening, right after the bullfight, a three-month-old female calf was released into the ring for the children's amusement. As the calf was run out of the ring, Tony stood up and grabbed his camera. "Come on. That's it! That's the end!" he said, sickened to the core.

"It's not," Vicki insisted. "Look at all the kids. There's something going on. Come on!"

They ran to the other side of the bullring, where all the children were dashing to the top row, then peering down over the edge to the ground outside. When they reached the top of the bullring, they saw the cause of the frenzy – some youths were stabbing the calf. Tony had used up his roll of film and Vicki's tape was full. He tried to keep calm and control his trembling fingers, while he put a new tape in her camcorder, and replaced his own film. Only then did he push through the crowd. What he saw was straight out of a horror movie. The calf was dead. They had chopped off its front legs and used them as wedges to hold it up on its back, while they skinned it. It would serve for a communal feast in the afternoon.

Due to the fresh climate in the mountains of the Sierra de Guardarama, Tony wore a check cloth cap, which would create some embarrassment for him. He had not realised that many of the bull breeders and impresarios wear such caps. They started dedicating the bulls to him and throwing their capes up in front of them. He found he was leading the applause; when he clapped, they clapped. So he decided to play a little game. When they did something wrong in the ring he clapped and they followed.

The fact that people have always said that Tony looked a little like Ernest Hemingway might also have contributed, although he insists that he looks nothing like him and is insulted even by the suggestion. Hemingway is still revered in Spain for making bullfighting popular all over the world with his novels. Without him, the bullrun in Pamplona would still be a squalid little fiesta, instead of the hyped-up, money-spinner it is now.

Also present in the bullring was the priest; not the only representative of the Church enjoying the bloody spectacle. A nun accompanying a group of mentally impaired people, also clapped enthusiastically.

Back in Madrid, a newspaper picture caught their attention showing a bullfight they had not come across before, in Campo Real, in which a donkey was used by the picador when he stabbed the bull in the back. Having sought out the newspaper's office, they purchased the photo. As usual, Tony tried to bring their latest trip to the attention of the media. The *Sunday Mirror* was interested and

Tony mentioned the picture of the donkey in the bullring but pointed out that it had not been taken by them, and not in Guardarama. A year later, the paper decided to do a piece on the atrocities committed on St Francis' Day. When the day arrived, Tony received a rude telephone call from the paper, accusing them of lying; there was nothing going on in the village, it was not even in fiesta. Tony was perplexed; there must have been some mistake. He asked where the reporters actually were. In Guadalajara, he was told. No wonder there was nothing going on. They were on the wrong side of Madrid and had got the name of the place wrong.

He could not believe his eyes when he saw the paper the next day. They had used the picture of the donkey in the bullring, claiming it *was* Guardarama. "Animals. Spaniards Kill a Donkey on Bull's Horns in Sacrifice to St Francis of Assisi" ran the headline. He called reporter Andrew Golden a few days later, and only then was he able to put together the pieces of the puzzle. When the reporters had finally arrived in the right village, there had indeed been a donkey used in the bullring. It was a so-called mock bullfight, which, for the unfortunate animals involved, turned out to be only too painfully realistic. Luckily, contrary to what the paper said, the animals had not been killed.

The *Sunday Mirror's* article was already going out that same weekend and 1993 still being pre-internet times, it was impossible to get the pictures back to England in time. So, inventive as ever, they had used the wrong picture instead. The photographer later sent him the pictures taken in Guardarama, showing a donkey being led up to the bullring. For mock protection from the young bull's horns, a blanket had been thrown over it. Trainers were put on each foot and he was blindfolded. His rider wielded a broomstick as a weapon. 'This was fact imitating fiction', says Tony.

A week later the paper did a follow-up on the report. Rather vaguely it stated that, due to the avalanche of protests from its readership, twenty-two villages in the area around Madrid had been fined. And who could prove them wrong?

# Scapegoat

If the inhabitants of Manganeses de la Polvorosa had a lot of stamina, so had Vicki. Thus she was back in the village once more on 23 January 1993. The day before the fiesta she met up with a British journalist in nearby Benavente, where she would stay at the Parador, which turned out to be packed with British press and international news agencies. It seemed they had been told that a British goat society would try to prevent the throwing of the goat.

With nothing much to do on the day prior to the fiesta, the press people decided it would be a good idea to check out the village and asked Vicki to come along. When they arrived, Mayor José Manuel Gil Barrio and Governor Gavilán happened to be in a bar for an informal meeting with some villagers. Vicki would have preferred to stay incognito, but the journalists pushed her forward and made the introductions. The governor must have recognised her anyway from previous encounters. She suggested not using a goat the next day, unaware that Gavilán had already come to an agreement with the town hall and the village youths – the Quintos. The use of the goat had been officially sanctioned; as long as it was lowered on a rope and not thrown from the tower, the fiesta could go ahead as usual. No wonder Vicki's suggestion was greeted with hoots of laughter. "We have banned the goat-throwing ceremony and sanctioned instead, a goat-lowering ceremony," Mayor José Manuel Gil Barrio proudly told the media. The goat would only drop on to the canvas from the height of a metre, otherwise sanctions would be imposed. But not everybody was satisfied with this compromise. "We're going tonight, once you lot [the media] have left, to chuck one off a roof or something. And we won't be using a sheet!" the reporters were told by one of the youths. Various expletives in English followed in Vicki's wake.

Undeterred, she managed to speak to the governor when he came out of the bar. "… he was in a bad humour and in no mood to answer questions or discuss anything. Virtually snarling, he said, 'The fiesta is the only thing that is important, the world is not important, the controversy is not important, only the fiesta.' He then refused to speak further and, surrounded by his entourage of police, councillors etc, went on his way." It was inconceivable that this high official had become a collaborator in the abuse of an animal but she knew that his votes in the next election depended on keeping the voters happy.

With time to spare, she tried to probe further into the origins of the goat-throwing event, asking the mayor at what point the fiesta had got out of hand and his explanation for this. At first he refused to answer. Asked a second time, he shrugged with annoyance saying he didn't know, it 'just happened'.

She also questioned the village priest, who confirmed that the goat had died in 1990, when Vicki first attended the event. He knew of no religious basis for the throwing of the animal and assumed that it started in 1976, when some drunken youths decided it would be a fun thing to do. While he absolutely opposed the abuse of the goat, he admitted that he feared personal repercussions. People hated him already, because in the past he had spoken to a local paper about it. He had given the Quintos the key to the tower, because it could not be entered from inside the church and was not consecrated ground. Vicki noticed that the tower had been altered since the previous year; the window from which the goat was thrown had had the bottom sill raised by about a metre, thereby adding this height to the original fall.

The Spanish press was full of speculation as to what might happen to Camila the goat. After all, nobody had yet paid their fines for last year's riot. And there was half-serious criticism too. "This is not a jump, this is an outright throwing", read one editorial, marvelling as to how, in this era of technology and cybernetics, anyone could still believe that all the sins of the village could be transferred on to a scapegoat. The author jokingly suggested throwing a modern scapegoat, such as a football referee, or something less noticeable, like a lizard, or a centipede.

The following morning, the day of the fiesta, the journalist informed Vicki that he would no longer be writing a piece about the fiesta. After all, he had a wife and children and should not be in the village risking his life. He would write an article for the *Sunday Times* colour supplement instead, using the interview Vicki had given him the day before. He then gave her a lift to the village, where all the British media were assembled in a bar. Vicki soon sensed that something was different. Usually, the media people were quite friendly but this time nobody involved her in conversation. She was soon to find out why. Her press companion apologetically told her that he had been appointed as spokesman for all the media present. Would she mind if they split up? She was simply too dangerous to be seen with.

By now, Vicki must have had an idea of things to come. She got up and walked out, finding another bar where she could keep warm until the goat was thrown. A young woman in a bar on her own is likely to be interpreted as some kind of signal by the male population and before long she was approached by a group of young men, whom she described as looking like 'desperados and thugs'. However, since they had no relationship with the locals, she decided to team up with them. After all, they might have the same intimidating effect on others and she could use some bodyguards.

The square in front of the church was packed with people, many of them in fancy dress, seemingly having a good time. Some even sported mock riot police outfits, complete with mock protective shields and helmets. On posters, and in graffiti on walls, the animal rights people, the 'ecologistas' were attacked. Many people wore orange stickers, which read "Cabra, SI!" (yes to the goat) Numerous television cameras and microphones were on view. While waiting for the goat to arrive, the crowd entertained themselves by bouncing people up and down on the green canvas and chanting the familiar goat song, 'La cabra, la cabra, la puta de la cabra'. A white official van with an orange light on top drew up in front of the church. Vicki assumed that somebody important must be inside. Then the tractor with the Quintos slowly made its way through the crowd, which by now had grown impatient and vociferously demanded the goat. The Quintos took their time to lead the animal up the stairs of the church tower, cheerfully waving at the villagers and swinging a bottle of cheap champagne. When they had reached the top of the outside stairs, the mayor, smiling broadly, unlocked the door to the tower and then relocked it, after the small group with the animal was inside.

The crowd down below was hysterical now, but again the youths intended to prolong their moment of glory and clowned around in the window, showing the visibly frightened animal to the crowd and then withdrawing it. This happened a few times before they finally laid the goat on the windowsill, the lilac ribbons on her horns fluttering in the breeze. One youth made a show of kissing and hugging the goat repeatedly. As the animal, wearing a harness, was lowered, it hung in the air rigid with fear. On reaching a tiny ledge, she desperately tried to crouch down on it, pressing herself into the wall. With a series of awkward manoeuvres using a long stick, the youths managed to dislodge her, so that she was dangling free again. In breach of the agreement, they let go of the animal at least ten metres from the ground.

The papers the next day printed the villagers' version of a 'controlled jump' in which the goat was said to have been thrown from a height of only three metres before being caught in the canvas. The goat was checked out by vets as well as Governor Gavilán, who saw for himself that it was alright. He would not impose sanctions this year. Vicki's video and stills tell a different story. "The canvas was held very, very low, and the goat did not appear to have been caught properly, probably hitting the canvas but because of its flaccid tension, hitting the ground through it. The animal could not walk." She shoved elbowed her way through the crowd to the goat. "A crowd of men, council officials, police in plain clothes, high ranking officers of the Guardia Civil, and Quintos, formed a close phalanx around the animal … so it was totally impossible to see her. She was carried up the steps from the yard of the church and into a small building, which serves as a municipal office. The door was slammed shut by police and no one was granted admittance."

After five minutes, the tractor pulling the goat's trailer drew up in front of the building. "The door opened and police and village officials pushed and shoved the crowd back. The motionless goat appeared in the doorway carried by the Quintos and was placed in the trailer. She did not stir and her eyes did not move. It was impossible to see if she was breathing, if she was, it must have been very faint. Her head lolled and she did not respond in any way to the crush, the noise, or the handling."

Vicki's video camera was still running and picked up an irritable male voice,

"The goat is alive!" She did not dare risk losing what she had filmed already, so used her tiny stills camera instead. The pictures show an animal more dead than alive, lying in the small trailer with someone holding its head up by one horn.

This was the moment when things got ugly for Vicki. Spain's *ABC* newspaper nonchalantly put it like this:

> *Present were several animal rights people, among them Vicky Moore from England. There was some tension with the villagers, because it is not the first time that she attends the festivity to denounce abroad, what in her opinion is a 'barbaric Spanish custom'.*

Barbaric it was. She was pulled away from the goat to find her bodyguards were nowhere in sight. She was suddenly surrounded by a seething, hissing crowd of fifty or sixty people, many of them women. They shouted and spat at her but she managed to keep her composure and walked straight through them. She believed that if one finger had been laid on her at this point, it would have broken the spell and she would have been seriously attacked.

Darkness was falling and she needed to get out of the village fast, but the British press corps seemed to have been swallowed up by the earth. With no transport, she was walking alongside the traffic queueing to get over the bridge to Benavente when she noticed that cars were being stopped on the bridge by some villagers who were shining torches inside every vehicle. She dared not go back to the village, so decided to hitch a ride in one of the queueing cars. But was anybody to be trusted? She scanned the queue and eventually found a car with a family inside, mother, father and two children. She knocked on the window and in her broken Spanish begged them to take her to Benavente. To add urgency to her appeal, she claimed she was pregnant and not feeling well. The family agreed to take her and with a sigh of relief she sat down between the children on the backseat.

The queue crept forward, much too slowly for her. When the car reached the bridge it was stopped by the villagers. Her heart in her mouth, Vicki reacted quickly. She held the toddler up in front of her and buried her face in his chest, tickling him. He appeared to be having great fun, chuckling away. After what seemed like an age, the torches moved on to the next car.

When they finally dropped her off at the Parador, Vicki expressed her gratitude to the family, convinced they had saved her from a severe lynching and maybe even death, but obviously she was not in a position to disclose this to them. Back in her room, her patience finally snapped. Livid with rage at the cowardice of the British press people, she tried to dial Tony's number, but her fingers were trembling uncontrollably and she kept forgetting to dial the country code. Eventually, she dialled British journalist Bill Bond's number in Madrid. He had been in the village with her when she rescued the two goats and she trusted him sufficiently to do a good spoiler on the other journalists. When they arrived back in the hotel, about an hour later, Vicki's version of the event was already a finished news item going out in a big way. She chose to spend the evening on her own.

Back in England, hunting with dogs and hare coursing had still not been banned, despite an Early Day Motion in Parliament to take immediate action, signed by one hundred and fourteen MPs in a very short time. A group of six MPs travelled from London to Altcar to see for themselves what hare coursing was all about. They returned resolved to put pressure on the government.

So they were back on the killing fields at Altcar once more to protest against the hare coursing. Again, the Waterloo Cup coincided with the donkey fiesta in Villanueva de la Vera. They could have split up as they had done so often before, but they felt that the behaviour of other animal protection groups in the Spanish village was counter-productive to the campaign and anyway, their budget was extremely tight.

On 25 May, Vicki entered in her diary, "Blackie, the little donkey from 1987 died in Devon." Even though this year's donkey had had a very rough ride, Blackie was still the big news and all the major papers printed obituaries. The donkey was believed to have been at least twenty years old and had had to be put down due to consequences of his old age. Vicki was truly sad about his death and regretted that she had not been able to see him again. "Going out to rescue him was a turning point for me. It changed my life … After the fiesta I can remember putting my arm around Blackie and he was trembling and rubbing his head against me."

The *Daily Telegraph* sent Stephen Pile to Southport to meet Vicki and Tony. "Writing the obituary of a well-known donkey is a tricky assignment, because little is known of Blackie's early life." Tony was very wary, thinking they might be ridiculed in the piece, when he first knew they would send Pile, who was known for his sarcasm and taking people to pieces. But as soon as he met the man in person, he no longer worried. The three of them seemed to hit it off, which can be deduced from the long piece he wrote. He was especially impressed with the authentic Spanish meal to which they treated him, and also with Vicki.

*I set off to the Southport charity shop that she runs to finance her animal rescues, expecting to spend the afternoon with a sweet, noble, grey-haired, tireless, but barking pillar of the local donkey sanctuary. Not a bit of it. If you walk past the racks of secondhand clothes and the household utensils that have seen better days, you are in for a surprise. Mrs Moore is a total stunner. She has glamorous waist-length hair, real intelligence and a good command of the Spanish language.*

Tony was so pleased with the article and the fact that they got their message out, that he forgave Pile for also writing:

*She married Tony Moore, a guitarist who looks like a cross between Ernest Hemingway and Terry Waite.*

# Dolphins in Distress

When the telephone rang in their home, it was rarely friends or family, but either the press, or a distressed member of the public who had just returned from abroad, as was the case in August 1993. A Crosby man and his family, holidaying in Malta, had come across three dolphins in a children's paddling pool. Even though there were no pictures to back up the story, Tony and Vicki immediately decided to help the dolphins because he sounded so genuine.

Vicki flew over to Malta, where she met journalist Alan Rimmer from the *Sunday Mirror* and immediately began the investigation at the Splash and Fun Park at the Bahar ic-Caghaq Marine Resort. What she found there reduced her to tears. The three bottlenose dolphins Hitcha, Pega and Budoan, were indeed stranded in the paddling pool. The dirty water was only a few feet deep and did not cover the large animals completely, so they had to lie on their sides all the time. They were literally roasting alive in the scorching Mediterranean sun. Next to them was a large swimming pool for tourists, and on the other side, visible to the dolphins, was the open sea, just a stone's throw away. The dolphins were originally from Russia, where they had been used by the military. When the Soviet Union broke up, the dolphins were no longer needed and were sold off. In 1992, a Maltese entrepreneur bought them for a dolphinarium he intended to build, selling the idea to the public by claiming they had been 'rescued' from unstable and war-torn Yugoslavia.

Even though Malta had signed the Convention on International Trade in Endangered Species (CITES), the government did not have a problem with the idea of a dolphinarium. It allowed the dolphins to be imported on two conditions: that they were not to be used for commercial purposes, and that an adequately large pool had to be made available before their arrival. A large pool for shows, with two connecting holding pens, had indeed been planned and the dolphins were brought to Malta accompanied by two Georgian caretakers. However, construction work had suddenly stopped, supposedly due to financial difficulties, so when the dolphins arrived, they were put into the paddling pool. Later on, they were transferred into a bigger pool, but when the tourist season arrived, they were moved back. All summer long they were stuck in the filthy swamp of a paddling pool. The Georgians genuinely cared for them, but could do nothing to alleviate the situation.

Due to the atrocious conditions, life for the dolphins was a continuous battle against disease. The large animals produce a considerable amount of faeces and urine per day and there was no adequate filtration system to keep the pool clean.

A fourth dolphin died soon after its arrival. Tony still grieves for the animal. "It is tragic, that the poor creature had to die before making it into the sea."

Vicki was shocked by the plight of the animals and, fully clothed, waded into the pool to examine them. She told the *Sunday Mirror*: "They were wallowing from side to side because the water was so shallow. It didn't even cover their backs. Their backs were scarred and there were scrapes and tears on their stomachs where they had been scraping along the bottom of the pool. I also noticed the flippers on at least one of the animals were infected with a fungal growth. The water was filthy, and even at feeding times the dolphins didn't appear to be enthusiastic."

Vicki warned the Minister of Tourism and Home Affairs that something had to be done, and fast, or the island would receive some very damaging publicity. She spent about a week in Malta meeting politicians and local animal rights people, who all agreed that things had to be resolved quickly. She was still on the island when a two-page spread in the *Sunday Mirror* came out with heart-wrenching pictures and the headline "Boiling Alive". The story spread to Maltese and international newspapers. The whole sorry affair was devastating to Malta. The headline in the *Maltese Times* read: "Tourists Told to Shun Cruel Malta". Malta had already been criticised for its cruel shooting of migratory birds; this was worse and they promised to do something about it fast.

And they did! Within ten days they finished one of the two holding pens. The Minister for the Environment had ordered the park's owners to complete the task within a week. Vicki and Tony had asked for the dolphins to be released into the bay, contained by a net, as a compromise. This was declined, but the holding pen, where the animals could at least swim, was a step in the right direction. They hoped local activists would succeed in pushing for improvements in the near future.

Tony received a phone call that the dolphins would be moved very soon and flew over. As he walked down Slima's parched streets the extreme heat bounced back off pavements and buildings and a fine coating of grey dust covered everything. Malta was in the middle of a heat wave making the transference of the dolphins a matter of urgency. On 5 September, at 6am, the complicated operation began, under the eyes of government officials, police and local and foreign activists. The paddling pool was pumped out, so that the dolphins could hardly move. In the blazing heat, four men in wetsuits tried to manoeuvre them one at a time into a sling. Each time the canvas was underneath it, the dolphin struggled and shot out like a rocket, knocking people flying. An older model was brought out and eventually they succeeded, hoisting up each dolphin and carrying it on two iron poles, threaded through the top of the canvas, which had holes for the dolphin's eyes and flippers.

One after the other the dolphins were placed into a box in the back of a lorry, and driven to the holding pen, where a tower crane lifted them up, swung them over the twenty foot deep pool and lowered them into the water. One of the Georgians, in wetsuit and flippers, was waiting for them and helped them out of the canvas. After several exhausting hours, all three dolphins were swimming up and down, going wild with pleasure. Even though he generally disapproves of dolphins being held in captivity, Tony felt a great sense of relief. His touching documentary about the dolphins was shown repeatedly on television around the world.

By 2003, the park had come under Italian ownership and one of the dolphins had died from stress but Pega and Budoan were still alive and performing their daily shows. Sadly, the situation had not improved for these highly intelligent animals, exploited for commercial purposes and tourists allowed to swim with them; better than being stuck in a paddling pool, but a travesty for animals who should have had the freedom of the open seas.

# Dirty Fighting

'A Life in the Day of', the article for which Vicki had been interviewed in Manganeses, finally appeared in the *Sunday Times* magazine on 17 October 1993. Aside from the usual inaccuracies, it gave a glimpse into Vicki's state of mind when in a fiesta.

> *You can't afford to get hysterical when things go wrong. When I was trussed up and thrown into a fountain, I tried hard not to panic. I kept thinking: how are you going to get out of this one, Vicki? I didn't! Having an irreverent sense of humour also helps me through the tough times. I used to be easily upset. Now I don't cry a lot, but I hurt a lot. The worst part is not the contretemps with angry people but seeing the animals suffer. Cruelty haunts me for days when I read about it. Having to record it makes it hard to be normal any more. If I've been to a horrid fiesta, I have a week of nightmares.*

While the feature did not generate any donations for her work, it did attract tremendous publicity. Amongst others, was a letter from Princess Catherine Aga Khan, a relative of spiritual leader, Aga Khan, "Your courage and perseverance set a fine example for us all. People like you give me strength to hope for the future of mankind." She was also contacted by publishers Souvenir Press, who felt she had an important story to tell. Their feral cat Sapphire had just died and maybe Vicki needed something to distract her from her pain, so she set about the task immediately. Without a computer, she typed and re-typed all thirty-nine pages of the first chapter. The publishers clearly recognised her writing talent but it needed more structure. Realising how time-consuming it would be, she abandoned the project. Her other work had to take priority.

The Waterloo Cup was cancelled due to heavy snow, so 1994 started peacefully for the hares. The media approached them, keen to spread the word about their work in Spain and each appearance or article led to further requests. One writer proposed a book about women working for animals, exploring their motivation. The New York University Press approached them to compile a book on blood fiestas. Already too busy, Vicki and Tony declined both offers. They were also approached by people asking if they would integrate their cats into their household, should anything happen to them. They accepted the commitment, especially since their beloved cats Natasha and Victoria died soon after one another.

An emergency call came from Greece. Bullfights were scheduled for 16 and

17 April 1994 in the Athens Stadium of Peace and Friendship; yet another attempt to export the 'fiesta nacional'. In 1991, the French bullfighting industry had tried to stage several bullfights in Poland. Due to strong protests, some were called off, but they took place in Szezecin, Poznan and Chorzów. Authorities in Chorzów had banned the corrida, but as the soldiers' trade union was somehow involved, it went ahead. Animal rights people picketed the entrance and were attacked by the police and the stadium guard. When some protesters managed a 'sit-down' in the ring, the organisers unleashed a bull, who was allowed to attack them. As the crowd chanted "Olé!" and called for more blood, another bull was released. When the police finally intervened, it was only to beat up the protesters. The result was several injured people, but luckily nobody got killed. A year later a bullfight was staged in Brno, in the Czeck Republic, provoking disgust amongst the Czeck people.

The Athens bullfight came disguised as a fundraiser for the poor; Helinas, the Hellenic Institute of Solidarity and Cooperation with Developing Countries, claimed that proceeds would be donated to Third World charities. The bullfights were promoted as bloodless, in the Portuguese style. The animal rights people of the Greek Animal Welfare Fund knew nothing about bullfighting; after all, they had more than enough on their plate with their own animal protection issues. They contacted Vicki and Tony for information. Vicki faxed page after page explaining the cruelty of the Portuguese corrida, and, anticipating all the arguments the organisers would use in favour of the bullfights, supplied all the right answers. Being heavily attacked in the media, Mara Levidi, general director of Helinas, accused animal rights people of exploiting the situation. "In Greece, some organisations think they have the monopoly on human sensitivity."

Then suddenly it was announced that the event would not be a bullfight per se, but a 'colourful fiesta' with bulls and horses, in which all the animals would leave the ring unharmed. The bulls would wear velcro patches on their backs on to which the darts would be thrown. To protect the horse, the horns would be shaved off. Reading this, Vicki saw red and sent graphic information about the suffering this caused the bulls. Helinas countered, "We hope that this alternative will be accepted internationally, and will contribute to the fight against bloody bullfights and other performances involving cruelty to animals which are so deeply integrated in the traditions of particular people … For this reason, animal rights groups should support the event."

With funding for FAACE still unresolved, flying to Athens and filming the corrida was out of the question, so it was agreed that Greek people would go in and film, but neither information nor tapes were made available.

Tony had committed himself to go to Italy. If Vicki had a fiesta she kept missing, this was his. Italian animal rights people told them about the small town

125

Calvello, which means 'calvary', where, despite a new law being in place, domestic animals were tortured to death during their village fiesta. Tony was told that the Carabinieri conveniently attended to other police duties outside the town during the sinister ceremony. Posing as a professor studying religious celebrations, he arrived in the village on 17 January, the celebration of St Antonio Abate. Someone had obtained an official invitation for him, so he was optimistic that he would get to see what he wanted. However, when he arrived with his translator and friend Merry Orling, they were too late. There was no hint of anything happening, so, with the promise that he would get to see the May celebration, they left.

When he returned in May, a celebration did indeed take place in the form of a procession honouring the Madonna del Saraceno. The Madonna was carried up the mountain to a small church, where she was to stay until September. Tony filmed extensively in the picturesque little town, asking many questions about the procession and other traditional events. His intention was to make a flattering video and send it to the town. In return, he was promised a copy of their video nasty, which had been shown to him when he arrived. It showed what he had missed on his last trip: live chickens, turkeys and even lambs strung up on a rope with blindfolded people hacking away at them with sickles. He kept his side of the bargain but never had a reply. The last thing he heard was that the person's car who had got him the invitation to the village, had been blown up.

Late in 1993, journalist Nigel Bowden contacted them from Spain. He was researching a programme on bullfighting for the *Cook Report*, with the intention of exposing fraud and corruption in the bullfighting industry. They would not have to do the undercover work themselves but simply be involved in the research and Vicki would be interviewed. Who could refuse when the programme attracted between eight and eleven million viewers? Despite a severe migraine, a pallid Vicki seized the opportunity to relentlessly bash the bullfighting industry.

When *Dirty Fighting* was aired on 9 June 1994, the programme showed no mercy for Europe's most brutal industry. Roger Cook and his team had posed as Hungarian entrepreneurs who wanted to introduce bullfighting into Eastern Europe. Before any deal was struck, they wanted to witness all the dirty secrets at first hand. With graphic pictures from behind the scenes, they documented the shaving off of the horns and proved that the fighting bulls were routinely tampered with. Naturally, the bull breeders were furious when the journalists disclosed their true identity. It was safe to assume that from then on they would be more suspicious when approached by foreigners.

On the home front, the anti-hunting movement was stabbed in the back when executive director James Barrington resigned from the League Against Cruel Sports and teamed up with the hunters. This came as no surprise to Vicki and Tony, as he had always had a very cosy relationship with the hunting lobby, as had Mark Davis, chairman of the League. One to take sides with the hares, was thirteen-year-old schoolgirl Renata Jackson. At a Tesco checkout a woman said to Tony: "You are my daughter's hero."

"Why is that?"

"Well, you saved the dolphins in Malta from dying."

Renata got involved, collecting three hundred and ten signatures at her school. At a press conference with a cross party representation at Altcar, she handed these over to West Lancashire MP, Colin Pickthall, saying, "The young generation feel concerned about what is going on around them and we would like to have something done about it."

Ralph James, Labour member of Sefton council explained how he wanted this year's demo to be conducted: "We also want to encourage and stress the need for a peaceful demonstration. I don't want to be disrespectful to those who have died for the cause of animal welfare but we must have a measured response and not play into their hands and alienate public sympathy."

On the demo, Renata carried a banner saying: "I'm thirteen and I know this is wrong and immoral! How old are you?" Tony wore a skull mask and a giant float from the League Against Cruel Sports, covered with graphic images, followed the demonstrators. However, it could not enter the mud path leading to the field and thus failed to attract the attention of the media.

The Waterloo Cup was founded in 1836 by entrepreneur and hotelier, William Lynn, to attract business for his Waterloo Hotel in Liverpool. He also left a second legacy for gamblers: the Grand National steeplechase in Aintree, near Liverpool. Horse racing and betting go hand in hand everywhere, but the Grand National is probably the most extreme challenge to horses. Even though, in 1989, organisers were forced to make changes to the most lethal jump, Becher's Brook, because too many horses died in the race, it is still considered dangerous by many people. Apart from injuries on the field, horses die afterwards from the effects of over-exhaustion. In countries like Germany the event is no longer shown on television, because viewers consider it too cruel. In this country, matters of conscience are easily ignored when there is money involved and thus the Grand National is feted by the media, which promotes it relentlessly. It is almost impossible to voice a different opinion. Only sporadically is the cruelty issue is addressed, as in 1991, when Vicki and Tony participated in Granada TV's *Upfront* programme. Opinions clashed between her and racehorse trainer Ginger McKain, whose legendary champion Red Rum had won the Grand National three times, making trainer and horse local celebrities. Ironically, in 2004, Vicki would beat the horse in the 'Southport's Greatest' competition!

Even though press releases condemning the race were dutifully sent out each year, only in April 1995 did Vicki manage to raise the issue again. Security was tight, since in the past animal rights protesters had managed to enter the field and prevent the race from starting on time. Vicki was interviewed on the premises by a television crew. However, she could not express on camera, what she really thought, that is that the RSPCA had not helped the cause very much, when they declared the changes to the dangerous fence sufficient. She and Tony agreed that, since it was on their patch, FAACE should do a high-profile campaign in the years to come.

However, life had different plans for them ...

# The Battle of Brightlingsea

1995 was the year in which animal rights hit the headlines. Animal rights people are often portrayed as the bad guys and the meat industry the good guys; after all, they feed people. But British consumers wanted to enjoy their steak without feeling guilty. The national conscience was rattled, early in 1994, by actress Joanna Lumley's emotional appeal to the government to ban live exports from Great Britain. The organisation, Compassion in World Farming, claimed that two million lambs and sheep and five hundred thousand calves, were exported from the UK in 1993 and after leaving the country, suffered from low transportation standards. Many died from a lack of sustenance during the hour- and even day-long transports. Those that made it alive to foreign abattoirs, were killed inhumanely, without prior stunning. In the following months, people who had never been interested in animal welfare, many of them pensioners, would become involved in the battle. Most accepted that beef cattle and sheep were raised humanely in the UK, so "It was a question of them against us, taking our poor little calves to the continent and torturing them," recalls Tony.

In June 1994, a letter bomb injured an employee of Stena Sealink, which, together with further protests, led the company to ban live transports. Rival P&O, followed by Brittany Ferries, also refused to transport animals to slaughterhouses across the Channel, so the beef industry came up with the idea of flying cattle out of the country. There were flights from Northern Ireland and Scotland but Coventry was to become the most infamous airport for two reasons. Firstly, in December 1994, a Boeing 737 hired by Phoenix Aviation, on behalf of veal exporters, crashed, killing all five of its crew. Secondly, because of the death of animal rights campaigner and single mother Jill Phipps, on 1 February, who literally gave her life for the animals, when she fell under the wheels of a lorry carrying calves, as she tried to block its way to Coventry airport. No less a person than Brigitte Bardot attended Jill's memorial service in Coventry Cathedral, saying that she was like a sister to her and was "the Joan of Arc of veal". She was not very proud of her country and was going to address the issue of veal crates in a meeting with the French Agriculture Minister.

A few weeks earlier, British agricultural minister William Waldegrave unwillingly entered the line of fire when it was disclosed that calves raised on his thousand-acre farm were sold abroad, while at the same time he called for a ban on veal crates on the continent. Journalists did not have to dig deep to find a cookbook, co-authored by his wife Caroline, praising the use of pale meat from Holland, which could only be obtained by locking up calves in semi-dark veal crates and feeding them a special diet. It was precisely these crates that had been banned by the UK government in 1990. It did not help Waldegrave's credibility when he claimed he no longer had control over where the animals went once they left his farm for the cattle markets.

The battle of the 'bunny-huggers' as the protesters were called in the press, spread to all major ports. Picketers faced the tough decision of how long to hold up the lorries, as it caused additional stress to the animals. They had to watch calves being thrown down from the upper deck of a lorry ramp, landing in a heap and then being manhandled on to a ship. They took pictures of injured sheep, some with eye infections and even one with an eye missing and sent them to the Ministry of Agriculture.

It was hard to keep infiltrators out. Most demonstrators wanted to keep it peaceful. While some simply abandoned their cars in the middle of the road to block the way, some got so caught up in the heat of the moment that they behaved very rashly. One man even threw himself out of his wheelchair and under a lorry.

Policing was very expensive; £6 million up to that spring. But those were not the only costs. As more and more people became involved, there were victims on both sides. Generally the police were criticised for being too tough. Essex Council compiled a list of complaints from peaceful protesters who were kicked, verbally abused and treated with utter contempt by officers in riot-style clothing. Many of those arrested posed no threat to anyone.

It was in this climate that Tony and Vicki were asked for support. They could not compete with large organisations such as the RSPCA, who regularly published large advertisements in the national newspapers, but they could contribute by having local cattle farmer Geoff Nicholls come along to the demo. "This Cheshire beef producer says No! to live exports," read his poster. They made the six-hour drive to Brightlingsea several times.

When the people in Brightlingsea thought the protests were losing steam, Tony got in touch with MP Tony Banks, who agreed to travel there on 20 April. He in Brightlingsea just before the lorries arrived. Tears sprang to his eyes when he saw the animals cramped inside. "It's only protests like this that actually get action in Westminster," he told the media.

While he certainly was not encouraging anybody to break the law, he insisted that the general public had a right to protest. "They [the exporters] say it is lawful, but what they don't understand is that when something is lawful but wrong, you have a right to do something about it." He soon had his own encounter with the police. When he pointed out that one of the lorries did not have a tax disc on it and thus was not licensed, the officer told him to mind his own f***ing business and to f*** off, thus proving to him that they were biased towards the exporters.

Tony's video, which he sent to the local activists, contained images of a mock funeral for the animals and images of a small boat circling the *Carolina* as its vast hold was being loaded up with sheep and calves. The police, in turn, circled their small boat, but eventually turned away. Tony's footage actually led to one of the protesters having her charges dropped, as it showed that she was suspended in the air and had a policeman on each of her arms and legs and was therefore not capable of causing harm.

Protests gradually spread to the continent. While protesters in Belgium faced water canons, the Dutch meat industry promised to keep British calves out of crates. Tesco was quick to inform their customers that they were moving veal production to England. Animal welfare groups would be consulted and the 'highest welfare standard' guaranteed. As this could not happen overnight, in the meantime Tesco's shelves would be filled with veal from Holland, where all calves were to be reared in groups with access to sunlight and roughage. None would be exported from England. Other supermarkets followed suit. But the aim of the animal rights lobby was to ban all live transports.

# Life on a Thread

And so, finally, came that terrible day which Tony will never forget – 25 June 1995. Vicki was in Spain once again, assisting in the making of a documentary on animal cruelty around the world for ITV. Producer Anthony Thomas had met them both to learn about Coria and had been advised strongly against going there, as the villagers were too used to having camera crews around and were adept at preventing them from filming what they wanted. But he insisted and it was agreed that Vicki would meet him and his team in Coria to give assistance.

The fact that Vicki had been to Coria twice already, and had even confronted the mayor, made it difficult for her to go there again without changing her appearance. Instead of wearing a wig, as she would normally do, she had blonde highlights put in her hair which changed her appearance quite dramatically. Tony took a picture of the new Vicki for a fake identity to be used in the village. She used the second of her first names, Lucille, and Haywood as her last name.

Just before leaving, Vicki said, "I don't want to go. I think there's something wrong. I don't feel safe." Of course, everybody knows what he, or she, is going to witness, yet they still go. So in the end she reluctantly agreed that she would have to go, because the tickets had already been bought. She flew to Madrid and then caught a train to Cáceres. On the train she met a student of Arabic descent who begged her not to go to Coria, she would not be safe he said, even though she had not disclosed her plans to him. She found his behaviour strange but did not take him seriously, so proceeded with her plans, catching a bus out of Cáceres to Coria. On the bus she said to herself, "If I see the church tower as I cross the bridge, it's all going to be wrong. If I don't, it'll be okay." At first she didn't … but then the tower loomed into view.

It was agreed that she and the television people would pretend not to recognise each other, even though they were staying in the same hotel, as the owner was very much involved in the fiesta. The crew soon encountered trouble. One night, before the actual filming, the crowd grabbed hold of a cameraman and dangled him over a fire. The message came over loud and clear – they did not want any more damaging reports about their village on television.

On 25 June, as they sat in the square filming one of the bulls being darted, the crowd shouted, "Fuera! Fuera!" (Out! Out!) The fiesta could not start before they had ousted the television crew. The crew realised that they were not going to capture the actual killing of the bull, so they asked Vicki if she could film it for them.

Around noon of that day, Tony got a call from Vicki which he felt was strange and out of character. She had witnessed the bull being tormented in the square and had broken away for a moment to call him from a public phonebox in a side street. "I'm being followed wherever I go," she said. "I've come out of the fiesta now. I'm not actually sure where the bull is … I don't know what to do … I don't know whether to go back, or stay away, because I don't feel it's safe at all … Something is very, very wrong."

They often used to phone each other for advice, so Tony said what he now considers to be the fatal thing and which he has regretted ever since, "You know, I'm not there. I can't tell you what to do. It's up to you whether you can go back or not. You've got to make a decision on that one, I'm afraid." He remembers that towards the end of the phone call she suddenly began speaking in Spanish, not very good Spanish, but enough to say, "It's quite interesting. I'm having a good time." They must have come right up to her.

An hour later, at about 1pm, Tony received that heart-stopping phone call from the village police, telling him that his beloved Vicki was dead.

"You like talk to eenglish man?" continued the policeman.

Stunned, unable to think straight, it was agreed that they would talk again in half an hour, when the devastating news had sunk in. As soon as he had put the receiver down, the phone rang again. It was Pilar. "Tony … I don't know how to tell you this … There's been a terrible accident …"

"I already know," said Tony, flatly, in severe shock, yet seeking comfort from her familiar voice. "But I don't know what happened."

Contradicting what the policeman had said, Pilar told him that Vicki was still alive. It was Pilar who had booked her hotel room, which was why she had been called by the police. She was told that Lucille Haywood had been very seriously injured and they did not yet know whether she was going to live or die.

When Tony put the phone down he felt his stomach flip and was overcome by a light-headedness, almost like fainting. He was also crushed by an overwhelming sense of responsibility, because it was he who had virtually told Vicki to go back into the fiesta, even though she had clearly felt unsafe.

Vicki's plans had been very different. She had proposed to film the children's encierro the next day, to find out if they used darts and banderillas on small calves, but until then she was in a quandary, unsure of what to do next and all the time with the strong feeling that things were very wrong. People were giving her funny looks and she was being followed around the village by two men and a woman. Wherever she went, they were there, talking to each other and following her. She later said in an interview on *Roscoe on 5*, "I have actually a rather jumbled mix of memories of that particular day. I remember ringing my husband and telling him that things were very, very bad in the village. There was a very bad atmosphere. What should I do? Because there had been a lot of difficult aggressive behaviour to anybody that was not of the village, any stranger. And he said, 'Well, I'm not on the spot, you're going to have to use your own judgement.'

And that, in a way, was a fatal thing, because FAACE, my organisation, works on a very slim budget. We can't afford to waste a fare to Spain. I knew – something told me – that it was very, very dangerous to actually follow the bull at that moment. But I also knew that we couldn't afford, as I say, to write off the expenses. So I went in."

Vicki told Linda McDermott on BBC Radio Merseyside, "I remember getting up to the bull, I'd been in the square where they were tormenting the animal. They were blowing darts at him, sticking banderillas in him. And then I wanted to get pictures of the activity in the street, which … these pictures are quite rare, because it's a dangerous thing to do. But I thought, well I'm going to try it this time, get some more stuff, you know.

"Now in the streets there are not barricades. It's lethal. People die in Coria very regularly … And the irony is that I had been to Coria, I think, on four occasions. I had a great deal of video material but unfortunately not on the format that we are now using. And I needed it on the new format to fill in the gap in the library, as it were."

Her decision was also influenced by the fact that Anthony Thomas had asked her if she could get pictures of the bull being killed, the crowd being too hostile to allow them to do it. "I got within about fifteen yards of the animal, who was at bay in one street. I've been doing this for nine years. I've been in some tight corners. So I think my judgement is quite skilful. Now he should go that way and I should be okay where I am, but there is a window grille nearby. I thought with the first sign of movement, I'm going to scramble up there. Of course, you always forget that there is somebody somewhere doing something that you do not expect … It was an idiotic action. Somebody from an upper window threw a bucket of water over the bull, which sent him in completely the opposite direction and right on to me. I was climbing up the window frame. Its grille wasn't fastened properly, which again was a nuisance. So it was sort of flapping against the window and as I was trying to climb up it, he was on me in a second and the whole horrible thing started.

"I felt the horns going into my hips, I looked down and I saw myself embedded on the horns and I was sitting on Argentino's head – Argentino was his name – and I was being tossed like a ball. Well, that's where my personal memory cuts out."

In private she admitted that she thought Argentino had been set on to her. Exactly how it happened she did not know. She thought they threw a firecracker under the bull and there was also a shout. When they control the bull they can actually shout at him to make him move. There was a very authoritative shout and the bull just came straight at her.

Video footage shows her trying to climb up the window, which proved impossible. Someone was reaching down to give her a hand up, but she didn't make it and Argentino attacked her, jabbing his horn right through her foot and pulling her off the wall. Then he rammed his horns into her and tossed her against the wall. He then threw her right up over his head, on to his back and down again, before flinging her against the wall once more. Vicki later recalled how lovely it felt when she landed on his back; a really warm beautiful animal smell – very comforting. But she also said that she could not believe the pain when his horns penetrated her body, so appalling that she wished she were dead.

Some witnesses claimed that he threw her ten times, after which she lay crumpled in the street, with the bull standing very near for at least four minutes. A little stream of blood trickled from her inert body along the centre of the road, around the corner and down another street. The horrified onlookers tried to entice the bull away by running and shouting at him, and running away again, but no one was quite brave enough to get too near, because he was such a dangerous bull. He had gored a young man some ten or fifteen minutes before Vicki's ordeal began. Argentino tossed him once but he was able to walk away and be rushed into first aid. Some men took a garrocha – a long stick with a metal point at one end – up into one of the buildings above where Vicki was lying and stabbed Argentino until he finally turned away and walked off. Then they rushed to her aid, picking her up between them. One of them threw a cloth over her, which they had been throwing at the bull to try and get him away from her.

They carried her into the town hall, which acted as a temporary first aid post, just as an ambulance was backing in. She was upside down when she was being carried and they had fastened her foot up in some way. The next time she was seen, she was on a stretcher with an intravenous drip in her arm being carried into the ambulance, then, with sirens blazing, the ambulance rushed away. She was in hospital within a very short time, so she was treated very quickly.

The telephone rang again. This time it was Anthony Thomas, calling from the police station; Vicki had been gored by a fighting bull and was critically ill in hospital. If it was any consolation, her face had not been touched, but the rest of her had been ripped apart, with horn wounds throughout her body. They could not say whether she was going to live or die. As he spoke she was being operated on in the hospital in Coria.

Then the policeman broke in again, "You must come today!"

"I can't come today," said Tony.

"Well, tomorrow will be too late!"

Whilst waiting for news of the operation, Tony tried to book a flight, but as it was a Sunday, it was impossible. He did not have a credit card at the time, so could not book over the phone. In desperation, he called a journalist friend. Shortly afterwards he was told that the *Daily Star* would like to accompany him. They would send a journalist and a photographer and, most importantly, a plane ticket would be waiting for him at Manchester Airport.

He did not sleep at all that night. On the motorway, the radio news said that Britain's most famous animal rights person was seriously injured and in hospital, which seemed somehow surreal to him. He met the team from the *Star* and they flew to Spain. At Madrid airport a flurry of newspeople awaited him, competing to drive him to Cáceres, where Vicki had been transferred. But Tony was driving with the team from the *Star*.

They drove without a break and arrived in Cáceres at 9pm "Donde está el hospital San Pedro de Alcántara?" Tony, who spoke hardly any Spanish, asked people in the streets. Nobody seemed to understand him, because he did not stress the correct vowel. He was desperate. They were losing precious time. At last, someone gave them some garbled directions, but although they could see the hospital across a field, they could not find the road leading to it. So they decided to drive right across the field, a decision which proved to be advantageous, since they entered the hospital through the maternity department, thus avoiding the press waiting at the main entrance. The Spanish newspaper *Hoy* had overstepped the bounds of decency by reporting in intimate detail the nature of Vicki's wounds. The whole nation wondered how she could possibly have survived.

In the morning Tony had rung the hospital to be told that Vicki was still alive, but it was doubtful if she would last till the evening. In 1995, mobile phones were expensive and not yet that common. He did not have one. When he arrived at the ward, he had no idea what to expect, so he was hugely relieved, to find Vicki still alive and better than he could have hoped for. The doctors told him that if she was going to last the next day, she would probably last another two, and if she lasted another two days, she would probably last a week. After a week, she would probably stay alive.

Tony went in to see her alone. He could barely recognise his darling wife; her head was swollen up like a football and was swathed in a green turban. A tangle of tubes and wires connected her to several machines, one of them to assist her breathing. She had received eleven horn wounds, the worst being the one in her groin area, the horns having entered her body from three different directions. Without taking his horn out, Argentino had nearly ripped her right leg off. She had a horn wound in the front and one in the back aperture of her body. This seems to be the place where most people seem to get horned, because it is easily accessible for the bull. A horn had pierced her chest and punctured her right lung, miraculously just scratching her backbone without breaking it. Two got in underneath her shoulder blade and she had one horn wound in each thigh, but again miraculously, the bull did not catch the tendon. Her right foot was very badly mangled, Argentino having flipped her off the wall by the foot and spun her round. Eight ribs were broken. There were also several smaller puncture wounds scattered all over her body. Even if she were to regain consciousness, the doctors could not say whether she would be able to walk again, or if she would be brain-damaged. Her life hung in the balance.

Feeling utterly helpless, Tony returned to his cheap hotel that night, where Pilar had booked a room for him. The next morning he rushed back to the hospital. Nothing had changed – Vicki's condition was still the same. There was nothing he could do, so he, Pilar and the *Star* team went to Coria to try and ascertain the truth about the accident. The journalist went to see Mayor José María Alvarez, who explained the security measures which had been taken prior to the fiesta and how the accident had happened. However, he did not feel the need to interrupt the fiesta in view of this tragic accident, and it was still in full swing. She asked if she could watch the bull in the square. The mayor was not keen, but finally assigned her a couple of bodyguards who led her to the square. Tony assumes that it was not so much to protect her, as to make sure she did not see the wrong things.

When she returned to the car later, she said she could not believe what they were doing to the bull. She was utterly disgusted, "Vicki is lying dying and there they are, still at it."

Argentino's breeder talked to the media. "I didn't know about Vicki before this," he said. "I just knew there was a girl dying. We tried to do our best for her with the doctor. It makes no difference who she is. The same thing happened before with another person and we did exactly the same. Everybody who goes in the bull run knows the risk they are taking." He showed no compassion for Argentino. "I am not sad. This is a wild animal – it has grown up for this." Nor indeed did the villagers see anything wrong in the animal's treatment. Juan Juanes, the town hall press officer, whose sister was killed in the fiesta a few years previously, was quoted in *The Times* denying there was any cruelty in the fiesta.

Pilar paid the bill in Vicki's hotel and picked up her belongings. Tony later found out that several rolls of film were missing and her video and stills cameras were badly dented after the accident and worthless. A roll of film which was still in the camera contained some pictures and there was a tape in the camcorder. Both would be used repeatedly by the media. Back at the hospital, the *Star* photographer was allowed to take a picture of Vicki.

Back home the headlines read: "Blackie the Donkey Girl is Gored by Crazed Bull" and "Blackie the Donkey Saviour Fights for Life After Horror at Fiesta". The media swarmed all over Tony's hotel, so the three of them decided to move to the expensive Melia instead but they were soon discovered. One journalist was sitting outside at a table with a glass of beer reading a book, trying to look inconspicuous. The only thing that let him down was that his book was upside down! Once, as Tony was leaving the intensive care ward, he bumped into two other press people. They wanted to take his picture but he covered his head and went back in. He called security and had them thrown out – they were not going to get to Vicki.

One evening he received a call in his room. A journalist from *The Times* was in the hall. He said, "I believe you are tied up with the *Star*, but couldn't you just come down and have a talk?"

"All right, provided you don't mind me bringing the *Star* people with me," he said.

He was not willing to divulge too much. He had to be careful. While Vicki was still in intensive care, he felt she was still very much at the mercy of the local people and did not want to cause any animosity. Among the doctors was a woman who was pro-bullfighting whom Tony did not trust.

After a while, the *Star* left and without their financial support Tony had to move back to the cheap hotel. Then, to his great relief, the doctors said that they were ready to allow Vicki regain consciousness. Until then they had kept her in an artificial coma, because she would have been unable to bear the intense pain. Vicki and Tony gave Linda McDermott an insight into that period on BBC Radio Merseyside.

Linda McDermott asked, "Were you conscious of Tony being there, even though you were unconscious?"

"I don't know. This is a strange thing, because I was in a coma for a while. And this is very interesting because you read of people being in comas and you have no real idea how much they can understand, or not. Yes, yes, I must have been. Because in the state that I was in I mixed dream and fantasy with reality. And I sort of identified in my dreams the people who were actually at my bedside, but I didn't know they were at my bedside, but yes I think it's very important when people are in that comatose state, that they should have the stimulation; people have to talk to them a lot, play music, even if there is no reaction. Having come from this situation, I think it is terribly important. And I think that is the thing that brings the person back, it gives them the sort of signposts back to life, even though it's all mixed up in this strange deranged mind wandering. It's there. So I could only say to people who have relatives in comas, for goodness sake, don't give up on it, because the person *is* aware. It is a strange awareness and they may not be able to communicate, but those are the things that bring the person back."

"What did you talk to her about, do you remember?" she asked Tony.

"When I was in there the nurses and doctors – and I must say they saved her life, without their help, she wouldn't be here – were with her all the time and constantly helping, doing small things, bringing in things of their own. Somebody would bring a radio in and get tapes that she might like and things like that. They said to me, just tell her what's happened to her, even though you don't see any reaction. Tell her, just keep telling her what happened, so eventually she'll know. She might even think she's at home. But she'll understand something and when she comes round, she'll know the situation and it won't be a shock to her. So I told her about everything. We had a lot of letters, wonderful letters too. And I read them all out to her. The nurse said, she does know, you know. Now and again a machine would flicker, which showed she knew you were there."

Vicki agreed, "When I finally came out of this thing and I was sort of conscious, yes I knew everything that had happened to me. I knew about the accident and where I was. Yes, it does work."

When Vicki first came round, after almost three weeks, Tony asked if she knew what had happened. She signalled in the affirmative. "And you know you're going to be better, don't you?" he added. Vicki was pleased with that. Tony understood that she wanted to know about Argentino. When he told her that they had shot him, she burst out crying. He thought she was sad because the bull had been killed but she told him later that she was glad that his suffering was over. She had cried for all the bulls still being tortured in Spain.

Vicki later told Tony that she had had terrible nightmares during that time. Once he told her a priest was coming round, hoping she would not get the wrong impression of the state of her recovery. She could not speak, but suddenly stared in alarm at a corner of the room, right behind Tony. Tony turned round and saw nothing. Vicki explained later that she saw St Valentine in Roman armour, looking at Tony. She spoke about her dreams to Sybil Roscoe: "I understand too, that in quite a strange way, you feel you've made up with the bull that injured you."

"Oh yes, very much so. I was in a coma for over three weeks. And when I first came out of it, I was nervous, really nervous of bulls. I was seeing hallucinations of bin bags in my room that sort of metamorphosed at night into a bull that was sitting there waiting to get me. But one night I had a dream in which Argentino came to me. During the attack I had a very good chance of seeing his face and there was this unremitting sort of obsession with doing what he was doing. His eyes were obsessed. Now in my dream, the bull came to me and his eyes were gentle; they were bovine, his soft wet muzzle, his lovely curly head. And he just came to my bedside and rested his massive head on my bed, looked at me and I said: 'Okay boy'. I put my arm over him and sort of gave him a weak little hug and then we both fell asleep together."

"Now some people listening might say to you, you're mad, Vicki. How could that possibly happen?"

"I think that was something within my subconscious that had overcome the fear that had been instilled in me. It was a dream and I think it really was perhaps some emanation from my subconscious that conquered the fear, because from then on, I knew I could go back to my work and I now only have love, great love and pity, for the bull that attacked me."

The doctors had predicted that Vicki would have a crisis after ten days, due to infection, as pieces of Argentino's horns and hair kept coming out through her wounds. She had been lucky in the first place, because surgeon Angel Prado, who operated on her in Coria for seven hours, had a lot of experience of gorings. His colleagues in the Cáceres hospital told Tony that his work was rough and ready but in perfect order. He saved Vicki's life and they both thanked him later on.

When the crisis came, it hit Vicki very hard. Her temperature suddenly soared, yet she was shivering from cold, so blankets were piled on top of her. The next morning it was the opposite, her temperature had plummeted, but she was sweating profusely. Bottles filled with ice cubes were packed around her body.

Another problem was the tube down her throat. Due to the fever, Vicki could not yet have a tracheostomy. On 5 July, however, her temperature was normal for an hour, so they rushed her into the operating theatre. They operated on her throat, the right lung and her foot at the same time. Doctors and nurses volunteered to help during this operation. The Spanish press reported widely on the successful outcome of the operation and the fact that Vicki had regained consciousness and was able to breathe on her own.

Vicki was indeed conscious, but exhausted, and due to the tracheostomy, still could not speak. She communicated with her eyes, then later, started to write little notes. For the first few days they were almost impossible to decipher.

Immediately after the accident, while Vicki was lying unconscious on the street, she had an extraordinary out-of-body experience. She saw herself sitting up against the wall, with her head to one side, while in fact she was lying flat on her stomach. Something came down from the sky, like beams of shimmering light, and what looked like a car with big fins, like an old, open-topped Cadillac. It came down beside her and her mother, who had died several years earlier, was sitting in it with two men whom Vicki did not recognise, but thought might have been relatives from the past. She also saw three of her cats, who were also dead. Topas, Vicki's favourite, a dark tortoise-shell, was sitting close to her head and licking her. The other was a black tom, Cassius, who had a big flat head. He used to sleep on Vicki's pillow at night. He had always been a tough cat, even breaking up a fight between Tony's dog and another dog, by sitting on his back and riding him with his claws in his flesh. Cassius was now going for the bull, but Argentino just stood there. The third cat was Victoria, a favourite of Tony's. She was running backwards and forwards and Vicki called her so she would not get too close to the bull.

There was also a tall figure, approximately about twelve feet in height, who seemed to be made out of laser lights. As the others were trying to pick her up and put her into the vehicle, he said, "No, not yet". Then the car suddenly disappeared and everything went dark. Vicki felt bereft, because it had been so warm and peaceful, then suddenly everything changed back into ugly life.

She did not remember being picked up and carried away by the villagers, but she did remember being in the ambulance. She had tried to sit up and said to the nurse, "Look, just ring my husband and tell him that I had a little trouble with a bull. Just get me back to my hotel. Call him and say everything is okay."

Someone held her head up to prevent her from seeing the state of her body. Then she sank into unconsciousness again.

When Vicki arrived at the hospital, one particular nurse declared that she was not going to let her die, even working double shifts without pay. Tony is still moved to tears when he remembers what this nurse said to Vicki, when they met again eighteen months later, "When you first came here you were on your way to heaven. We put a rope around you and pulled you back down."

Not everyone reacted with such affection and generosity. The British insurance company took the view that since Vicki had not stated what she intended to do in Spain when she took out the policy, her accident was considered almost self-inflicted. Tony had no choice but to ask them bluntly if they were going to pay up or not, whilst resorting to a little coercion by mentioning his press contacts and questioning what they might make of a refusal. Alternatively, he could praise the insurance company for doing a great job and so encourage people to take out insurance before travelling. The company decided to pay!

When the *Star* team went to see the Mayor of Coria the day after her accident, he had boasted to them that the village would take over all costs. Tony assumed this only applied to the hospital costs in Coria but the registrar of the Cáceres hospital would send his bill to the town hall too. He told Tony that even though the village took out insurance for the fiesta, they always sent the injured to the Cáceres hospital and they had to pay the bills. On 10 July, Pilar felt it necessary to sent a friendly reminder of his promise to the mayor.

While camcorders were not as common in 1995 as they are today, Tony was contacted by journalist Nigel Bowden who revealed that there was an amateur video of the accident. A man in the village had actually filmed the whole thing and wanted Tony to have the tape. However, when Pilar called the man, he wanted a great deal of money for it and Tony had to decline. The man subsequently sold it to Spanish television.

Tony went to the hospital on foot everyday, having breakfast in one particular bar, where he used to read of Vicki's condition in the papers. *El Mundo* published daily bulletins, even supplying diagrams of her back and front marking the location of the horn wounds. They got it all wrong! They questioned people on the street, "Conoce a Vicki Moore?" (Do you know Vicki Moore?) One man said he did not know her in person, but if you were doing this kind of thing you were bound to get into trouble. A barman thought that what she was doing was very important and that it was a pity that they were not doing it themselves. She was a very brave woman and should not have to do it. Others were of the opinion that such events should not happen in the first place.

Back home, the FAACE shop was under siege by the media. BBC's *Northwest Tonight* caught an incident on camera involving two Spanish students who had entered the shop and voiced their love of bullfighting. Staff politely asked them to leave. "It seems so awful that with Vicki so badly hurt, someone should come in and say they like bullfighting, or watching bullfights, which, as you know, is watching an animal tortured to death," volunteer Nora Fee told the reporter.

An article which had appeared in the *Daily Mail* was reprinted and translated by the *Periódico de Extremadura*. The article was very critical towards Spain. It implied that Vicki had come to Coria to stop the fiesta for good. Quotes were put into Tony's mouth which he did not recognise, as he had spoken to nobody but the *Star*. The paper insinuated that the villagers had deliberately tried to kill Vicki. On the same page, in the style of an obituary, they printed an article entitled: "Vickie, Leave Us Alone for Good!" It maintained that Vicki was the victim of her own hysterical urge to save animals and also listed the same tired old arguments that are routinely trotted out in defence of cruelty.

Tony felt it necessary to talk to the Spanish media to put things right and one of the nurse's cousins volunteered to translate. In the interview Tony faced three journalists, telling them to feel free to ask any question, with the proviso that they printed their questions and his answers verbatim. They asked him about the hateful newspaper article and he was able to defend himself. Despite fears over Vicki's treatment, he did not mince his words and told them that what they did to the bulls was a disgrace. "I can't understand how you can treat a three-month-old calf like a full-grown bull and stick banderillas in it. That is not very brave." Typically, in the article, the three-month-old calf somehow became a three-year-old bull, making Tony's statement sound ridiculous. The article was announced front page and was a whole page long. After that, Tony felt free to do interviews with his local British newspapers.

The media, however, were not his main preoccupation and his days were spent going back and forth to the hospital. On the third day after the accident, he had just got back to the hotel at lunchtime, when he received a call from the hospital telling him to come urgently. So he ran back through the heat. Out of breath, he put on his green hospital coat. A doctor met him saying, "Tranquilo, tranquilo." It turned out that they only wanted to ask Tony's permission to cut Vicki's hair off, so they could treat her head injuries. In the past they had been sued for cutting people's hair without permission. On another occasion he was met by a member of staff who told him that it was imperative that he go to a certain office before seeing Vicki. His heart in his mouth, he knocked on the door, imagining the worst. In the event, it was just to let him know that the hospital was flooded with letters and they wanted Tony to pick them up. Since many more were expected, would he pop into the office every morning? Over Vicki's four-week stay in hospital, she received hundreds of letters of support from all over the world. British MPs and MEPs, as well as animal rights groups and individuals, all wished her well. The letters gave them both strength and showed that they were not alone in this terrible situation.

Former Sefton counsellor Ralph James wrote: "… You are irreplaceable but never alone – everyone here is inspired beyond words …" One woman wanted to nominate her for an Order of the British Empire and sent her the forms. Vicki, who was not a royalist, never filled them in. Spanish nationals wrote too. One of the most notable was from a prisoner in Madrid's Carabanchel prison, who wished her well in her fight for life and the animals.

People also delivered handwritten notes at the reception. One that affected Tony deeply said, "May you be blessed by the Virgin of Guadalupe and may she preserve you and prevent you from further harm." While he read the note to Vicki, he could actually see the statue of the virgin on a hill opposite the hospital. Another letter Tony fondly remembers was from another local man, in which he enclosed a copy of his blood transfusion card stating that he had given blood in Coria the day before Vicki was gored and felt that blood ties now bound them together. Vicki used to joke later on when asked if she had any Spanish blood in her, because of her looks, that yes, she thought she might have and she had had it topped up several times in Coria and Cáceres.

Sometimes Tony was invited to lunch at people's homes, or restaurants, which helped improve his Spanish and broke his routine of living on cheese sandwiches. There was his hotel bill to pay for, as well as their flights back to England and with no money coming in, that was the only food he could afford. He was befriended by English teacher Pepe Morgan and his German artist wife Eva. Pepe told Tony that Vicki was entitled to some compensation – at least ten thousand pounds. For Tony this was out of the question. He did not want to be bought, or for them to be able to say, "Well, they took the money and that's the end of it now." To take the money would have been like saying it was all okay. Besides, in 1990, a bull took thirty-eight-year-old Jesus Martin's head right off. His relatives tried to sue the town hall for a million pounds but they still had not got the money.

*El Mundo* reported that the Spanish Society for the Protection of Plants and Animals from Tossa de Mar had rung up the town hall and demanded compensation for Vicki. Tony called them up and asked them to desist; if there was any suing to be done, he would do it. It was for Vicki to decide and she was still unconscious. Vicki later said, "The only compensation to me would be that they stop this cruelty. But if they start on the upward road to a different attitude to animals, then I think whatever has happened to me is a very small price to have paid. I don't want the animals' blood money. And that's what it would be. I don't think my accident is going to actually be the catalyst for that much change at this moment. But, in time, things will change."

# Going Home

When Vicki was well enough to go back to England, the insurance company at first promised to provide a helicopter, then changed its mind, saying she should travel to Madrid Airport by ambulance, which the hospital director strongly opposed. She was only fit to leave hospital if she could travel by air and he ordered a helicopter from the Air Rescue Ambulance Service. Tony was to travel with her, but on the morning of the actual transport he was not allowed on board. It was in the middle of a heat wave and there were already five people on board: a doctor, a nurse, the pilot, co-pilot and Vicki. They could not lift off carrying an extra person. Tony understood but was desperate – how could he make it to Madrid in time? Hiring a car was not an option due to lack of both time and money and a train, or bus, would take too long. Luckily, a nurse managed to get a good deal with a taxi driver.

A few days earlier the *Liverpool Echo* had rung Tony in Cáceres to ask whether they could send a reporter to travel with them back to England. Tony refused but it alerted him to the media frenzy that would greet Vicki's return. He rang Chris Johnson of the Mercury Press Agency and asked him to arrange a press conference on the day after his arrival and otherwise keep the media off his back. They booked the ballroom of Scarisbrick Hotel in Southport.

Everything was ready for Vicki; approximately twenty seats had been removed to make room, taking up nearly a quarter of the plane. Curtains were set up around her stretcher to protect her privacy and a doctor and a nurse had flown over from England to accompany her. Having fitted up all the drips and other technical equipment, they took over from their Spanish counterparts.

Contrary to Tony's wishes, a *Liverpool Echo* reporter was also on board and had attempted to sit next to him. The captain approached Tony and said, "I believe we have a reporter on board. Don't worry. Any problems, I open the door and throw her out!"

Vicki was still unable to speak due to her tracheotomy but she used to scribble notes for Tony. With a shaky hand she wrote, "ET going home" before the plane lifted off. This little note was published in the *Liverpool Echo* the next day, because Tony relented during the flight, not wanting to create any bad feeling with the press, as there was obviously some kind of symbiosis between them and FAACE. So when the reporter came to his seat and asked whether she could sit with him and speak to Vicki, he told her he would go and sit with her instead. That way he felt in charge of the situation. He did not tell her anything important, because there was the press conference scheduled for the next day, but he gave her the little note. She was thrilled.

It was already dark when the plane landed in Manchester and an ambulance was waiting on the tarmac, as were the press and television. Tony was angry but decided that, rather than have a confrontation, they would simply disembark and get into the ambulance as quickly as possible. The press did get some pictures and video footage of Vicki, but Tony would not speak to them.

On the way from Manchester to the Southport hospital, Vicki was given oxygen and painkillers and on arrival, taken straight into intensive care. Tony was relieved that everything had gone so smoothly. It was very late when he got home to the empty house – too late to retrieve the pets from the boarding kennels – but he did not have time to feel lonely. Instead, he went through the piles of cards and letters from well-wishers, which had arrived for Vicki. One was from former cabinet minister Dame Barbara Castle, who praised Vicki's campaigns and wanted to raise the animal cruelty issue in the House of Lords. Letters from Spain had arrived too. One had found its way, even though it was only addressed to 'Vicki Moore, England'.

When he walked into the intensive care unit the next morning, somebody said, "Hello there! I want a word with you. Where have you been?" It was Vicki, speaking to him for the first time for over a month. They had replaced the tracheotomy with a valve that allowed her to speak. Her voice was very weak but it was definitely hers. What joy! What utter relief, after all those dark days. Later that day, filled with a new optimism, Tony set off for the press conference.

There were quite a number of press people already waiting when he entered the hotel lobby. Reporters fired questions and cameras flashed all around him: "How is she?" "Exactly how do you feel?" "What did you think?" "Are you pleased to be back?" Of course, Tony was totally worn out and with some questions, he had trouble holding himself together. Some reporters seemed to be deliberately trying to upset him, to get the pictures they wanted. One headline read, "Tearful Tony Tells of Vicki's Bull Nightmare." He was described as being tired and emotional; indeed, he broke down several times and covered his face. When asked whether Vicki was going to be back on the campaign trail, he said that obviously it was impossible for the time being, but that mentally she was still very much in the fight. "I feel very, very contented, it is difficult to put it into words, but I just feel so relieved to have her here so that we can talk ... to know she is just there is wonderful."

The hospital had agreed that no reporters be allowed in but that was no deterrent and they were constantly ringing up claiming to be friends of the family. The hospital then initiated barrier nursing. Since Vicki had travelled from hospital to hospital there was a risk of contamination, so nobody except staff and Tony were allowed in.

Tony had yet to retrieve his car from Manchester Airport, where it had been since the day after the accident. He needed a lift and Chris Johnson from Mercury Press arranged for someone to drive him. The huge parking bill was a shock but he was in for a bigger one when he realised that he had left his keys at home, in his suitcase. Airport security staff offered to help and then the police arrived, also offering advice. They managed to open the window on the driver's side and then open the door, but the steering wheel was locked, so they broke it with a hammer. By sticking two wires together, Tony then managed to start the engine. He drove off but did not get very far before the car slowed down and then ground to a halt.

Lifting the bonnet, he saw that the petrol tube to the carburettor was leaking. It was like a sponge until halfway down. With a Swiss army knife he sliced it in two, and rejoined one end to the carburettor. Taking a Bic biro from his pocket, he took the ink tube out and then used the empty plastic casing to rejoin the two pieces of petrol tubing and so got the car running again. It took him about an hour to get to Southport and he had just passed the hospital when the car broke down again – the casing, eventually having succumbed to corrosive effects of the petrol, had melted. He was forced to abandon the car and return the next day to fix it properly.

Meanwhile, Vicki continued to make progress. The tracheotomy was reversed and her throat stitched up, though later she would have to have to have plastic surgery on her throat. When she swallowed, it was pulling and caused a choking feeling. She tried to cover up the scar with either a scarf, or a broad necklace. Her drip was removed and she was given her first meal: sausage, eggs and potatoes. She stared at it in disbelief. She had been a vegetarian for a long time and had had no solid food for over a month, but she ate a spoonful of potato, which tasted wonderful.

Due to the injuries to her foot, Vicki had to learn to walk all over again using the mantra, "good foot to heaven, bad foot to hell", when going up and down stairs. When she could manage about five of the hospital stairs, after about ten days, she was pronounced fit to go home. Tony had bought a single bed for her, because she had to lie absolutely still. It was put in their bedroom next to their double bed.

Even though her story was no longer hot news, many reporters still wanted to be the first to talk to her. The first person allowed in was Anthony Thomas and the next was David Dawson, from the *Sunday Express*. They had known each other for a few years and he was sympathetic to the cause. He spent a couple of days in town and came to the house for an hour each day to speak to Vicki. In a way, this proved therapeutic for her.

Television stations wanted interviews too. Tony allowed one short interview for the local ITV Granada, one for ITN and one for the BBC. Vicki must not be put under any stress, but on the other hand, it helped her to talk about the accident. She even showed her grizzly wounds and a painful bedsore to the cameras. For the first time the British public were given an idea of what she must have gone through and how much suffering still lay ahead. Vicki insisted that she did not blame the bull, "It wasn't his fault. I could have been a sack of hay, or anything. He was out of his mind. His place was with a herd in the field, not in the streets surrounded by crowds."

With intervals, more interviews would follow over the next weeks. Richard and Judy were still doing *This Morning* from Liverpool, when Tony wheeled Vicki into the studio early in September. Even though she still wore a cast on her right leg, a bandage around her throat and was very thin, she appeared relaxed and confident. She explained that she was still purple all over her body and that she had been told it would be at least six months before she would be back to normal.

A month later, the reality of her situation hit her with full force. In the segment 'Married to the Job' on the *Good Morning* show, she looked very depressed. Most of the time she looked down instead of speaking to the camera. "I realised how much I was dependant on Tony, because I couldn't sit up in bed on my own, I couldn't eat. He had to start me eating, because I'd been on a drip for a month. He had to do all the cooking and actually he has turned into a very good cook. In fact, the amount of dependence that I have had on him has been more than I would want, really. Although nurses can give you a tremendous lot and also have the skill and expertise, with Tony I can tap into his energy. It's an awful thing to say, because I feel like a vampire, but you can really tap into this other person."

Indeed, Tony looked haggard and hollow-eyed. Apart from being exhausted by Vicki's round-the-clock care, he was consumed by his guilty conscience, convinced that he could have spared her all the pain and heartache by telling her to get out of the fiesta. Vicki did not make it any easier for him, when she unwittingly said, "Well I thought, that it was a sort of implicit thing then … if I do what I want to do, which is to get the next bus back to Madrid, I'm letting everybody down. I'm letting FAACE down. I wish you'd just said, those are your orders, get out of the village, but …"

A few weeks later, on the *Selena Scott Show*, which went out on satellite for NBC, she had regained her customary composure. Determined to use her accident to improve conditions for the bulls in Spain, she had agreed to be driven to London for the show.

At first, Tony had to carry Vicki around the house. But she wanted to become independent as soon as possible and walked on her own within five days with the use of a Zimmer frame. Next, she progressed to crutches. Then she walked with two sticks for a while, although outside the house she used a wheelchair for quite some time. Whenever Tony wheeled her into town, people came up to her to wish her well.

They scraped by financially, with Tony as Vicki's full-time nurse. Vicki had sleep problems because her back was very badly bent. Argentino had twice thrust his horns into the rear left side of the spinal area, destroying the muscles, so that the backbone was no longer held in the centre of her back but had a twist in it and also stuck out. Vicki was very sad about this, because from childhood she had worked on a graceful posture. To compound her problems, she now also had excruciating bedsores on her actual backbone. Tony was shocked and dismayed by the state she was in. "The poor thing was skin and bones. She had no flesh on her at all. You know what it is like if you're lying in a hospital bed without eating. She hadn't eaten for a month. She'd only had the drip. And she was lying still, unable to move. She was like a skeleton and the skin was really thin. She was red-raw." To make matters even worse, her broken ribs made it impossible to sleep on either side. She also found that, other than lying on her back, she could not breathe properly.

To relieve the pain, Vicki resorted to acupuncture and Tony wheeled her to the acupuncturist around the corner. He was surprised when she decided to walk home on her own after only the second treatment. However, because of her foot, which was held together by four pins, she could only walk short distances and very slowly at that. These pins eventually worked their way up through the skin. The first appeared after a few months; the sharp point sticking out and puncturing her tights. When it was removed in the hospital, without any local anaesthetic, Tony held on to her shoulders, as the doctor used a pair of grips to extract it. He would not let her face it alone, as she had become terrified of hospitals since the accident. The next pin came out in May 1996, when they were on their way to Edinburgh to give a speech at the Advocates for Animals annual general meeting. In the car Vicki said, "Oh god! I think another pin is coming out." Settled into their hotel room, Tony went get something out of the car. When he came back, she said, "Look!" and held up a pin. She had pulled it out herself! In an interview with the *Edinburgh Evening News* she said, "I am out and about and walking but I reckon it will be another year before I am back to normal."

Luckily her face had hardly suffered, but the strain of her constant pain manifested itself around her eyes. A few months after her accident she said, "I have a little ambition, that I go back to Spain, walking properly again, looking not quite as scarecrowish as I have looked for a few months, restored to how I was before the accident and letting people see that there is life after a bull's horns and let them see, that not only have I survived, but that all my ideals about the animals have survived as well." A cosmetic surgeon who had read about her accident and wanted to help, fixed the comparatively minor problem of the wrinkled eyes for free, which boosted Vicki's confidence and for which she was very grateful.

Her soul needed treatment too. She underwent hypnotherapy to come to terms with the accident and her life afterwards, which depended so much on the support and care of others. However, when leafing through her personal organiser from after the accident, well into 1996, one would not have guessed what she suffered on a daily basis; it was packed with appointments for interviews and other work-related duties.

The *Cook Report* team wanted to do a follow-up programme on bullfighting and Tony gave them the name and address of the man who had filmed√Vicki's accident. A Spanish actor from the unsuccessful British soap *El Dorado* had persuaded the man in the village to let him be his agent. He pedalled the video around the world, getting a percentage each time. Every time Vicki made a television appearance, the producers got on to him. Tony was very annoyed, because he was prospering from Vicki's accident. To this day it is shown in full on international television and each time FAACE receives e-mails and phone calls from people who are shocked by the intensity of the images and the fact that this is still going on in Coria.

The *Cook Report* obtained the video and decided to do a programme about Vicki and expose bullfighting afterwards. They could not use the whole video because it was too shocking, but they showed an extract in slow motion. Tony received a copy in advance and watched it on his own in the office. "It was terrible. It was as if it was happening that moment. Although I knew Vicki was in the next room, either in bed, or sitting in a chair in the living room, or somewhere, I saw this happening as though it was happening at that moment. It was terrible watching it. And then, she was lying on the ground. She was lying there for a long time. I thought, God Almighty! Why don't you do something?" Eventually, when the bull moved away, after about four minutes, and they picked her up, I said out loud, 'Thank God! Thank God! They've got her at last; it's going to be all right now.' And it was so silly, because I mean, it all happened in the past but I was living it out now. And I lived it for a long time."

It was two months before Vicki could bear to watch it, the first time through half closed eyes. Then they both watched it again and again over a period of time. So often, in fact, that it did not mean anything to her in the end. Tony was convinced that the goring would otherwise have created a perpetual nightmare.

In December, the *Cook Report* was broadcast on ITV television, coinciding with a major article in the *Daily Mirror*, featuring a series of pretty graphic images from the video. People were amazed that after such an horrific experience, she could ever bring herself to go back to blood fiestas, but in many ways the accident had served to empower her. People had to sit up and take notice when she still persisted in her campaign. After the accident her message was amplified tenfold and that spurred her on. But apart from that, she was very determined; she wasn't going to let the fact of being nearly killed by a bull deter her.

Unbelievably, by February 1996, she was back on the campaign trail, convinced that she must not give in to her misery. Cocooned in warm blankets she appeared in her wheelchair next to the League's giant twenty-foot inflatable hare 'Harriet' for interviews. Once again she led the demo against the Waterloo Cup. Tony had made banners which could be attached to her wheelchair. The press called her 'brave' and 'valiant'.

She was still in a wheelchair when the *Liverpool Echo* presented her with the *Echo* Mersey Marvel Award at the Liverpool Aldelfi hotel. There were a number of steps, so Tony and others carried her up in the wheelchair to the ceremony. When they called her out to receive her award, he planned to push her up to the stage, but instead she forced herself to her feet. It was about a twenty metre walk to the stage. She received her award and walked back to her table, then collapsed in the wheelchair. The effort left her exhausted for a couple of days.

She never admitted to people that she was in constant pain, preferring the focus to remain on the animals rather than on her. She told the *Sunday Express*, "We must go on. At times ... the pain was excruciating. But it has also helped me to understand better what the animals go through. Now I know what it feels like."

# Inner Demons

Even though animal rights people are generally regarded as killjoys by the world media, after the accident Vicki was in great demand. She was already known in the USA before her accident but NBC's *Dateline* programme was the first to cross continents to meet her. Not only had they travelled to Coria to get pictures of the infamous metal window grid, but they arrived in Southport with two camera crews in tow. It was the middle of June, so Southport's botanic garden, being in full bloom, was selected as a location. Tony wheeled Vicki across the park, where she met interviewer John Hockenberry, who was in a wheelchair himself. "Be warned, this is no trip to the petting zoo," he warned the television audience before showing footage of her accident. There was a good chemistry between him and Vicki. She appeared relaxed and laughed out loud, when he incredulously asked her, "You put your mom in a rest home to save a *donkey?*"

She insisted on walking during the programme. With super-human strength she managed to suppress the pain in her foot and avoid a limp, as she was filmed walking their dog Susie with Tony. She was determined not to reveal any weakness on camera. Her daily reality at home was depressing enough, without showing it to the world. She was still not able to accomplish the things she wanted, such as finishing the Spanish landscape which still adorns the hallway today.

The next request came from Carlton Television (now ITV). For the *Big Story* programme they wanted Vicki to go back to Coria. Vicki and Tony agreed, partly because they welcomed the opportunity to express their gratitude to those people who had helped save her life and partly because it would serve to direct the media spotlight on to the animal cruelty once again. On 30 August, even though Vicki was still far from fully recovered, they flew to Madrid, hired a car and drove to Cáceres. They were booked into the expensive *Melia* hotel by the television people and when they came down into the lobby, the Spanish press had arrived in force, somebody having alerted them. Tony refused to disclose the purpose of their visit and tried to impress on them that Vicki needed to rest. He and the researcher then drove to Coria to see the mayor. Tony told him that they wanted to see as many people as possible who had been involved in Vicki's care. "I haven't come here particularly to castigate, but I am not here as a friend either," he explained. The mayor told him not to worry, because it had been very good publicity for the village.

Next morning there was a press conference in the town hall. Quite a crowd had gathered, including people working for the Red Cross, doctors and security people. Vicki was very moved and had tears in her eyes when she was introduced to the young man who had first pulled her away from the bull. Yet she would not sell out on her conviction. "This is a short truce in a battle. I have come here to thank you for what you did to save my life. And for the moment ... we forget that what you're doing is wrong." Together they revisited the place where the accident had taken place.

In a bar outside the walls of Coria they were surprised to see pictures of Vicki on the wall, as well as newspaper clippings. The owner asked her to sign the pictures, which she did. Wherever they went, she was treated like a star. Tony needed something out of their car and went on ahead, because Vicki could still not walk well and would follow slowly. Half an hour later she had still not arrived and worried, he started to look for her. When he finally found her he asked where she had been. "It's incredible! Wherever I've gone, people have run up to me. Women were holding up their children for me to touch for luck. They invited me into their houses to have a drink." They had held a mass for her every day while she was in hospital and were genuinely pleased to see she was still alive. Their friend Pepe Morgan joked, "You'd better be careful. They would love to kill a bull, or have a fiesta in Vicki's honour."

Right after Vicki's accident Argentino's breeder, Jesús Pérez Escudero, had wanted to meet Tony, but he had refused. The television crew now wanted Vicki to meet him, so they went to his ranch. They followed him across fields until they came to the one in which he kept the fighting bulls. He opened the gate for them to walk amongst the bulls – everybody declined, especially since one of the animals was Argentino's half brother. Tony took pictures and later used them for FAACE's anti-bullfighting leaflets. The producer prompted Vicki to ask the bull breeder what he felt about the bulls he had reared dying in such a way. "What do I ask him that question for? I know what the answer is. You know too what the answer is." But the producer insisted. Vicki, who was normally very patient with people, turned and got into the car. It took the producer quite a while to convince her to come back out to resume the interview. She posed with the bull breeder for a brief moment for the camera, but would not speak to him again.

Friction with the producer built up. Young and ambitious, she was unused to the imperfections in the Spanish way of life and was also keen to keep costs down. With the filming complete, Tony and Vicki were suddenly dispensable. No matter that she was still recovering from very serious injuries. Had it not been for presenter Dermott Murnaghan's intervention, they would have even been left without a car.

Of course, the papers had announced that Vicki was back. Apparently, *El Periodico de Extremadura* did not like the fact that Tony had refused them an interview in the hotel lobby. In their article they said, "She has come back in a very nice way. But you should be aware that beneath the fleece of the sheep, there are the teeth of a wolf."

In October 1996, Tony set foot in the USA for the first time and the pair of them set off on a lecture tour, beginning and ending in New York and taking them down the East Coast. For once, they were able to do some sightseeing, albeit limited by Vicki's mobility problems. One day, however, one of their acquaintances took pity on them and offered to chauffeur them around. Vicki chose to see Trump Towers and Tony the Twin Towers – to be demolished into 'Ground Zero' in 2001.

The decision to fly to Los Angeles just before Christmas, was not an easy one. In fact, it took a lot of convincing on the part of producer Shannon Fenady of FOX television's *When Animals Attack 3*. This highly popular programme, with an audience of over thirty million viewers, was repeated worldwide. It reported on people who had survived violent encounters with animals and featured attacks by sharks, alligators, lions, elephants and even male deer. Tony was very much against Vicki participating in such a programme. So far they had succeeded in using Vicki's accident as a vehicle for exposing Spanish blood fiestas, but this sounded suspiciously like some kind of freak show. He requested a tape of one of the earlier programmes. He was disgusted by it and said so quite openly but he underestimated the producer's dogged perseverance. Not only was he offering a club class ticket for Vicki, but also a donation of five thousand dollars to FAACE. Even though the money would have been highly appreciated, Tony still played hard to get; they could not be involved in the programme if it simply focused on Vicki's accident. It took three months of telephone calls and faxes until they finally came to an agreement.

Vicki found it strange being with the three other women around the breakfast table in the Sportsmen's Lodge Hotel. One had been attacked by a bear, one by a lion and one by a bull. Though all of them looked presentable and recovered from their gruesome experience, they all still suffered from the consequences. Vicki envied the ongoing quality of their medical treatment, because the doctors had worked wonders on them.

Tony watched a tape of the programme and was pleasantly surprised. Against all the odds, they had produced what he described as the ultimate animal rights piece. The programme is certainly quite powerful and the last segment is dedicated to Vicki and contains a lot of fiesta footage. In it, she says, "Even though I was the victim in this case, the animals are the victims every day, every month, every year, as it has been for centuries. It must change ... When we allow animals to be hurt and degraded, we hurt and degrade ourselves." Presenter Robert Urich echoed these sentiments when he finished with the line, "In the end, each of us must preserve and protect the rights of animals and when we do, we are all the better for it."

There were some lighter notes on Vicki's trip too. In an open convertible the three women were ferried around Los Angeles, ending up in a restaurant, which took pride in its singing waiters. When it was time to say goodbye, Vicki was handed an envelope, which supposedly contained her cheque. When she opened it a little later there was certainly a cheque inside, but only made out for ten dollars. In disbelief, and with little time on her hands, she inquired where the company's offices were and set off to sort the matter out. She was told it must have been some kind of mix up and that nothing could be done about it now. But she was adamant and would not leave, because she feared she would not get the money once she had left the country. If they had intended to dupe her, they had picked on the wrong person. Probably just to get rid of her, they sorted the problem out and she proudly handed the cheque over to Tony upon arrival in Manchester.

# A Class All by Herself

Shortly before Christmas 1996, Vicki received a letter from Los Angeles. "Please accept our enthusiastic invitation to you to be the Guest of Honour at our Eleventh Annual Genesis Awards …" The ceremony would take place in April 1997. Far from being flattered, Vicki initially reacted with suspicion. After all, in modern society one was flooded with dubious offers, so-called business opportunities and prize notifications. She had never heard of this award before but the letter was accompanied by some background information. She learnt that the Genesis Award had been given, since 1986, to honour 'outstanding individuals in the major media who have increased public awareness on animal issues'. The event's organisers, the Ark Foundation, knew about Vicki because the NBC Dateline's *Raging Bull* programme had been aired a few weeks earlier and had made a huge impression. While she would not receive an award herself, as this was reserved for producers, artists and writers, she was invited as Guest of Honour, "because of your bold and courageous actions, exposing yourself to the barbaric 'traditions' of the Spanish people, which led to you having been gored by a bull … and now having returned in fine form, physically and spiritually, with renewed commitment to publicise these atrocities to the world."

As much as Vicki appreciated the gesture, she would not write back until she had spoken to her American contact Ron Scott, who knew the people involved. He endorsed it wholeheartedly. The round trip, including her hotel accommodation, would be paid for by them. She and Tony both felt that he should not miss out on this important moment in their lives. It took some faxing between Southport and Los Angeles to figure out which were the cheapest connections, so they could fly together without having to change planes too often. The long-distance flight, change of climate and time difference would already put too much strain on Vicki.

However, Vicki was getting restless. She needed to prove to herself that she could do things on her own and pick up on her life. Even though the accident would always be part of that life, she had talked enough about it. There were more fiestas to expose and she was impatient to get started. A bull fiesta was out of the question, but in January there were many fiestas involving chickens in the Salamanca area. After lengthy discussions, Tony conceded that she should go but it was imperative that she be as safe as possible. He therefore arranged for her to fly to Madrid, where, after a night's rest, she would be picked up by journalist Bill Bond, who had known her before and after her accident. He liked and respected her because she was not a fanatic, just determined and absolutely committed.

They would drive to the village of El Pego, observe the fiesta and drive straight back. Vicki was thrilled to see that dead chickens, which had been humanely killed beforehand, were strung up on the rope instead of live ones. Revolting as the idea of the mutilation of dead birds was to her, she accepted that it was a mark of progress, not just in El Pego but in the whole region. Bill Bond acknowledged that Vicki had played a part in changing the law. He didn't get his story because they stuck to the law, but Vicki was delighted … her campaign had borne fruit.

It was also a relief that the trip had gone so well for her personally. "It seems to me like years ago now, but I suppose it's a quick recovery when you think I am back to where I was before, although I still have to take painkillers." She also had some good-humoured advice: "It is strange that I am trying to root-out animal cruelty in a country whose doctors and nurses certainly saved my life. If you are going to be gored by a bull, for goodness sake, make sure it is in Spain."

"Range Rovers, Rioja and a Race for Life", ran the *Daily Post* headline announcing the 1997 Waterloo Cup. Animal rights groups and many newspapers were convinced that this would be the last Cup. Tony Blair tried to win the support of animal rights groups in a pre-General Election speech in London, prefacing it with his usual, "Trust me …" Back in 1997 the anti-hunting lobby certainly felt that their voice was being heard by politicians and FAACE teamed up with the League and IFAW in a national newspaper advertising campaign in which full-page ads showed a hare being ripped apart by two dogs, with the caption, "It's not the hare being brutally savaged by two dogs that upsets people. It's betting on the wrong dog". Readers were asked to lobby their MPs urging an end to such legalised cruelty. At the same time, ninety MPs demanded a bill to protect the hares, because their numbers had gone down by eighty per cent. Newspapers ran telephone opinion polls, in which an overwhelming majority voted in favour of a complete ban. The coursers also tried to take advantage of election time, retaliating with postcards to Tony Blair urging him to rethink his policy pledge.

April arrived and finally it was time to pack their bags for Los Angeles. The flight from Manchester via Paris to Los Angeles was a strain on Vicki, despite five-star treatment. They were picked up from the airport in a Cadillac and dropped off at their plush hotel. Vicki was unable to go to a get together in the evening but wanted Tony to be there. A limousine took him up into the hills and when they arrived at their destination, people in uniform rushed up to park the cars. The luxurious house was the height of kitsch; a mix of all kinds of styles. It would have been a bit chilly, but for the fact that great gas stoves heated the entire garden. The swimming pool was an imitation lake with a jacuzzi in the same style. A vegan buffet was provided and everybody was introduced.

The next day, the day of the awards, Vicki felt refreshed and was looking forward to the ceremony. Choosing what to wear had posed problems. On the one hand, evening gowns were very expensive and on the other she wanted to conceal her scars. While in London on business she had found a dark brown velvet dress in a dress agency, which was relatively short, but closed right up to the neck. It had gold sparkling decorations on the front and she looked very glamorous. Her hair was back to shoulder-length and was full and shiny. There was no outward sign of the terrible injury to her foot, but she must have been in acute pain when she squeezed into her high-heels. They made a handsome pair when they were picked up by director Anthony Thomas, who had been nominated for his documentary *To Love, or Kill: Man vs Animal*, for which Vicki had made that fateful journey to Coria.

The lengthy ceremony, with all the awards and customary acceptance speeches, took place at the Century Plaza Hotel. Before the awards, Gretchen Wyler introduced the guests of honour to the audience and Vicki received a plaque, which, together with other awards, still adorns the office wall. The whole show was videoed to be broadcast on the Discovery Channel and Animal Planet. The presenter for *Raging Bull* was actress Joan Van Ark, who presented the award to producer Robert Buchanan saying, "All over the world, thousands of people are engaged in a struggle to save animals from cruelty, exploitation and even extinction. Many are selfless and dedicated. Some are even willing to risk their own lives. But one elegant British woman, Miss Vicki Moore, may be in a class all by herself." An extract of the documentary was shown, ending with Vicki saying about the bull who had gored her, "I excuse him totally … we were just two victims".

In his acceptance speech, Robert Buchanan said, "Vicki's story was no easy sell. We thought at first, how could we put the story on network prime time television? We were going to show animals being maimed, animals being mutilated. But after we talked about it, we realised that was exactly the reason why it should be on prime time network TV … I am very pleased to announce that Vicki has come all the way from England to be with us tonight. Please welcome Vicki Moore."

Vicki rushed across the stage, kissed him on the cheek and said: "Thank you very much. And my thanks now to Rob and to John and to all the wonderful Dateline team. They are changing things, because in Spain, I recently went back to fiestas that I exposed nine, ten years ago and those fiestas don't exist anymore. Things are happening."

The ceremony was a memorable event in their lives but it did not make much difference to their work, as neither new media contacts, nor potential sponsors, came out of it. Vicki was asked to fly to San Francisco for a short television interview and a radio programme, but she did not feel well enough to squeeze the flights into their already tight schedule. Mentally she was already focusing on their next projects on the old continent.

# A Close Call

Several more approaches were made by American television companies but they would only agree to go if they felt the result would be a positive one for their cause. They were always struck by the producers' change in attitude before and after filming. Before, they could not do enough to help them, afterwards, it was a case of "Who are you?" The trips were always gruelling for Vicki yet no account was taken of her injuries, or fragile physical condition.

In November 1995, the year of her accident, Vicki received a call from Hong Kong. Local animal rights people of the Hong Kong RSPCA, EarthCare and IFAW asked her to attend their protests against the bullfights scheduled to take place in the Portuguese enclave of Macao for the Chinese New Year's celebrations in February 1996. Vicki was simply not capable of flying to the other side of the globe and Tony couldn't go either, because she still needed his help around the clock. So they sent lots of material over instead. Since the last known bullfights in Macao had taken place in 1974, hardly anybody could remember what a Portuguese bullfight entailed. The 'tourada' is wrongly described as a bloodless bullfight. The bulls are not killed in front of the audience but their death is only postponed until they reach the abattoir. The bulls have their horns sawn off and covered in leather so as not to hurt the horses ridden by the bullfighters, the 'cavaleiros', who stick three barbed metal spear-like weapons, the so-called 'farpas' and six banderillas into the animal's shoulders, causing great loss of blood. A team of eight 'forcados' immobilises the animal for a short time. One hangs on to the bull's tail and spins him round until the others are clear and then lets go.

Since tickets sales were low outside of Macao, the organisers came up with a bizarre strategy to endear the Chinese audience to bullfighting. It is traditional in China to give 'lai see' to the people one cares for on New Year's Day. Lai see is Cantonese for a red gift envelope with a bank note inside. So a red envelope would be pinned between the horns of a specially selected fighting bull and people from the audience would be invited to prove their courage by grabbing the envelope containing three thousand Hong Kong dollars. However, concerns over safety scotched the plan.

The campaign failed, and the bullfights took place, although the six thousand-capacity bullring was only a third full at any one time. The bulls were released directly from their crates on a truck into the ring and then lassoed back via a ramp after the fight. The sides of the ramp were so narrow that the weapons were ripped out of at least one of the animals' flesh. The audience's opinion was surveyed and most people thought it cruel and would not be repeating the experience. Many people voted with their feet and left before the end. Veterinary surgeon Dr O W Young, who witnessed the bullfights, concluded that they should be banned. So, when, in September 1997, another call for help came from Hong Kong, Vicki and Tony were shocked. With the touradas of 1996 a clear financial and moral flop, everybody was convinced that bullfighting in Macao was a thing of the past.

Five bullfights would take place between 27 September and 5 October. Again Dr Stanley Ho and his casino syndicate Sociedade da Turismo e Diversoes de Macau invested heavily in the show and had twenty-four bulls, as well as horses and bullfighters, flown to the island. He did not seem to recognise any conflict in having been the former honorary president of the Hong Kong RSPCA and self-proclaimed animal lover.

This time Vicki decided she felt well enough to go. Tony borrowed the money for the tickets and accommodation was arranged in a private home with a British family. A few days before the flight, Vicki came down with a bout of 'flu but decided that cancelling the flight was out of the question. On 23 September Tony took her to Manchester Airport. As the plane came in to land on the narrow landing strip squeezed between Hong Kong's skyscrapers, she felt so ill that she took herself to the Hong Kong Adventist Hospital, where she was diagnosed with pneumonia. The doctors wanted her to stay in but she had work to do, so she was given antibiotics and left.

She could not rest, because the family she intended staying with had to go away suddenly and she was asked to stay at their friends' home instead. The family's children were very lively and she got no peace. Hong Kong hotels are outrageously expensive, so it was out of the question to move out and she felt far too poorly to explore the impressive city.

Mustering all her strength, she went on Hong Kong television and did newspaper interviews. She challenged the Macao people by asking them whether they did not have any cultural heritage of their own. Why did they have to adopt the so-called cultural heritage imposed on them by an imperialist power? A heritage that was dying out in their own country, so they were forcing it on to Macao. Macao should be returned to China without this horrific legacy and she outlined the cruelty they should expect.

Meanwhile, back at home, Tony was busy faxing data out to the Macao and Hong Kong press on how BSE had hit the Portuguese cattle industry. The original plan was to sell the meat from the dead fighting bulls to hotels as a delicacy. Suddenly, nobody wanted to be associated with the idea any longer, removing another important source of income for the producers.

Veterinary surgeon Gail Cochran and Jill Robinson of IFAW accompanied Vicki to Macao, an hour's boat ride away. Vicki was not impressed with the island, best known for its great variety of gangster-run casinos. On the day of the bullfight, the bullfighters paraded through the streets escorted by the police. A group of Chinese animal rights people tried to break up the parade by bravely jumping in among them with their anti-bullfighting banners and were dragged away by the police.

The parade ended in front of the temporary bullring, which was festooned with huge green and red plastic sheets. Spanish paso doble music blasted away, while the international press did interviews with the activists and people buying tickets. A lorry containing wooden crates was parked in front of an entrance. The bullring itself was dwarfed by Macao's skyscrapers. In the ring there was a Chinese band playing and all advertisements were in Chinese. As the bullfighters and their teams entered the bullring, two people jumped inside two huge lion costumes and danced around the bullfighters, after which, the start of the bullfight was announced in Chinese and Portuguese. Vicki filmed the small number of spectators and the many empty seats. She even crawled behind the scenes and filmed a huge electro shocking device used to coerce the bull run into the ring. A policeman tried to stop her, but she continued filming, asking, "What do you have to hide?"

The five bulls showed obvious signs of fatigue and were already stumbling and collapsing. Vicki attributed this to drugging and being attacked by two horsemen simultaneously. The bullfighters on foot tried to impress the audience with cheap stunts, but the occasional 'Olé's' were rather weak. After three hours, the injured animals were painfully lassoed and locked up in their crates before being driven to the slaughterhouse.

Under cover of darkness, Vicki and her companions followed the truck. Apart from one man locking up the pens, the slaughterhouse appeared deserted. It was too risky to park in front of the complex, because they sensed danger, but they discovered that the slaughterhouse would remain closed until after the weekend. This meant the animals were locked up with no treatment for their wounds for two whole days, before enduring the horrible ordeal of being slaughtered. It was impossible for Vicki to get in and take a picture of the animals.

There was even less interest in the second bullfight on 28 September; the arena was less than a quarter full and torrential rain put an end to the show after an hour. About five hundred angry people demanded their money back and started a row. The organisers' spokesperson responded by saying, "... they should ask God. Maybe Jesus Christ Superstar will deliver it to them."

In an ouspoken television interview for an Asian television channel, before heading back to Hong Kong, Vicki alleged that the bulls had been drugged, which was confirmed by vet Gail Cochran. She also implied that the whole corrupt operation was run by the Chinese mafia.

After the interview, Vicki and Jill Robinson quickly jumped on to the ferry.

But Gail, who had to catch a ferry to a different part of Hong Kong, was stopped and taken into custody. She was told that she had been stopped because of a passport irregularity concerning Vicki Moore. On the screens of the passport control she read, "Apprehend Vicki Moore and Gail Cochran before they leave Macao". She rang her husband, who passed it on to Jill by mobile phone. Vicki hid in the toilet until the boat was out to sea, but they did not look for her on the boat, convinced that she had not yet embarked because the first name on her passport was Lucille. She wondered whether they were looking for her films and video, or if they were angry about the television interview. Back in Hong Kong, the Macao bullfights received a very bad press. On 29 September the Hong Kong *Standard* concluded its editorial with, "... our message to the authorities in Macao is: let that be the last one."

The successful, but energy-sapping trip left Vicki exhausted and she returned to England in very poor health, but after a period of recuperation, she travelled to Strasburg to show the Macao video to the European Parliament and warn against the expansion of bullfighting. She found an ally in Simon Murphy MEP, who asked the European Parliament to act against the spread of bullfighting outside of the EU. To this day, there have been no more bullfights in Macao but there have been several partially successful attempts to have corridas on mainland China.

Autumn that year was a rather gloomy period for Vicki and Tony. Triggered by the deaths of her beloved cats Fleur and Pepe, Vicki tried to come to terms with loss and what might come after death: "I feel numb and stone-like between big bursts of hot tears," she wrote in her diary. I am lying in bed and for the first time in many years, Fleur is not trotting about over me. She has, since my accident, been most religious in her insistence to sleep on my stomach, or chest, or even throat. I am dreading the empty weightless sensation that tonight's sleep, or rest, or whatever, will bring ... One doesn't become more stoic with age, or more accustomed to loss. The diminution of our existence is like so many branches and roots being lopped off ... We took Fleur to Leyland [the pet crematorium]. It was an October day that fulfilled the description – golden with clear skies, frosty bright sun, the crisp edge and snap of an autumn apple. In the car Fleur lay on her little flower-decked bier. Her garden had yielded its last blooms to strew her little body. The sun warmed as it filtered through the car windows. And I drew back the muslin cloth and Daddy's old jumper that covered her to let the warmth and light fall on her little head. It was for a last few minutes, as though she lay just sleeping. We passed a pair of shiny chestnut-rumped police horses in Croston and the fields were full of sheep and cattle and in my fanciful mind it seemed they watched her passing when a wraith of smoke rose from the chimney as her poor little mortal remains were consumed. A bird flew in graceful ark across the lower sky and two jets like shooting stars as they twinkled in the frosty sun drew icy vapour trails in perfect symmetry. A huddle of ponies stood in a nearby field, very much amid the animals and nature that seemed so much a part of her, our Fleur was transmitted into a little closely-hugged box of ash. Please let there be more than that! I know there must be more than that."

In another entry she wrote, "Eleven days after Fleur we have said goodbye to our lovely stoical old Pepé ... I remember, especially after my accident, Pepé and Fleur nursing me together, at any rate cuddling up to me, one on either side and sharing all my meals. We watched blanket wall-to-wall television and dozed away the afternoons and a good time was had by all.

"We took Pepé to Leyland, strewn around with red flowers ... It was a sullen November afternoon with a sky the shade of iron, or dull steel. In the ten days since we made this journey with Fleur, the autumn had stripped the leaves from most of the trees, carpeting the roads with swathes of yellow and gold. The old familiar lace-work of bare branches were etched against the sky, but some trees remained foliated and there were brilliant primary splashes on the drear scene – red, saffron, acid yellow, sepia and copper. Pepé lost all her age and look of beetle-browed intensity that she had worn for the last few years and lying in our sitting room, swaddled like a baby in towels, she looked like a young kitten, delicate, untroubled, in a sweet and gentle dream sleep. I felt that, for all the deep sadness and loss, she was truly at peace and set free from her struggles and in my heart could not wish her back in pain. I hope she is reunited with Fleur, Victoria, Fenny, Mimo and the gang and also her little baby kitten, that she lost so long ago in the days of her litter under our care ... how empty everything seems without her presence and that of my Fleur. Bless and protect them both and all our little ones."

# Mysterious Ways

"There are few things as grey and chilling as November in the North of England," wrote Vicki. "On a cold dank afternoon my telephone rang and a voice in very halting broken English said, 'You must know, bullfights now in Egypt'. A burst of crackling interference rattled in my ear and the line went dead. I didn't think this was a hoax – Egypt was an unlikely venue, but having fought campaigns against the export of bullfighting to Russia, Greece and Czechoslovakia and only recently returned from Macao, nothing would really surprise me any more."

It transpired that the corrida, accompanied by flamenco dancing, would take place in the Sun Club in Heliopolis, northwest of Cairo. There would be two shows on both 20 and 26 November, with bullfighters from Spain and Portugal and authentic Spanish fighting bulls. The event was backed by the Egyptian Ministry of Culture and the Cairo Opera House. Vicki recognised the usual pattern, "Normally the participating countries have only the vaguest idea of bullfighting. The potential bookers are gullible and greedy, and those locally who oppose the imported bullfights lack the knowledge and strategies to fight them effectively."

They contacted an Egyptian journalist, who spoke good English and appeared to be on their side. Over the coming weeks he would inform them about what was going on on the Egyptian side. Word of the event spread and other animal rights organisations became involved. Egyptian animal lovers tried to take the organiser to court, involving the highest religious authorities. The Grand Mufti of Egypt, Sheik Nasr Farid Wassel, was of the opinion that bullfights were sinful and so was eating the meat, because the bulls would not be killed according to Islamic laws. This was devastating for the organiser, who postponed the corrida while he secured the opinion of another important religious authority. This postponement, however, was mistakenly interpreted as a cancellation by people outside Egypt. Large organisations like the World Society for the Protection of Animals, and the Humane Society International, prematurely announced their success.

Tony, who had learned from experience to be more sceptical where a lot of money was involved, called the Sun Club requesting tickets. No problem, they were still on sale. The organiser had been informed that while it was still wrong to torture animals, their meat could be used, if bled in the traditional way, so removing an important stumbling block. It could be arranged in the Portuguese style and turned into a charitable event by donating the meat to hospitals. The bullfights were now scheduled to take place on 4 December.

Then Vicki had one of those little inspirations, those sideways ideas that she got – lateral thinking, you might call it. She pointed out that there was a very famous and influential Egyptian person right here in Britain, in the person of Mohammed El Fayed, and she wondered if he might help. In 1990, she had already written to the owner of Harrods on a different matter, because she felt he had been treated unfairly. He had replied and thanked her for her kind comments and words of support, which he greatly appreciated.

In Vicki's experience, powerfully placed people may be prepared to use their influence unstintingly in crisis situations, if they can be sure their involvement will not reach the media. A direct approach was needed, rather than going through the normal channels via Harrods, as they were running out of time. Max Clifford appeared to be El Fayed's public relations man, so Vicki rang him and asked if he could help. While not giving her a definite answer, he did give her the phone number of Jeffrey Lyes, of Lowe Good Relations. This PR company had just been hired by the Egyptian authorities to try and improve the image of the country after the massacre of sixty tourists near Luxor by gunmen, which had all but wiped out the Egyptian tourism industry. The English advisors were horrified by the idea of bullfights, even more so, since Vicki insinuated that there might be a call for a tourism boycott should the corrida take place. As with rumours, boycotts are hard to stop. Vicki faxed over all the information they had at their disposal and hoped they were on the right track.

The day of the corrida came without a single bullfight taking place. Their Egyptian contact from a Cairo newspaper told them it was due to security reasons and they would now take place on 18 December and continue after Christmas. Tony kept pressurising their English contacts but nothing seemed to be happening. He was wrong. Even though details were not disclosed to him, he knew that the night before the event, there were a number of meetings and telephone calls made. Lyes told him that he had never ever spoken to a customer like this before. He had used the most appalling language and felt thoroughly ashamed of himself when he put the phone down, but the upshot was that he was pretty sure that it would no longer take place.

Tony was still not convinced. Two hours before the start of the corrida, he rang up an Egyptian journalist hoping for confirmation. "It's all off. It's finished," he was told. The Grand Mufti had put out a death threat on the bullfighters. The Spanish and Portuguese might as well pack their bags. If the Egyptian Government had banned the bullfights, the organisers would have found a way round it and still gone ahead. But when the Grand Mufti issued a fatwah decreeing a death sentence, there was nothing they could do.

# New Arrivals

"New Labour – Old cruelty", read Tony's banner. Using uncharacteristically strong language, Vicki called Tony Blair 'Judas', accusing him of betraying voters by putting off the ban on hunting. Whilst admitting that they had not won the battle, they had not lost the war. Organisers of the Waterloo Cup defended themselves with a huge advert: "Next week at the Waterloo Cup the usual bunch of animal rights activists will tell you coursing should be banned ... Animal rights activists are wrong, they've always been wrong."

Ex-Beatle Sir Paul McCartney spoke out on behalf of the hares and gave his support to the League Against Cruel Sports by backing a petition to Lord Leverhulme to stop the Waterloo Cup taking place on his estate. However, the big name made no difference. Several veterinary practices from the Formby area entered the debate and their spokesman addressed the Prime Minister, calling on him, as the leader of an animal-loving nation, to allow the majority to be heard and openly support the ban.

Hoping for the umpteenth time that this would be the last Waterloo Cup, Vicki and Tony turned their attention back to their work in Spain, to a matter they dreaded most – dogs' homes. This time, however, the call did not come from the Spanish mainland, but from ZOE, a group from Tenerife. FAACE was asked to alert the international media to a situation which was being widely ignored by the local authorities and the media.

As usual, they delivered. In the middle of March, Vicki, accompanied by a team from the *Daily Mail*, arrived in Santa Cruz de Tenerife, the capital. There was no time to enjoy the sunshine, or the impressive volcanic landscapes and the next morning, they were confronted with the most horrific sight. One hundred and sixty dogs, twice its capacity, were crammed into the shelter of Valle Colino, in the north east of Tenerife. Not only were they afflicted with all sorts of illnesses, they were also so starved that they had begun to eat each other. Dead dogs were simply dumped in a bin. The depressing situation was all too familiar.

The shelter belonged to the council, but it was run by one of Tenerife's animal protection groups. There was talk of irregularities in the handling of donations and because there were no records of dogs entering or leaving the shelter, their was suspicion that some were being sold on to vivisection laboratories. Volunteers who had helped in the past, signed written statements describing the conditions, supporting their complaints with a report compiled by a private investigator. This resulted in them being banned from entering the shelter, while the authorities closed their eyes to the dogs' suffering.

Vicki took a lot of pictures; a good idea, as the *Daily Mail* did not run the story after all. She had been home for a week, when Tony decided to hold a small press conference in their office. Northwest papers and the *Sunday Mirror* carried the story, copies of which were sent to Tenerife and taken up by the local press.

Back in Southport, they collected one thousand five hundred signatures and were about to fly to Tenerife again, when Channel 5 decided to send a team. Nothing had changed. The volunteers kept the dogs alive by secretly feeding them after the workers had left but, due to lack of funds, they only managed to provide food three times a week. They had to cut the fence each time in order to recover the dead dogs and stop those left from fighting over the food. Vicki exposed to the camera what the workers fed them: long-expired cornflakes and cat food. Even though Tony had already seen Vicki's footage, he was unprepared for the sickening sight he was about to witness. He managed to rescue three very sick dogs and took them straight to the vet's. Sadly, they were beyond help and had to be put down immediately. Eva, one of the volunteers who spoke English, made a touching statement on camera, "They just need the same things that you or I need: care, food and some love." Vicki and Tony met with officials and handed over the signatures. Euro MP Richard Corbett submitted a parliamentary question to the EU-Commission calling for the situation to be investigated.

However, things only changed very slowly. Some of those who ran the shelter were fined for breaking the law by neglecting the animals and plans were made to build a more modern shelter. However, it took until October 2005 for it to open, next to the site of the old shelter, which was still in operation.

There was nothing more FAACE could do in Tenerife, so they accepted an invitation to Amsterdam. Even though there is a Dutch bullfighter, unknown within Spain, as are most of the foreigners who take up the cape, Dutch people generally are strongly opposed to bullfighting, due to a strong anti-bullfighting group, the Comité Anti-Stierenvechten, which supports campaigns in Spain and elsewhere and educates the general public to stay away from bullrings.

Tony had compiled a graphic sample of Spanish fiestas and Vicki made quite an impression when she appeared on the popular Dutch television programme *Heb Ik Dat?* showing the actual weapons used in the ring. Having watched film extracts of her accident, the audience were amazed, not only by her survival, but also by how well she looked. Were the people who did this crazy? she was asked. She explained that they had been brainwashed, having witnessed such gruesome events from early childhood, but opposition was definitely growing in Spain.

Even though Vicki appeared to be in good health, she still suffered enormously from the massive trauma to her foot. In Amsterdam she had hardly been able to make it up the steep stairs to their hotel room and could only manage short walks around the canals. Some pins needed to be taken out and a toe straightened, in order for her to have any chance of walking normally again.

Hating the thought of yet another painful operation, but determined to get back to full mobility, she reluctantly checked into a Liverpool hospital on her return from Holland. The pain and suffering involved was worth it, because the operation was a success.

Barely recovered, they were thrust back into the fray once more, this time joining an international anti-bullfighting demonstration in Gerona. Friends provided a wheelchair for Vicki but, as usual, she refused to use it. Tony bought her a pair of large men's sandals and cut one to fit her foot comfortably. She even tried to mix in the crowd and bravely danced the traditional dance, the Soldana.

A few days before the August bank holiday, someone gave Tony three magnets in the shape of black kittens, which he stuck on the fridge door. He now considers this an omen, because in the morning of the bank holiday he received a call from nearby Formby. Two abandoned kittens had been found in the front gardens of two adjoining houses. Something must have happened to the mother, whom they suspected to be a semi-wild black and white cat, who didn't seem to belong to anyone. Tony advised the caller not to touch them, that the mother was probably just shifting them, and if left alone, might come back for them. As it was a fine day, the kittens were in no immediate danger. However, Tony rang again in the afternoon and found that they were still there. At 8pm, dark thunder clouds were gathering, so he rang again. The mother still hadn't returned for them and they were now lying on their stomachs, 'swimming' and crying, so Tony and Vicki took a cat carrier and went to pick them up.

When they arrived, a third kitten had been discovered in a garage nearby. Scooping up the little scraps and putting them in the basket, they took them home. The kittens were lucky, because all the necessary equipment and food formula were available in the house and they were fed every two hours. Kittens were the last thing they would have chosen at that time, because Vicki was far from well and Tony was not getting any younger.

The next morning, Tony called all his contacts to try and find someone who would nurse all three, but nobody from the local cat protection society was willing to accept such an onerous task. So they continued to feed them themselves at short intervals. At first getting up together at night, later on taking turns. Of course, this bonded them to the kittens and after a week there was no longer any question of anybody else taking them; they were totally hooked. They already had their individual personalities and were christened Tolly, Tiny and Thomas Chip. Their Spanish cat Alita was the only survivor of their many other cats and enjoyed being the only star in the family. She did not conceal her disgust with the three black kittens and soon showed them their place in the household.

# Into the Firing Line

Autumn can be quite chilly in Spain, as Vicki and Tony were to find out in November 1998, when they travelled to Medinaceli, in the province of Soria, about 70km north east of Madrid going up the motorway to Zaragoza. Strategically placed on a mountainside plateau in the valley of the River Jalón, Medinaceli has the potential to become a major tourist attraction, with its Roman and Arabic monuments and archeological museum in which old mosaics are still being restored. Yet the village is strangely deserted and the tourist office never seems to function.

Once a year, however, on a Saturday night close to 13 November, the village becomes the centre of a nationwide controversy. A fire bull fiesta – the so-called 'Toro de Jubilo', (Jubilation Bull) – takes place within the Cuerpos Santos fiestas, the local patron saints' festivities. Several legends abound, most of which conclude that it is of Celt Iberian origin. One version maintains that it is a symbol of the fight between the hero and the totem-animal of the Celt Iberians, the bull. Another, that it is an initiation rite. The most colourful version dates back to the war against the Carthaginians, when the village was under siege. When there was nothing left to eat except for a bull, they decided to impress the enemy with a clever manoeuvre. They set fire to the bull's horns and sent him down into the valley. The frightening spectacle gave the impression that the siege was having no effect; the villagers must still have so much food that they could afford to sacrifice the bull. The ruse worked and the siege collapsed. Either version makes not a jot of difference to fate of the poor animal.

Having booked into a hotel at a nearby village, Tony and Vicki set off to explore Medinaceli. Vicki felt up to the challenge; though still in pain every day, things had improved physically, although no one was sure what the ultimate psychological reaction to such trauma would be. They drove up a precipitous winding road for quite some time, until they came to a parking area. The streets and most of the houses seemed deserted. The large main square, however, was bustling with activity, with men erecting fencing and stands for the evening's entertainment. Half the square would be fenced-off for the bull to be run in. Carts had been positioned around the fenced-off area, on to which people could climb. They briefly deliberated as to whether it would be a good idea to talk their way on to the town hall balcony but decided against it. Tony then spotted the place where the pole to which the bull would be tied, would be placed. That was the best place to be and they would come early and hold their places.

A large, six-door black limousine suddenly rolled into the square. They did not recognise the man who got out of the car but from all the handshaking, concluded that he must be an important person. Accompanied by some local people, the man inspected the area. Tony refrained from taking pictures, because he wanted to keep a low profile.

After leaving the village they drove around the area killing time, stopping at a transport café for a bite to eat. The wait must have seemed endless to Vicki. By now she was feeling very apprehensive, because it was her first bull fiesta since her accident. After dark, but still early for the fiesta, they went back to Medinaceli, by which time the temperature had dropped dramatically and they had to keep moving to stay warm. The entrance to the square was filled with the aroma of roasting chestnuts and they bought some to keep warm. They sat in the car for a while with the heater on full, before resuming their positions close to the post.

By now, the square was thronged with people, one of whom nodded to Tony with the usual greeting, "Hola". He did not know any of them, but was reassured by the friendly smiles. Vicki was not so sure. Although she had protected her identity with a chin-length platinum wig, too many pictures of her had appeared in the Spanish press at the time of her accident. Apart from that, just being English in Medinaceli was risky, because the fiesta had been banned during the Franco era from 1962 to 1977, due to reports of animal cruelty made by English journalists. Tony took a picture of her in the crowd. Her shiny blonde wig stuck out like a sore thumb. Her hands were bright red from the bitter cold.

A murmur of excitement rippled through the crowd as a lorry backed into the square carrying the bull. It stopped close to one of the doors of the Aula Arqueológica. It took a while to fix a rope around the bull's horns as he kicked and bucked inside the transporter, bellowing in terror. He was dragged out and put into a makeshift stable inside the building. In the fenced-off area, five fires, representing the village saints, were lit. By this time, people were trying to push Tony out of the way, but he stood his ground.

At around 11.30pm, the end of a long rope, which came out of the place where the bull was tethered, was passed through a hole in the post. A game of tug-of-war ensued, with several men trying to drag the bull on to the square. This took a very long time; the terrified animal was not moving voluntarily and was using all his power to resist, as if he sensed the bloody fate that awaited him in the square. His terrified screams could be heard before he came into view, backwards, being relentlessly dragged towards the post by the rope around his horns. On his other side, men tried to hold him in place with the end of the rope, ready to run, should he suddenly charge at them.

Eventually, they had him where they wanted, ensnared in their lethal trap. Several men forced his head down and tied it closely to the post, while others yanked his tail to keep him in position. Vicki, who was using their new Super VHS video camera for the first time, had problems using the viewfinder and had to guess whether she was aiming in the right direction. The men began to daub the animal's head and shoulders with clay, supposedly to prevent his skin from being burned. Then the so-called false horns – a contraption to hold the torches made of hemp soaked in wax and paraffin – was screwed on to his head. This done, the hemp was set on fire, the men bashing at it to make it burn brighter. Soon the flames were shooting high up in the air. They all piled out, except for three or four of them whose job it was to cut him free. The bull's terrible screams echoed round the square but they fell on deaf ears, the villagers perceiving the tortured creature, not as an object of pity, but as the night's star turn. It took several attempts to cut the bull from the post, as when they let go of his tail, he started kicking frantically. They danced around him, trying to cut him free without being kicked, or burnt by the fire.

Finally, some youths managed to cut the rope, sending the crowd into uproar as the bull broke free and ran off. But his freedom would not last for long and the real torment had only just begun. People leapt out in front of him to prove their bravery, firecrackers were thrown at him and he was beaten with a stick. Soon his snout and legs were streaming with blood. Demented, he charged into the fire, sticking his head into it, as if trying to fight fire with fire. Records of earlier years describe the bull being so exhausted that he broke down in the square and would not get up, another had simply withdrawn into a corner and refused to move.

In this fiesta, the bull simply wanted to get out, away from his tormentors. The crowd screamed as the bull charged, dislodging the top bar of the fence and trying to jump over at exactly the spot where Tony and Vicki stood. For Vicki this must have been the ultimate nightmare; a full-grown bull charging straight at her again! But, fearless as ever, she did not run away, determined to report the animal's plight to the world.

When the flames died down at last, it was easy to see the damage the fire had done to the bull. His mouth was bleeding badly and his horns so charred and blackened that they looked as if they would shatter if you hit them. He was covered in sparks and had small burn holes dotted all over his back. He was panting heavily when a deafening firework display was triggered, adding to his terror and confusion. Some men managed to get a rope around his head and dragged him back into the Aula Arqueológica. Several historic reports suggested that the bull would be killed later, but the mayor insisted, as they always do, that the next day he would be happily grazing in the pastures. This was ludicrous; even if he survived, the poor thing could never graze again.

All the old feelings of depression and disgust came flooding back as they drove back to their hotel. Tony described his sentiments, "It affects you, doesn't it? I felt like I always do. When I walk away I don't want to know anything about it. I feel dirty somehow, as though I have been involved in it, even though I haven't. In fact, I try to do the opposite, but I still feel as though I have taken

170

part." They ran through their video footage; they had got enough to denounce the cruelty, which was some consolation.

The *Sunday Express* published the story, "So Cruel, but the Spanish Just Love It" ran the headline above a huge picture of the bull with his head on fire, bleeding heavily from the mouth and front legs. In January 1999, Vicki reported on the fiesta in the European Parliament in Strasbourg. But due to the lack of power where animal abuse for traditional or religious reasons is concerned, nothing more than an official letter of complaint to the governor was the result.

With the beginning of democracy after Franco, the fiesta was tolerated but not officially sanctioned. In 2000, Alfonso Chillerón and Gustavo Saleh, president and vice-president of ANPBA, filmed the fiesta and denounced the village. The government of Castilla y León issued a laughably small fine of three hundred euros. In 2001, they were fined three hundred and seventy euros due to another complaint by ANPBA. By 2002, the village had got their act together and had the fiesta legalised. On 18 September, hardly two months before the return of the fiesta, the Junta of Castilla y León, the regional government, declared the event a 'festejo taurino tradicional'. To qualify for such ranking, the village had to prove that it had been going on for two hundred years without interruption. ANPBA questioned the proceedings and was able to present documents which proved that it had not taken place for several years. The ombudsman took their side and asked the junta to revise the process. However, to this date, the fiesta continues. It is even promoted as a fiesta 'de interés turístico', on the official website of the Soria province. The fenced-off area where the bull is let loose has even been enlarged considerably to accommodate more spectators.

Despite Members of the European Parliament being strongly opposed to the fiesta, money was claimed from the European Social Fund to renovate the Aula Arqueológica, which doubles as the makeshift stable where the bull is kept and manipulated before and after the spectacle. Such contradictions are not uncommon in the EU. When the *Sunday Express* asked Vicki for her feelings when the bull charged at her, she admitted that it had brought back terrible memories but she also felt that she had been blessed with enough stamina to be back in the front line.

Why was she still carrying on after her accident? "The fact that I had such a narrow escape means I have to prove myself worthy by not wasting my life."

# What the King Saw

Six months later, Vicki's health had deteriorated even further. Apart from having to take more and more painkillers, which had unpleasant side effects, she felt generally unwell, but refused to go and get checked out. After having been in constant pain for such a long time and repeatedly going in and out of hospital, she had developed a phobia of anything medical. Injections, blood tests, operations, even the very smell, or sight of a hospital used to consume her with dread. Tony is sure that she knew she was going to die. "Of course, we all know we'll die, but she knew her death was coming up a lot sooner than most people's." She spoke dispassionately about her death, but there were moments of sheer desperation. Would it be a good idea to make her exit in a big way? In a very public gesture, by attacking one of the bullfighters or impresarios? It would not matter if they shot her, she was going to die anyway. It might even save her a lot of slow dying later. Tony is sure he was right to talk her out of it. Neither the animals nor the movement would have benefited and she would simply have been ridiculed as a crazy woman. Anyway, he was in denial and could not bear the thought of losing her. Vicki did not dwell on her worries and despite her ill-health, she never lost her sense of humour. While in Santa Cruz de Tenerife, she went to the Museo de la Naturaleza y el Hombre, where she found a portrait of Admiral Horace Nelson, who lost his right arm in the battle of Santa Cruz in 1797. On her ticket she scribbled, "Nelson's loss of an arm during the attack somewhat pointedly was causing me to reflect that we Brits do rather seem to be in the habit of losing bits of our anatomies up and down the peninsula and islands."

They tried to just get on with their lives – with one important alteration. Travelling solo was no longer possible, since she couldn't carry her luggage anymore and needed to be looked after. And so, at the end of June 1999, they flew to Barcelona and drove down the coast to the Castellón province. Their map of Spain was circled in many places round that area, each circle indicating a fiesta involving bulls. Even though it was already high season, they found an empty hotel in Oropesa and got a room very cheaply. During the day they took pictures of cattle fiestas and the infamous pony roundabouts in various locations. They had received many complaints about these from British tourists. The ponies are forced to walk round in circles all afternoon in the blazing heat and well into the night without a break. Their heads are fastened on either side to rigid metal bars, which keep them in the same position. In the main, they are not well looked after and are usually to be found in the middle of a fairground with loud music blasting out all around them.

One such pony roundabout was in the seaside town of El Grau. Having taken their pictures, they strolled into the town and watched in despair as a group of young children played with a mock fighting bull on wheels. There were also real bulls for the grown-ups. There were two posts available to which bulls could be tied in the large square, used alternately, because they had a lot of bulls. Some of the animals were locked up on the side of the square in a small shed with metal on the inside and plywood on the outside. Children were hammering, banging, kicking, screaming, shouting and throwing things over terrifying the poor animals. It was unbearably hot and must have been even more suffocating inside the shed. It is impossible to imagine the effect on the bulls of being snatched from their fields and thrust into this living hell.

The fire bull event was about to start, so Vicki and Tony squeezed into the tightly packed stands, much to the irritation of the people already sitting there. The bull turned out to be a huge disappointment to the youths taunting him. He just stood there and wouldn't chase around, a real spoilsport. Even the so-called traditional fiestas manage to catch up with new technology; in this one they used three hand-held lasers, aiming them directly at his eyes. When the bull still refused to perform, he was killed on the spot, loaded up and driven away.

By now, thanks to Vicki and Tony, the British press and their readers were well aware of all aspects of Spanish fire bull fiestas, so the story was no great news item but this did not apply to other countries. In June 2003, Harald, King of Norway, participated in a regatta, which brought him to El Grau. He accepted an invitation to the first fire bull of the celebrations of Sant Pere. Accompanied by his bodyguards, he sat in the front row and watched the whole ugly spectacle. One of his bodyguards was even slightly injured by the bull. A few days later, the local press reported that the King had enjoyed the experience and that there was hope that he would return the following year with his son Haakon and Mette-Marit, his wife. Tony could not live with the idea that, due to the Norwegian King's presence and absolution of the fiesta, Norwegian tourists might be drawn to such events in the future. He wrote a letter of complaint to the King, asking him to distance himself from the fiesta but received nothing more than a mere confirmation of receipt. So he transferred his footage on to video tape and sent it to four major Norwegian newspapers. "What the King Saw", was the title of the accompanying information. The response was swift and massive. Norwegian journalists contacted Tony, one of them repeating the King's argument that he had been there in private and not as King. "No more can he say he is a private citizen than I can say I am a King," replied Tony, dismissing the argument.

A major television station then requested the video and Tony was coached over the telephone by a technician on how to send his footage via the internet, so that it could be used in a late afternoon newscast, as well as in later news. The video arrived just in time. Several newspapers also put the footage on the internet. The general public was enraged. Neighbouring Sweden also took up the story and Tony and Vicki alerted the Spanish press about events in the two Nordic countries. The King was under pressure and begrudgingly ordered one of his press officers to admit that he had had 'a negative reaction'. Tony was under the impression that the King had wanted to return to El Grau in the future, because it had an attractive marina and along the front there were several exclusive shops and restaurants. All this in contrast to the sordid proceedings around the corner. It was like two separate worlds.

# Living Target

While still in the Castellón area and looking for a hotel, they stopped at a bar in a small village called San Juan de Moro. As they walked into the cramped little bar, they were greeted by bulls heads everywhere and Tony picked up a small leaflet detailing the village's fiesta schedule. However, what attracted their attention were not the various cattle events, but the 'Tirada de Cordoñiz' or quail throwing. More than twelve years ago a friend had told them about this little known event and even shown them poor quality pictures, but they had never witnessed it. While researching for this chapter I contacted several Spanish hunting associations but no one volunteered information about this so-called sport. No one seems to be proud of it.

At the advertised time, they asked a villager for directions, which turned out to be endless and confusing; apparently the shooting range was quite a way from the village. For more then two hours they drove around, asking for directions, ending up on what was more like a dry river bed than a proper road and eventually finding the place in the middle of nowhere. The shooting on the bone-dry terrain was already well under way in the sweltering afternoon sun. Vicki was not feeling well, so Tony did most of the talking in his poor Spanish. They were the only people there, other than those taking part and Tony asked could if he could take photographs. Thinking he wanted a gun, they said he could shoot for one thousand pesetas (seven pounds fifty) for ten birds. "No, I do my shooting with a camera," he replied, which seemed to amuse them.

Vicki sat down in a good vantage point and started filming, while Tony moved around and took still shots. Tiny birds were taken out of eighteen plastic containers delivered by a factory farm. There were thirty birds in each container. The launching device was similar to that used in clay pigeon shooting, but had been adapted for the quails. The chicks were squeezed into the tube, one at a time, then a large spring was pulled back, catapulting the quails up into the air. Each time they ran out of their living targets, a man would go over to a shed and fetch more plastic crates. Tony walked up with him to take pictures and recognised him as the fellow who had first given him directions in the village and who was now eyeing him with suspicion. He shouted something to the other participants, and seemed to be trying to stir up trouble. It was pointless to be there and not get good footage, so, rather than retreating from the situation, when the man came out of the hut, Tony shouted, "Stay there!" and took his photograph. This caught the fellow off guard, so Tony quickly seized his chance and lifting the lid, was about to take a photograph of the chicks inside, when he suddenly realised he needed a flash. "Un momento, por favor!" he said, took out the flash, and pressed the button.

When he was satisfied with his shot, they walked over to the gun, where the ground was now littered with tiny feathered corpses. Most of the chicks did not meet their deaths by being shot in the air, but by crashing to the ground, because they could not fly. Any chick seen alive was either bashed on the head, flung against a wall, stamped on, or shot on the ground. Vicki observed one chick running across the fenced off area. It kept stopping and then running a little bit further. She stood up. "I'm going to get it," she announced. "I'm going to save that one." She had just set off, when a small child raced over, picked up the chick and twisted its neck, which deeply upset her and Tony had to restrain her. She later told the *Daily Post*, "Watching the Tirada de Cordoñiz, without being able to do anything, was like having my guts put through a mangle. It was very gruelling."

When all the birds had been used up by late afternoon, the winner received his prize money and stood proudly while Tony took his picture. Everybody was packing up and Tony and Vicki were loading their gear into the car ready to drive off, when he realised that there was one last shot he must get, that of the dead birds and the handling of them. So he went back again. The dead chicks were being stuffed into plastic bags to take home for supper. "I saw one really solid looking bloke tipping a pile of chicks into the back of his van. So I got right behind him and took some fantastic pictures."

British expats in Spain were particularly outraged by their subsequent report, which was covered widely in the British press.

# Sparky

On a hot August afternoon in 1999, Vicki and Tony passed through a place called Morata de Jalón, about 65km south west of Zaragoza; a small town consisting of scruffy concrete buildings and narrow streets. The usual fiesta outfit – metal barriers and flags – immediately drew their attention. It turned out to be the local patron saint's day and they walked to the main square to find out what was going on. As they neared the square, they heard the instantly recognisable sound of a calf screaming.

The plaza had been transformed into a makeshift bullring, scattered with sand and littered with garbage, most of it empty soft drink cans. There were barriers made from wood and corrugated iron where people could jump in and out. Sprayed on to one of the barriers, in big red letters, was the message, 'Toreros Asesinos' (Bullfighter Murderers). On the shaded side of the ring there was a stand where a band of about twenty youths, wearing white shirts with blue epaulettes, was playing the usual pasodobles. The village beauties, the mayoress with her young child and the police, were also seated there and people were looking out from their windows and balconies into the square. On the far side there was a building around which barriers had been erected. The animals were let into the square from a small pen behind where Tony suspected they would be killed afterwards.

They found a seat on the stand and, as usual, Vicki videoed while Tony took stills. Cows were run into the ring and very young calves were chased around. Children targeted their eyes with rubber bullets and threw cans at them. Tony estimated that some of the animals were no older than three months. Leaving his place, he made his way round the back and climbed up scaffolding to look over the pen. The man handling the animals turned out to be none other than the mayoress' husband.

A little group of calves came out. One of them, a bull calf, was in a terrible state, screaming with over-excitement. One moment he careered round the ring, where people kicked him repeatedly, at other times he kicked the sand, indicating that he wanted to stand his ground. He displayed little interest in the dirty oversized pink and yellow cape the kids were trying out on him. Strings of saliva poured out of his mouth.

After a while, the calves were all put back in, but because the little bull had reacted so strongly and thus promised to be good fun, he was released for a third time. Terrified, he ran around the ring, desperately searching for a way out. He got his head wedged in the rails right beneath Tony. The kids were pulling at him and somebody on the other side was kicking him in the head, trying to knock it back out again. After what seemed like an eternity, they succeeded and the little bull was thrown back into the pen. Even though he had no obvious injuries, he was sweating and frothing.

Suddenly, Tony felt a movement behind him and turned around. "Vicki was behind me. I don't how she did it; she had climbed up the scaffolding. She could hardly walk, but she had willed herself to climb and there she was standing behind me. When it came to getting down, I virtually had to carry her."

In order to get back into the square they had to take back streets. By the time they got back there, they had independently decided to try and rescue the little black calf with the white legs and belly and white dot on his back. The calves were already being loaded up into a trailer, so Vicki approached the caretaker and expressed an interest in buying a calf, which immediately attracted the attention of the by-standers. Tony demonstrated with gestures to the breeder that he wanted a small calf, one that was still suckling. They took the breeder's mobile phone number and his address. The animals were being taken back to his ranch near Zaragoza. Had any of them been killed or damaged in the fiesta, the village would have had to pay more.

Tony and Vicki drove back to their hotel, retrieved their belongings and relocated to another hotel nearer the ranch. With the help of journalist Nigel Bowden, who spoke good Spanish, they made arrangements for the deal to be finalised. On the ranch Tony told the breeder he wanted the little bull calf with the white patch on the stomach and white dot on his back. He was told the bull's name was 'Chispita' (Little Spark), because his mother was called 'Chispa' (Spark). They re-christened the calf 'Sparky'.

There were a lot of taurino cómico bullfights happening in the area and since Sparky had no ear tags, it would have been easy for him to disappear without trace, so Tony immediately made arrangements for his transport. It occurred to him to seek help from an English couple whom he knew from an anti-bullfighting demo in Gerona, who lived near Lloret de Mar. They were very committed to animal rights and what was more important, trustworthy. When Tony rang them, they were delighted by the good news, but asked for an hour or so to come up with a solution. In due course they rang back saying Sparky could go to a riding stable for a limited period and they had even found transport. Although this would be expensive, it turned out to be the cheapest alternative. And so they eventually set off for Gerona, approximately 400km away, following their new pet in their car. They arrived late at night and Sparky was put into a stable. One of the helpers asked Tony, "What are you going to do with him? Have some fun?"

Since the stable was expensive, Sparky had to be brought to England quickly. The vet of the riding stable agreed to do the paperwork on the Spanish side and Vicki and Tony left to sort things out with the Ministry of Agriculture back home.

Sparky was going to live on a farm on the Wirral, about an hour's drive from their Southport home. The farmer, Geoff Nicolls, who had inherited the organic beef farm from his father, had recently started growing organic vegetables and kept the remaining cattle as pets, so Sparky and his new pals would never end up in the food chain. FAACE would pay for his keep. Sparky would serve a purpose too; schoolchildren and the general public would be educated on the cruelty of bullfighting. Vicki put it like this, "Sparky coming to England is very important … His importance apart from the attendant publicity for the issues involved, is an educational one. To have a fighting bull and be able to demonstrate to the world that he is not a fiend or demon, but essentially an animal totally vulnerable to mankind's cruelty, will be important. We want people to see Sparky and through him, all the thousands of animals who are tortured to death each year. He is a lovely animal, intelligent, and during the time I spent with him at the stables, I was amazed by the wonder in his eyes, as he watched the horses and the dogs, and listened to the cocks crowing … I spent time talking quietly and softly to him, and certainly seemed to get a positive response."

What had seemed relatively straightforward at first, proved to be a never-ending and ill-fated story. Even though Sparky had no ear tags, which were required to move the animal within Europe, a new set should be issued fast, since they had the ear tag numbers of Chispa, Sparky's mother.

Two weeks after Sparky's arrival in Gerona, they returned to Spain with a hired four-wheel drive. Since he was only young, an ordinary horse trailer would do and somebody had loaned it to them for free. Brittany Ferries had given a discount too. Nevertheless, the cost for this one trip amounted to over £1,250. They took the overnight ferry from Portsmouth and arrived in St Malo in the early morning. Tony drove straight through western France and they arrived near Gerona at night, exhausted but in good spirits, looking forward to seeing Sparky again.

They were in for a shock. The Gerona branch of the Ministry of Agriculture had remained closed over the endlessly long Spanish holiday season, which paralyses the whole country each year. Nothing had been done. In addition, Sparky would have to return to Aragón, his birthplace, for his papers. The vet in Gerona was furious, Sparky would not have to go back. It would be sufficient for Vicki and Tony to collect the papers and eartags from the breeder. He would insert the tags, do the necessary health checks and issue the corresponding certificates. They would still be able to take Sparky to his new English home as planned.

In the summer of 1999, Spain was plagued by tremendous thunderstorms which turned their journey to Aragón into a nightmare. Visibility during the drive was appalling with torrential rain and lightning flashing all around them. Determined not to waste any more time, Tony drove straight through it all.

They were in for another unwelcome surprise when they arrived at the ranch. The breeder was away delivering a set of fully-grown bulls to a series of major bullfights. The foreman explained that he alone could sign the documents and deliver the ear tags and he would not be back for two weeks. Parked by the roadside in the continuing deluge, they felt more than a little shell-shocked. The breeder was obviously trying to cover up malpractice in the registration of his animals. They had always known that bullfighting was crooked, but this provided a very personal insight into the type of corruption involved.

They decided to cut their losses. After arranging for Sparky to remain at the stables for a few more weeks, they returned to England to curtail the vehicle hire charges and conserve every penny, as they would have to make this journey again. Sparky was safer in Gerona than on the ranch, because there were many fiestas in the area until October. According to official statistics, in the Aragón province alone, approximately one thousand three hundred cattle fiestas took place annually. The calves were mostly rented and returned to the breeders. Only if they were severely 'damaged' were they killed. Damages cost extra.

When they felt it was safe for Sparky to return to his place of birth, they flew to Spain again. They had to settle outstanding bills, which by now were quite high, because the calf had been there for two months instead of the intended two weeks. The same people would take care of his transport. Their price was the same. In fact, they were not sure they would do it because Sparky was now so much stronger and bigger, although still very much a calf. However, the awful mythology of the 'fighting bull' had done its work and everyone was claiming to be frightened of him.

The little bull seemed happy to be with cattle again rather than horses and Vicki and Tony returned to England in good spirits. In theory, by mid-November, Sparky would be given his blood tests, health certificates, and ear tags, by a team of veterinary officers. If his and the whole herd's tests came back fine, they could bring him home by the end of November.

However, it was not yet meant to be and the saga continued when a huge agricultural scandal erupted in Aragón. A three thousand-head herd of dairy cows was found to have never received any tuberculosis testing, or any other check, so all hands from the Ministry veterinary team had been sent to deal with the mess, postponing all their routine visits. Yet another illustration of how irregular everything can be in Spain. Thwarted once again, they fervently hoped to be able to bring Sparky home before Christmas, or at the latest, early in the New Year.

Sadly, Vicki was never to see Sparky again.

# Goodbye

By now, Vicki could no longer ignore the gnawing pain in her stomach and in autumn 1999, she reluctantly went to the Royal Liverpool Hospital to have it examined. They found a huge lump which Vicki thought had been caused by Argentino's attack in Coria. There was no rush, she was told, but eventually she would need to have an operation. So they set off for Spain as planned, for yet another attempt at bringing Sparky home. Whilst there, Vicki fell seriously ill; the pain became unbearable and she grew weaker and weaker. They returned to England and she went back to the hospital. This time the doctors realised the gravity of her condition. Ironically, before this, she had been asked by Southport newspaper *The Midweek Visiter* how she intended to spend New Year's Eve and the start of the new Millennium. "I'll be taking the opportunity to catch up on a bit of quiet with my husband, Tony, and continue the work I'm doing with the animals. This is a good time to reflect over the past years and hope the world moves to become a more peaceful and enlightened place." But it was not meant to be.

Vicki was wheeled into the operating theatre on 30 December. The sheer size of the lump complicated the operation, but after a couple of days she started to look a lot brighter. However, an abscess had formed after the operation and a drain was put in. Tony grew more and more concerned when the leakage would not stop and she was getting visibly weaker again. It did not help his state of mind when he overheard hospital staff referring to Vicki as "the one whose stomach's rotting away". He spent every day at the hospital, driving the forty-five minutes back to Southport to feed the four cats, getting changed, and driving back to Liverpool again. Around the middle of January, just as he arrived home, the hospital called him. Vicki had had a haemorrhage. Could he come back in?

When he rushed into the ward, Vicki was still in the operating theatre. A major blood vessel had burst and they had already given her about eight blood packs. Consumed with dread, Tony sat down in the waiting room. "I suddenly felt Vicki in the room with me. I felt an actual presence, I almost said hello. I thought she had died, because she had suddenly come to me." As soon as the operation was over he insisted on seeing her. The doctor eventually agreed, but warned him that she was covered in blood. "I don't care, I want to be in there with her!"

With legs like lead, Tony stepped into the recovery room and took hold of her hand. She opened her eyes. "Are you all right?" he asked and she smiled. One of the medical staff told him that her heart had actually stopped shortly before. "I know, because she came to me," he said simply. Vicki was taken straight from the recovery room back into intensive care.

Much later, as Tony was on his way back to Southport again, his mobile rang. It was one of the doctors who had wanted to speak to him, but had missed him in the hospital. He pulled over and listened as she told him they were not going to resuscitate Vicki if the same thing happened again. They would not put her through all this stress again, she was too weak.

From that moment, Tony knew that he was going to lose Vicki very soon. She had difficulty breathing and he had noticed, when he brushed her hair every day, that it was falling out in clumps. Eventually, she was moved from intensive care into a single room and Tony decided to rent a room in the hospital. He paid in advance for a couple of nights, but never used it. He sat at her beside night and day, clinging to her hand. Deprived of sleep, he finally dropped off at around 11.30 on the morning of 6 February 2000. He was woken up by a voice saying, "She's gone ..."

He deeply regretted not being awake when she died – she might have wanted to say something ... He was gently asked to leave the room while they took out the drips and tidied her up. When he saw her again for the last time, she looked very tranquil, and very beautiful, just like the young woman he had first met.

He was not yet given time to grieve. Not only did he have to sort out all the paperwork in the hospital, but when he entered the parking lot in front of the hospital he found that his car had been stolen, despite security guards and cameras. Utterly dejected, he reported the theft to security and took a taxi home. His whole body felt numb and he just wanted to be alone, but his answering machine was full of messages. Against his expressed wishes, someone at the hospital had leaked the news of Vicki's death to the media. Feeling unable to handle them on his own, he called a journalist friend for help, who put the word out that Vicki had died from cancer. There were many tributes to her; a minute's silence was held at the European Parliament in Strasbourg and a memorial service was held outside the British Embassy in Washington DC.

He arranged for a small funeral at the local crematorium, which he managed to keep private. As her coffin was taken in 'I Pini del Gianicolo' by Ottorino Respighi was played, one of Vicki's favourites. Friends Geoff Nichols and Ralph James said some words and Reverend John Kelly took the service. During a few moments of contemplation before the mourners filed out, the 'Adagio' from the 'Concierto de Aranjuez' by Joaquín Rodrigo filled the room.

In death, as in life, Vicki hated fuss and had wanted a do-it-yourself funeral, telling Tony to put her in a cardboard box. Although he respected her wishes, he felt he could not do this to all the people who had loved and supported her. So a memorial service, followed by a vegan meal to celebrate her life, was arranged at the Liverpool Anglican Cathedral for 8 April 2000. A free bus from Southport for people wanting to attend was made available. Right Reverend Rupert Hoare, the Dean of Liverpool, presided over the service. Among the speakers were animal rights people from Great Britain, the USA and Spain, and the Reverend Andrew Linzey, who said, "… Up to the last, she minimised her own sufferings lest she, rather than the animals, became the focus of media attention. Vicki died when she was only forty-four years old. It is not enough to marvel at Vicki's personal qualities. Her remarkable bravery, her patient endurance of suffering, her steadfast refusal to abandon hope, her total and unswerving dedication to achieving some alleviation of suffering. Neither is it enough to say that she demonstrated in her life how facile and repugnant is the common media perception of animal protectionists as human haters, or advocates of violence. Here was someone who put her life on the line, who sacrificed everything she had in pursuit of a vision of a cruelty-free, violence-free world … Vicki stands in a long tradition of saints and seers, poets, philanthropists and thinkers who have championed the cause of animals."

Dr Manuel Cases, vice-president of the Spanish animal rights group ADDA said, "We were united by the universal language of the love for animals, for which we wanted to do more and better things. But to follow Vicki was very, very difficult, as she had an inner strength that outdid us all … Her fight has helped, and will continue to help … put a stop to cruel festivals in Spain … Tony and Vicki worked wonderfully together but now Tony will have to continue alone, there is plenty to be done."

Many people who were not able to attend personally, had sent statements. Tony Banks, MP, whose sudden and early death in January 2006 was a shock to Tony, wrote: "Vicki was a very courageous, determined woman who inspired thousands by her example in caring for animals. We must honour her and all her work by keeping up the campaign to improve the welfare for animals, not just in Europe, but around the world."

Comedian and author Alexei Sayle wrote, "To me, she will always be an outstanding heroine – a truly brave, inspiring person who achieved so much. She really did make a difference."

Vicki did not live to see some of the successes of her crusade for the animals. However, she was aware that after years of exposing the goat fiesta, FAACE had found an ally in the Madrid animal rights group ANPBA who had only formed in 1999. In January 2000, only a few days before her death, they managed to have the goat fiesta banned. The goat was not thrown. As she lay in her hospital bed, Tony was able to tell her that they had stopped Manganeses de la Polvorosa. And despite being very weak, she managed to smile and hold up her thumb.

# And What Happened to Sparky?

Throughout these dark and lonely days, Tony stayed in touch with the bull breeder by telephone. In March 2000, he was told that the bull had been issued with ear tags at last and that new tests were coming up. After that, he would have ten days in which to sort out the export permits and take Sparky out of Spain. The mere thought of the trip was depressing. It would be the first time he had travelled without Vicki to see the little bull. Even though he was accompanied by a cameraman from BBC Northwest, he was filled with sadness as he journeyed through the towns and villages where they had been together. Every turn in the road brought back painful memories. He missed her terribly.

He had come to expect the worst where anything to do with Sparky was concerned and so was hardly surprised when he arrived at the farm to find that two animals had reacted positively to the tuberculosis test. Thwarted once again!

In May, he returned once more, accompanied by the same cameraman. There was no four wheel drive available, so he was given a twenty-seater bus instead, which made it awkward to pull the horse trailer. They took the ferry to Santander and as they were disembarking after a twenty-four-hour trip, Tony's mobile rang. What was it now? Nigel Bowden had been trying to ring for a while but there had been no signal at sea. He had spoken to the breeder – the herd had had another bad test result. This time, the tests had come up with bovine contagious pneumonia. They decided to abort the mission and try to make the evening ferry from Saint Malo. The empty trailer triggered the curiosity of French customs officials, who went through it with a fine-toothed comb, but they still made the ferry.

Meanwhile, Sparky continued to grow and gradually changed colour. He was of the Cardeno type, which meant he would end up being light grey all over. Tony made sure he would not be branded, as this is very painful and stressful to the animals.

Tony returned to the ranch yet again at the beginning of September. This time he brought a journalist from the now defunct Channel 1 Cable TV. She was going to make a report not only on Sparky but also on the whole environment of bullfighting.

First, however, they were faced with a problem that was to spread like a wildfire throughout Europe. Towards the end of August, French fishermen blocked the Channel ports to protest against high fuel prices, leaving thousands of passengers stranded. Lorries were stuck at the British ports and the ferry companies started to re-route to Holland and Belgium. Clearly misjudging the situation, British Deputy Prime Minister John Prescott complained to CNN: "It is totally unacceptable that Britain could be held to ransom in this kind of blockade rising out of a dispute in France." The French government came to an agreement with the fishermen, but now French farmers, taxi and lorry drivers staged a protest. Oil refineries throughout France were blocked off and fuel stations ran dry. After a six-day protest, French Prime Minister Lionel Jospin agreed to a fifteen per cent cut in fuel tax.

The strike spread to the UK, the Northwest being hit worst, when a Shell refinery near Liverpool was blockaded, prompting panic buying. The government ruled out any concessions and the strike was eventually called off. The protests had spread across Europe. Blockades, or similar strike action, albeit to a lesser extent, were reported in Belgium, The Netherlands, Germany, Poland, Hungary, Norway, Spain and Italy. Eventually, OPEC agreed to increase oil supplies by eight hundred thousand barrels per day.

Tony managed to board the ferry with a full tank, just before the crisis hit hard. On arrival in France, the petrol stations were just about to be re-fuelled and it took them many hours and a huge detour to find a functioning petrol station to refill their tank. He felt under pressure because they had to pick up another journalist at Bilbao airport. They drove on to Spain, unsure of the situation there. At points on the way, the journalists made Tony stop several times, doing little takes on him, asking him questions such as, "How do you feel now that you're going to get him?"

When they arrived in the village, the railway bridge which led to the ranch was damaged and closed for repair work. It seemed as if every possible obstacle was standing in their way. Tony tried in vain to find a crossing, eventually coming across an old man walking in the general direction they were going. When they asked him the way he gestured that he wanted to go with them. He led them to a long narrow tunnel under another railway bridge. The trailer only just squeezed through. So, after having overcome endless problems and delays, the three of them were at the farm at the agreed time. The breeder did not show up. It was clear to Tony that this was not just one of his usual delays but clearly intentional but he managed to reach him on his mobile. The herd had failed the tests yet again. New tests would be carried out in two weeks time. It was embarrassing having to explain this to the two journalists as Tony drove them to Barcelona Airport, before returning to the village.

After they had said their goodbyes, he was rearranging his luggage in the car boot when a man appeared in front of the car, signalling wildly. Tony took a few steps towards him but could make no sense of his garbled Spanish, so he turned back to the boot, locked it and drove off. Only later, when he stopped for a break, did he find that his best stills camera, with all the expensive accessories, was missing. Gone also were his maps and hotel guide. It is not hard to imagine the depths of his despair when, a short time later, he came across a place where he and Vicki had stopped by the roadside. A lesser man would have broken down and cried.

Such dark moments only spurred him on to carry on the fight in her memory. His tenaciousness was just as strong as hers and despite all the setbacks, he was determined to rescue that special little bull. Watching every penny, he lived in a cheap hotel and ate at a truck stop. During his eight week stay, he spent a lot of time on the ranch studying their innermost workings such as breeding, feeding, the conditions in which the animals were kept and the way they were handled and transported, gathering interesting information and pictures, which would be invaluable in the future. He was accepted as an interested harmless foreigner, some days even being taken to fiestas riding in the cab of the ranch's cattle trucks. Luckily, the animals that were taken to the fiestas in these instances came back alive. Yet time dragged and the days seemed endless. Every morning he spent a lot of time waiting for the breeder and his farm hands to show up. Hours were spent in a cheap restaurant at lunchtime, forced to eat meat to protect his identity. After lunch, everybody disappeared, only showing up again at around 5pm.

The farm's working practices got to him too. One of the cows was left to die a slow death. The skeletal animal was too weak to stand and thus unable to drink from the bucket put next to her. Instead of calling a vet to put her down and spare her further suffering, the farm hands carelessly watched her dying over four days. When she had finally died, she was hoisted on to the front loader of a tractor, her horns chopped off with an axe and dumped into a hole in the ground outside the farm's corrugated iron fence.

There was nowhere to go and no money to spend, so every evening Tony returned to his miserable lodgings. He extended his dinner of overcooked vegetables and the odd piece of meat over half a bottle of wine for as long possible, before retiring to his tiny stuffy room. He watched unfunny shows on the small television set suspended under the low ceiling with a clothes hanger for an aerial. He lay awake sweating in the airless night, worrying about his four cats, who were in a shelter and his good friend Nora in the charity shop on her own during his prolonged absence. Above all, he felt a yawning emptiness without Vicki by his side.

Without warning, the weather suddenly turned bitterly cold. Not expecting such a long stay, Tony had not packed for cold weather. He yearned to go home, but still hoped to take Sparky with him. On the day of the results he was devastated to learn that, even though Sparky himself was healthy, other animals in the herd had tested positive and had had to be slaughtered. This meant that Sparky could not be moved and would have to wait for the next round of tests. Anybody else would have given up hope, but not Tony. Frustrated and disappointed, he returned home leaving the trailer on the ranch in anticipation of his next journey.

At the end of 2000, BSE was beginning to spread throughout Europe and restrictions on cattle movement were imposed. The appearance of a Foot and

Mouth epidemic at the beginning of 2001 did not help either. He considered flying Sparky out, but chartering a plane turned out to be impossible. He could not ask the general public for donations, because he wanted to keep Sparky's whereabouts secret for as long as possible.

So it was April 2001, when he finally returned to the ranch to retrieve Sparky and the trailer. By now he was considered a friend by the bull breeder and his staff and he took pictures and videos of his bull, who had grown to quite a size. Even though the herd's test results came out badly again, Tony was still determined. He was aware that people questioned his perseverance against all odds but when Vicki had lain dying, he had vowed to bring Sparky home to England away from certain torture and death.

When I came into the picture I understood and respected their attitude towards this mission impossible. As an international animal rights activist myself, I was concerned with the same issues that had consumed them both during most of their life together. When I first met Tony in Salt Lake City in late November 2001, as a German member of the same campaign to try and stop a rodeo at the 2002 Winter Olympics, I was immediately aware of an aura of overwhelming sadness surrounding him and I knew a little about Vicki and her tragic death in February of the previous year.

Tony described our first meeting as love at first sight on his part. We certainly hit it off, but I think at first I reminded him of Vicki and it was this which drew him to me. Our second meeting in Lausanne, Switzerland, just before Christmas, to meet the Medical Director of the International Olympic Committee, cemented our relationship. With a free afternoon at our disposal, we strolled by Lake Geneva and simply enjoyed each other's company. At dinner that evening, Tony told me that he still had all Vicki's belongings around the house; he couldn't bring himself to part with them. This saddened me, because I felt that he would never get on with his life until he freed himself from the past. He and Vicki had been as close as a couple can be and her untimely death had devasted him, but she would not have wanted him to go on grieving forever.

We hugged and cried together. That night, our future together began, although it would take a while before I could move to England. Only then did we have time to get to know each other. Many nights, after one of Tony's delicious vegan dinners, the story of their life together slowly unravelled from his amazing memory. I also found documents written by Vicki herself and, of course, many newspaper articles and a great deal of video footage. Tony and Vicki had been asked to write about their lives before, but had declined, not considering themselves that important. Granada Television had wanted to do a documentary on Vicki's life, but again she had declined, fearing that her identity would be stolen from her. So I took it upon myself, with Tony's blessing, to let people share their unbelievably strange and courageous lives. This book is an expression of my love and admiration for two exceptional human beings and, hopefully, it will inspire people to take action, when injustice is done to living beings – human or animal.

So, while I could fully understand and respect Tony and Vicki's campaign to save Sparky – and indeed it had now also become my campaign – from my many phone conversations and personal visits to the ranch it was soon clear to me that they had selected one of Spain's sloppiest bull breeders. On numerous occasions we waited anxiously for the test results, packed and ready to go to Spain, but instead of improving, the cattle's health deteriorated. The breeder confided that he had been advised by the veterinary officers to consult another bull breeder in another province on how to keep his cattle in better conditions and so avoid illnesses.

What I saw in May 2002 on the ranch was in sharp contrast to the myth of the fighting bull happily roaming the fields, never being handled by people. In order to load them up into the transporter, electro-shocking devices were used. The full-grown fighting bulls were kept in corrugated iron compounds, standing on bare ground, and were fed from a tractor. The food came from a great, foul-smelling heap, which turned out to be a mixture of sugar beet, chicken manure and chicken remains – the feathers clearly visible. One of the farm hands explained to me the origin of the feathers: ground-up chicks from battery farming – a clear breach of EU laws. Because of the BSE crisis, it had long been forbidden to feed animal parts to cattle.

We took samples of the filthy feed, which we split in half, having one half analysed in the Laboratorio Regional Agragrio de la Comunidad de Madrid and the other in the Lancashire County Laboratory in Preston. Both samples came out positive for animal components and the certificates specifically mentioned feathers. We also snatched several different empty medicine containers – so much for the 'organic product fighting bull'! However, Tony decided not to go public with our discoveries, fearing it would jeopardise our chances of getting Sparky out alive. All we could do was hope that he was not going to be used in fiestas, or in a competition called a 'Concurso de Recortadores', in which the animals were jumped over by youths. Sparky's breeder had actually introduced that particular pastime into the area and the first national competition took place in the farm's neighbourhood. When we read about it in the *Diario de Navarra*, in August 2002, it was too late to fly over.

At the beginning of February 2003, the River Ebro flooded the area repeatedly. We read the regional newspapers on the internet and were shocked to find a picture of Sparky's village, reduced to a tiny island in a huge lake. The *Diario Vasco* reported that dykes had burst and that several villages had had to be evacuated, some by force, and that the river had risen three thousand one hundred cubic metres per second, reaching a level of nearly six metres. When I rang a few days later, I was told that many animals, mostly calves, had drowned, but the bigger ones had fled to a nearby hill. Tony fervently hoped that Sparky was amongst them.

A few weeks later, the good news came. Sparky had been spotted alive, but he and his friends were now on a shooting range belonging to the Spanish military. The breeder would not be allowed in to retrieve the animals before the military shut the range down over the long summer holidays. There was also another problem. The farm had been destroyed and he no longer had any space to house the animals. Besides, he needed to make money fast and was too busy. Due to rising insurance costs, many villages could no longer afford to have cattle fiestas and there had been a decline in demand of fifteen per cent.

In December 2003, he and his men finally retrieved some cattle from the shooting range. They found the few fully-grown bulls and cows had started a new herd and now had lots of calves in tow. Not all the animals could be captured because some were too wild. Sparky was amongst these. They intended to have another attempt after the Christmas holidays using anaesthetics.

However, a new governmental order loomed on the horizon. 'Real Decreto 1047' would be enforced in 2004 and decreed that no cattle which had left a farm could return alive. The whole bullfighting industry was in turmoil and feverishly tried to negotiate with the government. We were told that, once retrieved, the animals would be hidden somewhere to escape being destroyed. Tony was worried that it would be impossible to get an export permit for Sparky if he did not officially live on the ranch.

Due to the 'mañana' syndrome, things move very slowly in Spain and so, on 11 March, when the terrible Madrid bombings took place, the animals were still at large on the shooting range. After that, due to increased levels of security, civilians were no longer allowed on to military ground and The Ministry of Defence gave the order to kill the supposedly ownerless cattle. Sparky, his mother Chispa, and some thirty head of cattle, were shot on 24 July 2004 and taken directly to the incinerator.

Tony was very sad when I broke the news to him but he consoled himself with the thought that because they had adopted him, he had been safe for the rest of his life. During his last seventeen months Sparky had lived completely freely, roaming the countryside in his small herd, not being handled by anyone and that, in a country like Spain, is as good as it gets. Nobody could possibly have done more than he did to help the little bull.

# A Rough Beginning

Before I could finally settle down in England, I travelled back and forth to my home country a few times. At the beginning of March 2002, I flew back to Germany for the last time. When I said goodbye to Alita, the Spanish cat rescued by Vicki, I was not sure I would see her alive on my return due to her declining health. I knelt down and asked her to please hang on until I came back and she lifted her head and looked up at me. It felt like a promise.

I had intended to bring both my cats over to England. The recently introduced Pet Scheme made it possible for them to spend their quarantine period at home but, sadly, my cat Cuy died while I was getting everything ready. When I returned to England two weeks later, Alita was in a very bad way, but still alive. I thanked her for hanging on. The next morning we found her dead in the kitchen. Her death hit Tony very hard, as she had been one of his favourite cats. Two dead little creatures within two weeks almost seemed like a form of punishment for breaking up my marriage in Germany.

Alita's death also meant a final goodbye to Vicki. What I had not known before was that Tony still kept Vicki's ashes, her mother's and those of their cats Trigger and Fleur, and their dogs Susie and Fritz. Vicki had wanted her ashes to be scattered in Brontë Country. So on 20 March 2002, we drove to Wycoller and in those lovely surroundings, said goodbye to each of them.

In October 2002, we rented a car and Tony drove all the way across France and Germany to bring my cat Lunes home. Our family seemed complete again, with the three black cats Thomas Chip, Tiny and Tolly, and it has since grown. In February 2003, we adopted run-away cow Bluebell, who sought refuge in a friend's woods and survived on her own all winter. It turned out she was in calf and she gave birth to Belana in July.

But 2003 was not a happy year. Tony was diagnosed with prostate cancer, which left us devastated, although he was lucky, in a way, because he was diagnosed early. Radiation was suggested as the best treatment option, so for many weeks we travelled back and forth to Clatterbridge Hospital on the Wirral on a daily basis. While he underwent his treatment, I sat in the waiting area and with headphones, transcribed the audiotapes of his life. Neither the treatment nor its effects made him slow down for long and Vicki and her work continue to be part of our lives. They had both recognised that there was always a danger that something might happen to one of them and had an agreement that if anything did, the survivor would carry on. In memory of Vicki, and for all the tortured animals, Tony's work and that of FAACE continues.

Only a few days after her death he went on the annual Waterloo Cup demo. Many of the demonstrators were also still in shock over Vicki's death and a minute's silence was held in her memory. Animal rights campaigners had hoped the coursing fraternity would show some sign of respect for her, but they refused. In fact, some of them openly gloated on the fact that she was no longer there, shouting at Tony, "One down and one to go".

However, there was no turning back the clocks and the Hunting Act was forced through using the Parliamentary Act in November 2004. The animal rights lobby around Southport was jubilant. Everybody was confidant that there would not be another Waterloo Cup but Tony, myself and the other faithful lovers of the British hare stoically attended the very last demo against the Cup just four days before the ban, when the organisers decided to move the event forward to have one last go at the hares. The Ormskirk police were not pleased, because with both sides knowing that this would be the very last Cup, emotions were running high.

It proved to be a very tough policing job indeed. The protesters were led into a corridor between the coursing field and the catering area, and once inside were surrounded by the enemy. Insults were exchanged between the two parties, with some members of the press actually urging protesters to be a bit more provocative. Freshly-torn and still warm hare's limbs were thrown at us. Wearing a gruesome deathmask, I picked up a leg and held it up to the many cameras. This inflamed the coursers, who responded by throwing handsful of mud and fire crackers into the ranks of protesters, among them small children. Police horses reared up in the chaos and for several tense moments the protesters worried whether the police had underestimated the situation. However, the officers regained control and nobody was injured.

When the ban finally came into force on 18 February 2005, Tony said, "It was inevitable. It was a progression that had to come. Why did we have to wait so long? All the hares, all the foxes, all the stags, have all been chased to death needlessly. All the people who have died, who fought for the end of hunting and failed to see the success of their work. You can't be triumphant about it. You can be pleased it happened, but sad it took so long."

Apart from his trips to Spain to bring Sparky home to England, he has assisted in Tenerife in yet another case of a troubled dog shelter and participated in a big demo in Barcelona. He was also involved in the campaign against rodeo in the Salt Lake City Winter Olympics, where we met and together we have travelled to investigate rodeos and blood fiestas in Europe and to demonstrate against hare coursing in Ireland.

Vicki's legacy lives on and she is still constantly in our thoughts. In moments of crisis and when faced with difficult decisions, I frequently turn to Tony and ask, "How would Vicki have handled this?" certain in the knowledge that she is still there to guide us in our continuing quest to help the animals who suffer at man's hands.